29	Supporting a thesis	105
30	Avoiding plagiarism	107
31	Integrating nonfiction sources	110
32	Integrating literary quotations	118
33	MLA documentation style	121
34	MLA manuscript format; sample pages	155

APA Papers — 163

35	Supporting a thesis	164
36	Avoiding plagiarism	166
37	Integrating sources	169
38	APA documentation style	173
39	APA manuscript format; sample pages	195

Chicago Papers — 207

40	Supporting a thesis	208
41	Avoiding plagiarism	210
42	Integrating sources	213
43	*Chicago* documentation style	217
44	*Chicago* manuscript format; sample pages	235

CSE Papers — 243

| 45 | CSE documentation style | 244 |
| 46 | CSE manuscript format | 256 |

Glossaries — 259

| 47 | Glossary of usage | 260 |
| 48 | Glossary of grammatical terms | 270 |

Index 279
Documentation directories
Charts and lists for quick reference
Checklist for global revision
List of excerpts from student papers
Visiting the writing center
Revision symbols

Washtenaw Community College

WCC1	ENG 090: Writing Fundamentals I	2
WCC2	ENG 091: Writing Fundamentals II	4
WCC3	ENG 111: Composition I	7
WCC4	ENG 226: Composition II	9
WCC5	The Writing Center	11
WCC6	Venues for the Literary Arts	14

WCC1 ENG 090: Writing Fundamentals I

WCC1-a Course Objectives

1. Develop topic through prewriting using a variety of prewriting methods (e.g., cluster, list, outline).

   Methods of Evaluation

   Class attendance, Participation, or Work Paper(s)

   Matched Outcomes

   a. Demonstrate satisfactory-level competency on multi-paragraph writing when asked to write in class independently under the observation of the instructor without the benefit of electronic or other means of tutorial intervention.

2. Identify and write thesis statements and topic sentences.

   Sections 29a-29c, Thesis statements (MLA)
   Sections 35a-35c, Thesis statements (APA)

   Methods of Evaluation

   Class attendance, Participation, or Work Paper(s)

   Matched Outcomes

   a. Demonstrate satisfactory-level competency on multi-paragraph writing when asked to write in class independently under the observation of the instructor without the benefit of electronic or other means of tutorial intervention.

3. Complete multiple drafts of assignments applying essay structure (introduction, body paragraphs, conclusion).

Methods of Evaluation

Class attendance, Participation, or Work
Paper(s)

Matched Outcomes

a. Demonstrate satisfactory-level competency on multi-paragraph writing when asked to write in class independently under the observation of the instructor without the benefit of electronic or other means of tutorial intervention.

4. Edit drafts for coherence and unity, adjusting style for appropriateness with regard to subject, audience, and purpose.

   Chapters 1-9, Clarity (For appropriate voice, see Chapter 9.)
   Chapter 29, Supporting a thesis (MLA)
   Chapter 35, Supporting a thesis (APA)

Methods of Evaluation

Class attendance, Participation, or Work
Exams/Tests
Paper(s)

Matched Outcomes

a. Demonstrate satisfactory-level competency on multi-paragraph writing when asked to write in class independently under the observation of the instructor without the benefit of electronic or other means of tutorial intervention.

5. Proofread for grammar/usage errors.

   Chapters 1-9, Clarity
   Chapters 10-16, Grammar
   Chapters 17-21, Punctuation
   Chapters 22-24, Mechanics
   Chapter 47, Glossary of usage
   Revision Symbols (See endpapers.)

Methods of Evaluation

Class attendance, Participation, or Work Paper(s)

Matched Outcomes

a. Demonstrate satisfactory-level competency on multi-paragraph writing when asked to write in class independently under the observation of the instructor without the benefit of electronic or other means of tutorial intervention.

6. Revise edited drafts.

    Checklist for Global Revision (See endpapers.)

    ### Methods of Evaluation

    Class attendance, Participation, or Work Paper(s)

    ### Matched Outcomes

    a. Demonstrate satisfactory-level competency on multi-paragraph writing when asked to write in class independently under the observation of the instructor without the benefit of electronic or other means of tutorial intervention.

WCC2 ENG 091: Writing Fundamentals II

WCC2-a Course Objectives

1. Develop topics through prewriting using a variety of prewriting methods (e.g., cluster, list, outline)

    ### Methods of Evaluation

    Class attendance, Participation, or Work Paper(s)

Matched Outcomes

a. Demonstrate "C" level competency on minimum college-level entrance writing when asked to write at least a five-paragraph essay independently under the observation of the instructor without the benefit of electronic or other means of tutorial intervention.

2. Identify and write thesis statements and topic sentences

   Sections 29a-29c, Thesis statements (MLA)
   Sections 35a-35c, Thesis statements (APA)

Methods of Evaluation

Class attendance, Participation, or Work Paper(s)

Matched Outcomes

a. Demonstrate "C" level competency on minimum college-level entrance writing when asked to write at least a five-paragraph essay independently under the observation of the instructor without the benefit of electronic or other means of tutorial intervention.

3. Complete multiple drafts of assignments applying essay structure (introduction, body paragraphs, conclusion)

Methods of Evaluation

Class attendance, Participation, or Work Paper(s)

Matched Outcomes

a. Demonstrate "C" level competency on minimum college-level entrance writing when asked to write at least a five-paragraph essay independently under the observation of the instructor without the benefit of electronic or other means of tutorial intervention.

4. Edit drafts for coherence and unity, adjusting style for appropriateness with regard to subject, audience, and purpose

   Chapters 1-9, Clarity (For appropriate voice, see Chapter 9.)
   Chapter 29, Supporting a thesis (MLA)
   Chapter 35, Supporting a thesis (APA)
   Checklist for Global Revision (See endpapers.)

   Methods of Evaluation

   Class attendance, Participation, or Work Paper(s)

   Matched Outcomes

   a. Demonstrate "C" level competency on minimum college-level entrance writing when asked to write at least a five-paragraph essay independently under the observation of the instructor without the benefit of electronic or other means of tutorial intervention.

5. Proofread for grammar/usage errors

   Chapters 1-9, Clarity
   Chapters 10-16, Grammar
   Chapters 17-21, Punctuation
   Chapters 22-24, Mechanics
   Chapter 47, Glossary of usage
   Revision Symbols (See endpapers.)

   Methods of Evaluation

   Class attendance, Participation, or Work Paper(s)

   Matched Outcomes

   a. Demonstrate "C" level competency on minimum college-level entrance writing when asked to write at least a five-paragraph essay independently under the observation of the instructor without the benefit of electronic or other means of tutorial intervention.

6. Revise edited drafts

Checklist for Global Revision (See endpapers.)

Methods of Evaluation

Class attendance, Participation, or Work Paper(s)

Matched Outcomes

a. Demonstrate "C" level competency on minimum college-level entrance writing when asked to write at least a five-paragraph essay independently under the observation of the instructor without the benefit of electronic or other means of tutorial intervention.

ENG 111: Composition I

WCC3-a Course Objectives

1. Rhetorical Context—Audience, Purpose, and Evaluation

   Matched Outcomes

   a. Identify reasons why people write and value writing.
   b. Use appropriate forms and strategies to address varied audiences and occasions.
   c. Demonstrate an ability to question, explain, interpret, and evaluate the writing of others, as well as their own.

2. Writing Process—Prewriting, Drafting, Revising, Editing, and Proofreading

   Matched Outcomes

   a. Demonstrate knowledge of prewriting techniques.
   b. Formulate, develop, and support effective thesis statements.

Sections 29a–29c, Thesis statements (MLA)
Sections 35a–35c, Thesis statements (APA)

    c. Use a variety of organizational strategies.
    d. Use appropriate conventions of style in establishing levels of formality and tone.

Chapter 9, Appropriate voice

    e. Write 4–7 polished final essays throughout the term, at least 40–50 pages, including rough and polished essays.

Revision Symbols (see endpapers)
Checklist for Global Revision (see endpapers)

3. Critical Thinking

    Matched Outcomes

    a. Use writing for inquiry, problem solving, and making discoveries about themselves and their world.
    b. Use tools of problem solving, including observation, analysis, and reconstruction.
    c. Support a position with reasons and evidence.

    Chapter 31, Integrating sources (MLA)

    d. Evaluate counterpositions and arguments.

    Chapter 27, Evaluating sources
    Sections 29c (MLA) and 35c (APA), Using sources to inform and support your argument

4. Research and Documentation

    Matched Outcomes

    a. Use a variety of resources available for credible research and documentation.

    Chapter 26, Finding appropriate sources

    b. Assess source material for validity.

    Chapter 27, Evaluating sources

c. Document sources using MLA style or another appropriate research documentation style.

> *Chapter 33, MLA documentation style*
> *Chapter 38, APA documentation style*
> *Chapter 43, Chicago documentation style*
> *Chapter 45, CSE documentation style*

WCC4 ENG 226: Composition II

WCC4-a Course Objectives

1. Analyze argumentative texts in a variety of academic and professional disciplines, such as essays, proposals, videos, images, and multimedia.

   Matched Outcomes

   a. Demonstrate critical thinking skills.

2. Evaluate the strength of rhetorical strategies within argumentative texts.

   Matched Outcomes

   a. Demonstrate critical thinking skills.

3. Make effective choices regarding the formulation of claims and explanation of reasoning in creating a range of argumentative texts such as academic essays, presentations, informal writing, and Web-based genres.

   Matched Outcomes

   a. Write a competent academic argumentative essay.

4. Make effective use of rhetorical strategies in creating a range of argumentative texts such as academic essays, presentations, informal writing, and Web-based genres.

Matched Outcomes

a. Write a competent academic argumentative essay.

5. Discover and incorporate evidence from a variety of relevant, credible sources, using MLA or APA formatting when constructing argumentative texts.

   Chapter 27, Evaluating sources
   Chapter 31, Integrating sources (MLA)
   Chapter 33, MLA documentation style
   Chapter 37, Integrating sources (APA)
   Chapter 38, APA documentation style

   Matched Outcomes

   a. Write a competent academic argumentative essay.

6. Demonstrate audience-awareness through appropriate language, evidence, and other rhetorical choices in creating arguments and argumentative texts.

   Chapter 9, Appropriate voice
   Chapter 29, Supporting a thesis (MLA)
   Chapter 35, Supporting a thesis (APA)

   Matched Outcomes

   a. Write a competent academic argumentative essay.

7. Engage meaningfully with multiple perspectives and counterarguments in creating arguments and argumentative texts.

   Section 29c, Using sources to inform and support your argument
   Section 31c, Synthesizing sources

   Matched Outcomes

   a. Write a competent academic argumentative essay.

WCC5 The Writing Center

LA 355
(734) 973-3647

If you need help with any kind of writing, the Writing Center (LA 355) is the place to visit. The Writing Center has friendly and knowledgeable instructors and tutors on duty who are happy to help you out. Tutoring is free and available on a walk-in basis, and the hours of operation are extensive. Visit us soon!

You can find the Writing Center on Facebook at **www.facebook.com/thewritingcenter**; on YouTube at www.youtube.com/user/wccwritingcenter; and from the WCC home page by typing "Writing Center" in the search box.

WCC5-a For WCC Students Enrolled in ENG 000: Writing Center

A special welcome to you! You are the Writing Center's biggest customers! Because you're enrolled in one of the following writing courses—ENG 050, ENG 051, ENG 090, ENG 091, ENG 100, or ENG 111—you have a required Writing Center (ENG 000) component consisting of a series of writing assignments that will count as 25 percent of your final grade in your writing course.

WCC5-b Getting Started in ENG 000: Writing Center

■ 1. Come to the Writing Center during the first week of the semester for orientation.

■ 2. Listen to the orientation presentation and read this brief introduction to the Writing Center.

■ 3. Complete the orientation assignment and have it checked by a Writing Center staff member.

■ 4. Buy the Writing Center workbook for your writing course—ENG 050, ENG 051, ENG 090, ENG 091, ENG 100, or ENG 111. These workbooks are available at the WCC Bookstore on the first floor of the Student Center building.

■ 5. Note your Writing Center assignment deadlines.

WCC5-c Things We'd Like You to Know about ENG 000: Writing Center

■ 1. You're welcome in the Writing Center any time that it is open.

■ 2. You may complete your Writing Center assignments at home or in the Writing Center.

■ 3. You must have your Writing Center assignments checked by the Writing Center on or before the deadline dates. You can work ahead as fast as you want; some students complete all of their assignments by midterm.

■ 4. We recommend that, instead of making a special trip to campus just for Writing Center, you come to get your assignments checked on a day when you're already on campus for class—as long as you meet or beat your deadline dates.

■ 5. Please bring hard copies of your writing assignments to the Writing Center. It is difficult for instructors or tutors to help you if your writing is on your laptop. If this is the case, the best we can do is offer you suggestions on a sheet of paper. Instructors and tutors cannot type on your laptop for you or tell you what to type on your laptop.

■ 6. Late Writing Center assignments will not be accepted. If you have a late assignment, talk with your writing course instructor.

■ 7. Beware of bringing in an assignment less than a half hour before closing time. A half hour may not be sufficient time to check your assignment.

■ 8. Your Writing Center assignments are graded pass/fail and count as 25 percent of your final grade in your writing course. Your instructor receives frequent updates on your progress.

■ 9. Some Writing Center assignments must be typed. You may use the computer lab in LA 354 if a class is not in session there.

■ 10. If there is a line, you're limited to fifteen minutes with a Writing Center staff member who is helping you.

■ 11. At the Writing Center, instructors and tutors are committed to providing friendly, compassionate, and knowledgeable support that will help you become a better writer.

WCC5-c How to Pass Assignments in ENG 000: Writing Center

■ 1. Be aware of your assignment deadlines.

■ 2. Follow the directions in your Writing Center workbook and write the best you can.

■ 3. Fill out the cover sheets for assignments legibly and accurately—including your name, your instructor's name, your writing course section number, and the date.

■ 4. Make sure you have completed all of the items on the assignment checklist.

■ 5. When you come to have an assignment checked, bring your Writing Center workbook.

■ 6. When you pass an assignment, we tear the completed cover sheet out of your Writing Center workbook and file it. We also sign your checklist sheet, which you keep.

■ 7. If you don't pass an assignment, don't worry. We'll tell you what to fix and how you might want to fix it. Remember, though, your revised work must still be checked on or before the deadline date.

■ 8. Ask questions. Talk with the Writing Center staff member who is checking your work. All instructors and tutors at the Writing Center want you to succeed.

WCC6 Venues for the Literary Arts

WCC6-a The Huron Review

WCC's Literature and Arts Magazine
Winner of 54 National and Regional Awards Since 2002

Open to submissions of poetry, fiction, nonfiction, artwork, and photography from September through January.

Contact Information
E-mail: hrr@wccnet.edu
Web: thehuronriverreview.wordpress.com

WCC6-b The Big Windows Review

The WCC Writing Center's
Web Zine of the Beautiful and the Strange

Contact Information
E-mail: orange@wccnet.edu
Web: thebigwindowsreview.wordpress.com

WCC6-c WCC Poetry Club

Meetings are poetry workshops held in the Writing Center (LA 355) on Fridays at 5:00 p.m. during the fall and winter and on Fridays at 1:00 p.m. during the spring and summer.

Contact Information
E-mail: tzman@wccnet.edu
Web: wccpoetryclub.wordpress.com/

WCC7 Notes

A Pocket Style Manual

A Pocket Style Manual

Sixth Edition

Diana Hacker

Nancy Sommers
Harvard University

Contributing ESL Specialist
Marcy Carbajal Van Horn
St. Edward's University

Bedford/St. Martin's
Boston ◆ New York

For Bedford/St. Martin's

Executive Editor: Michelle M. Clark
Senior Editors: Mara Weible and Barbara G. Flanagan
Production Editors: Lindsay DiGianvittorio and Rosemary Jaffe
Senior Production Supervisor: Jennifer Peterson
Production Assistant: Laura Winstead
Senior Marketing Manager: Marjorie Adler
Editorial Assistant: Kylie Paul
Copyeditor: Linda McLatchie
Indexer: Ellen Kuhl Repetto
Permissions Manager: Kalina K. Ingham
Senior Art Director: Anna Palchik
Text Design: Claire Seng-Niemoeller
Cover Design: Donna Lee Dennison
Composition: Nesbitt Graphics, Inc.
Printing and Binding: Quad/Graphics Leominster

President: Joan E. Feinberg
Editorial Director: Denise B. Wydra
Editor in Chief: Karen S. Henry
Director of Marketing: Karen R. Soeltz
Director of Production: Susan W. Brown
Associate Director, Editorial Production: Elise S. Kaiser
Managing Editor: Elizabeth M. Schaaf

Library of Congress Control Number: 2011932253

Copyright © 2012, 2008, 2004, 2000 by Bedford/St. Martin's

All rights reserved. No part of this book may be reproduced, stored in a retrieval system, or transmitted in any form or by any means, electronic, mechanical, photocopying, recording, or otherwise, except as may be expressly permitted by the applicable copyright statutes or in writing by the Publisher.

Manufactured in the United States of America.

6   5   4   3   2
g   f   e   d   c

Distributed outside North America by PALGRAVE MACMILLAN, Houndmills, Basingstoke, Hampshire RG21 6XS

For information, write: Bedford/St. Martin's, 75 Arlington Street, Boston, MA 02116 (617-399-4000)

ISBN: 978-0-312-54254-2

Acknowledgments

Acknowledgments and copyrights can be found at the back of the book on page 278, which constitutes an extension of the copyright page. It is a violation of the law to reproduce these selections by any means whatsoever without the written permission of the copyright holder.

How to use this book

A Pocket Style Manual is a quick reference for writers and researchers. As a writer, you can turn to it for advice on revising sentences for clarity, grammar, punctuation, and mechanics. As a researcher, you can refer to its tips on finding and evaluating sources and to its color-coded sections on writing MLA, APA, *Chicago*, and CSE papers.

Here are the book's key reference features.

The brief or detailed contents The brief table of contents inside the front cover can help you identify broad areas of helpful coverage. To target specific sections, check the detailed contents inside the back cover.

The index If you're not sure which topic to choose from the tables of contents, check the index at the back of the book, which includes user-friendly terms like "*I* vs. *me*" to point to common problems like pronoun case.

Charts and checklists If you need quick advice on revising a draft or preparing for a writing center visit, you can find key strategies for improving your writing in the charts and checklists throughout the book and at the end of the book, after the index.

MLA, APA, *Chicago*, and CSE papers Color-coded sections help you focus on the kind of research paper you are writing. You can refer to discipline-specific advice on supporting a thesis, avoiding plagiarism, and integrating sources in MLA, APA, and *Chicago* styles. Directories to documentation models in MLA, APA, *Chicago*, and CSE styles appear on the first pages of each section and in the back of the book.

The glossaries When in doubt about the correct use of commonly confused or misused words (such as *affect* and *effect*), consult section 47, the glossary of usage. For brief definitions of grammatical terms such as *subordinate clause* or *participial phrase*, turn to section 48.

Web references Check the bottoms of pages for references to practice exercises or complete model papers on the book's companion Web site (hackerhandbooks.com/pocket). See the next page for more about these free online resources.

How to use the companion Web site

Throughout *A Pocket Style Manual*, you'll find references to models, practice exercises, and additional support at **hackerhandbooks.com/pocket**. The resources listed here are free.

Exercises Practice online with more than 1,400 interactive grammar and research exercise items with immediate feedback. Unique research exercises help you integrate and document sources and avoid plagiarism.

Model papers More than thirty models of student writing in five documentation styles provide cross-curricular examples of writing and formatting various types of documents. Model papers are listed by genre and by documentation style.

Revision Check out papers in progress and models of global and sentence-level revisions.

Research and Documentation Online Consult guidelines and models for finding and documenting sources in more than thirty academic disciplines.

Multilingual writers and ESL Check out charts, study help, sample papers, and exercises designed for writers who speak languages in addition to English.

Writing center resources Make the most of your writing center sessions with revision checklists and helpsheets for common writing, grammar, and research problems.

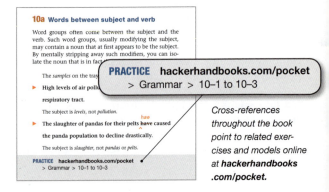

*Cross-references throughout the book point to related exercises and models online at **hackerhandbooks.com/pocket**.*

Clarity

1 Wordy sentences 2
2 Active verbs 3
3 Parallelism 5
4 Needed words 6
5 Shifts 8
6 Mixed constructions 9
7 Misplaced and dangling modifiers 10
8 Sentence variety 13
9 Appropriate voice 15

1 Tighten wordy sentences.

Long sentences are not necessarily wordy, nor are short sentences always concise. A sentence is wordy if it can be tightened without loss of meaning.

1a Redundancies

Redundancies such as *cooperate together*, *yellow in color*, and *basic essentials* are a common source of wordiness. There is no need to say the same thing twice.

▶ Daniel ~~is employed~~ **works** at a private rehabilitation center ~~working~~ as a physical therapist.

Modifiers are redundant when their meanings are suggested by other words in the sentence.

▶ Sylvia ~~very hurriedly~~ scribbled her name and phone number on the back of a greasy napkin.

1b Empty or inflated phrases

An empty word or phrase can be cut with little or no loss of meaning. An inflated phrase can be reduced to a word or two.

▶ ~~In my opinion,~~ **O**ur current immigration policy is misguided.

▶ Funds are limited ~~at this point in time~~ **now.**

INFLATED	CONCISE
along the lines of	like
at the present time	now, currently
because of the fact that	because
by means of	by
due to the fact that	because
for the reason that	because
in order to	to
in spite of the fact that	although, though

PRACTICE hackerhandbooks.com/pocket
> Clarity > 1–1 to 1–4

INFLATED	CONCISE
in the event that	if
until such time as	until

1c Needlessly complex structures

In a rough draft, sentence structures are often more complex than they need to be.

▶ Researchers ~~were involved in~~ examined ~~examining~~ the effect of classical music on unborn babies.

▶ ~~It is imperative that~~ All night managers must follow strict procedures when locking the safe.

▶ The analyst claimed that because of volatile market conditions she could not ~~make an~~ estimate ~~of~~ the company's future profits.

2 Prefer active verbs.

As a rule, active verbs express meaning more vigorously than their weaker counterparts — forms of the verb *be* or verbs in the passive voice. Forms of *be* (*be, am, is, are, was, were, being, been*) lack vigor because they convey no action. Passive verbs lack strength because their subjects receive the action instead of doing it.

Forms of *be* and passive verbs have legitimate uses, but if an active verb can convey your meaning as effectively, use it.

BE VERB	A surge of power *was* responsible for the destruction of the pumps.
PASSIVE	The pumps *were destroyed* by a surge of power.
ACTIVE	A surge of power *destroyed* the pumps.

2a When to replace *be* verbs

Not every *be* verb needs replacing. The forms of *be* (*be, am, is, are, was, were, being, been*) work well when you want to link a subject to a noun that clearly renames it or to

PRACTICE hackerhandbooks.com/pocket
> Clarity > 2–1 to 2–4

a vivid adjective that describes it: *Orchard House was the home of Louisa May Alcott. The harvest will be bountiful after the summer rains.*

If a *be* verb makes a sentence needlessly wordy, however, consider replacing it. Often a phrase following the verb will contain a word (such as *violation*) that suggests a more vigorous, active verb (*violate*).

▶ Burying nuclear waste in Antarctica would ~~be in violation of~~ *violate* an international treaty.

▶ When Rosa Parks ~~was resistant to~~ *resisted* giving up her seat on the bus, she became a civil rights hero.

NOTE: When used as helping verbs with present participles to express ongoing action, *be* verbs are fine: *She was swimming when the whistle blew.* (See 11b.)

2b When to replace passive verbs

In the active voice, the subject of the sentence does the action; in the passive, the subject receives the action.

ACTIVE   The committee *reached* a decision.

PASSIVE   A decision *was reached* by the committee.

In passive sentences, the actor (in this case *committee*) frequently does not appear: *A decision was reached.*

In most cases, you will want to emphasize the actor, so you should use the active voice. To replace a passive verb with an active one, make the actor the subject of the sentence.

▶ ~~The~~ *The contractor removed the* debris ~~was removed~~ from the construction site.

▶ ~~The land was stripped of timber before the settlers realized~~ *The settlers stripped the land of timber before realizing* the consequences of their actions.

The passive voice is appropriate when you wish to emphasize the receiver of the action or to minimize the importance of the actor. In the following sentence, for example, the writer wished to focus on the tobacco plants, not on the people spraying them: *As the time for harvest approaches, the tobacco plants are sprayed with a chemical to retard the growth of suckers.*

NOTE: Scientific writing often uses the passive voice to emphasize the experiment or the process rather than the researcher: *The solution was heated to the boiling point and then reduced in volume by 50 percent.*

3 Balance parallel ideas.

If two or more ideas are parallel, they should be expressed in parallel grammatical form.

A kiss can be a comma, a question mark, or an exclamation point. —Mistinguett

This novel is not to be tossed lightly aside, but to be hurled with great force. —Dorothy Parker

3a Items in a series

Balance all items in a series by presenting them in parallel grammatical form.

▶ Cross-training involves a variety of exercises, such as running, swimming, and *lifting* weights.

▶ Children who study music also learn confidence, discipline, and *creativity.* ~~they are creative.~~

▶ Racing to work, Sam drove down the middle of the road, ran one red light, and *ignored* two stop signs.

3b Paired ideas

When pairing ideas, underscore their connection by expressing them in similar grammatical form. Paired ideas are usually connected in one of three ways: (1) with a

PRACTICE hackerhandbooks.com/pocket
> Clarity > 3–1 to 3–4

coordinating conjunction such as *and*, *but*, or *or;* (2) with a pair of correlative conjunctions such as *either . . . or*, *neither . . . nor*, *not only . . . but also*, or *whether . . . or;* or (3) with a word introducing a comparison, usually *than* or *as*.

▶ Many states are reducing property taxes for home owners and ~~extend~~ ^extending^ financial aid in the form of tax credits to renters.

The coordinating conjunction *and* connects two *-ing* verb forms: *reducing . . . extending*.

▶ Thomas Edison was not only a prolific inventor but also ~~was~~ a successful entrepreneur.

The correlative conjunction *not only . . . but also* connects two noun phrases: *a prolific inventor* and *a successful entrepreneur*.

▶ It is easier to speak in abstractions than ~~grounding~~ ^to ground^ one's thoughts in reality.

The comparative term *than* links two infinitive phrases: *to speak . . . to ground*.

NOTE: Repeat function words such as prepositions (*by, to*) and subordinating conjunctions (*that, because*) to make parallel ideas easier to grasp.

▶ Our study revealed that left-handed students were more likely to have trouble with classroom desks and ^that^ rearranging desks for exam periods was useful.

4 Add needed words.

Do not omit words necessary for grammatical or logical completeness. Readers need to see at a glance how the parts of a sentence are connected.

4a Words in compound structures

In compound structures, words are often omitted for economy: *Tom is a man who means what he says and [who]*

PRACTICE hackerhandbooks.com/pocket
> Clarity > 4–1 to 4–3

says what he means. Such omissions are acceptable as long as the omitted word is common to both parts of the compound structure.

If a sentence defies grammar or idiom because an omitted word is not common to both parts of the compound structure, the word must be put back in.

▶ Some of the regulars are acquaintances whom we
  who
  see at work or live in our community.

  The word *who* must be included because *whom live in our community* is not grammatically correct.

▶ Mayor Davidson never has and never will accept a
       accepted
  bribe.

  Has . . . accept is not grammatically correct.

▶ Many South Pacific tribes still believe and live by
                                       in
  ancient laws.

  Believe . . . by is not idiomatic English.

4b The word *that*

Add the word *that* if there is any danger of misreading without it.

▶ In his obedience experiments, psychologist Stanley
                    that
  Milgram discovered ordinary people were willing to
  inflict physical pain on strangers.

  Milgram didn't discover people; he discovered that people were willing to inflict pain on strangers.

4c Words in comparisons

Comparisons should be between items that are alike. To compare unlike items is illogical and distracting.

▶ The forests of North America are much more
               those of
  extensive than Europe.

Comparisons should be complete so that readers will understand what is being compared.

INCOMPLETE   Brand X is less salty.

COMPLETE   Brand X is less salty than Brand Y.

Also, comparisons should leave no ambiguity about meaning. In the following sentence, two interpretations are possible.

AMBIGUOUS   Kai helped me more than my roommate.

CLEAR   Kai helped me more than *he helped* my roommate.

CLEAR   Kai helped me more than my roommate *did*.

5   Eliminate confusing shifts.

5a Shifts in point of view

The point of view of a piece of writing is the perspective from which it is written: first person (*I* or *we*), second person (*you*), or third person (*he, she, it, one,* or *they*). The *I* (or *we*) point of view, which emphasizes the writer, is a good choice for writing based primarily on personal experience. The *you* point of view, which emphasizes the reader, works well for giving advice or explaining how to do something. The third-person point of view, which emphasizes the subject, is appropriate in most academic and professional writing.

Writers who are having difficulty settling on an appropriate point of view sometimes shift confusingly from one to another. The solution is to choose a suitable perspective and then stay with it. (See also 12a.)

▶ Our class practiced rescuing a victim trapped in a wrecked car. ~~You~~ *We* were graded on ~~your~~ *our* speed and ~~your~~ *our* skill.

▶ ~~Travelers~~ *You* need a signed passport for trips abroad. You should also fill out the emergency information page in the passport.

PRACTICE   hackerhandbooks.com/pocket
> Clarity > 5–1 to 5–5

5b Shifts in tense

Consistent verb tenses clearly establish the time of the actions being described. When a passage begins in one tense and then shifts without warning and for no reason to another, readers are distracted and confused.

▶ There was no way I could fight the current and win. Just as I was losing hope, a stranger ~~jumps~~ *jumped* off a passing boat and ~~swims~~ *swam* toward me.

Writers often shift verb tenses when writing about literature. The literary convention is to describe fictional events consistently in the present tense. (See p. 29.)

6 Untangle mixed constructions.

A mixed construction contains sentence parts that do not sensibly fit together. The mismatch may be a matter of grammar or of logic.

6a Mixed grammar

You should not begin with one grammatical plan and then switch without warning to another.

▶ ~~For~~ *M*ost drivers who have a blood alcohol level of .05 percent increase their risk of causing an accident.

The prepositional phrase beginning with *For* cannot serve as the subject of the verb *increase*. The revision makes *drivers* the subject.

▶ Although the United States is a wealthy nation, ~~but~~ more than 20 percent of our children live in poverty.

The coordinating conjunction *but* cannot link a subordinate clause (*Although . . .*) with an independent clause (*more than 20 percent . . .*).

PRACTICE hackerhandbooks.com/pocket
> Clarity > 6–1 to 6–3

6b Illogical connections

A sentence's subject and verb should make sense together.

▶ Under the revised plan, ~~the elderly, who now receive a double personal exemption,~~ ^the double personal exemption for the elderly^ will be abolished.

The exemption, not the elderly, will be abolished.

▶ We decided that ~~Tiffany's welfare~~ ^Tiffany^ would not be safe living with her mother.

Tiffany, not her welfare, would not be safe.

6c *Is when, is where,* and *reason . . . is because* constructions

In formal English, readers sometimes object to *is when, is where,* and *reason . . . is because* constructions on grammatical or logical grounds.

▶ Anorexia nervosa is ~~where people~~ ^a disorder suffered by people who^ think they are too fat and diet to the point of starvation.

Anorexia nervosa is a disorder, not a place.

▶ ~~The reason~~ ^T^he experiment failed ~~is~~ because conditions in the lab were not sterile.

7 Repair misplaced and dangling modifiers.

Modifiers should point clearly to the words they modify. As a rule, related words should be kept together.

7a Misplaced words

The most commonly misplaced words are limiting modifiers such as *only, even, almost, nearly,* and *just.* They

PRACTICE hackerhandbooks.com/pocket
> Clarity > 7–1 to 7–6

should appear in front of a verb only if they modify the verb. If they limit the meaning of some other word in the sentence, they should be placed in front of that word.

▶ Lasers ~~only~~ *only* destroy the target, leaving the surrounding healthy tissue intact.

▶ I couldn't ~~even~~ *even* save a dollar out of my paycheck.

When the limiting modifier *not* is misplaced, the sentence usually suggests a meaning the writer did not intend.

▶ In the United States in 1860, all black southerners *not* were ~~not~~ slaves.

The original sentence means that no black southerners were slaves. The revision makes the writer's real meaning clear.

7b Misplaced phrases and clauses

Although phrases and clauses can appear at some distance from the words they modify, make sure your meaning is clear. When phrases or clauses are oddly placed, absurd misreadings can result.

▶ *On the walls* ~~There~~ are many pictures of comedians who have performed at Gavin's. ~~on the walls.~~

The comedians weren't performing on the walls; the pictures were on the walls.

▶ The robber was described as a six-foot-tall man *170-pound,* with a mustache. ~~weighing 170 pounds.~~

The robber, not the mustache, weighed 170 pounds.

7c Dangling modifiers

A dangling modifier fails to refer logically to any word in the sentence. Dangling modifiers are usually introductory word groups (such as verbal phrases) that suggest but do not name an actor. When a sentence opens with such a modifier, readers expect the subject of the next clause to name the actor. If it doesn't, the modifier dangles.

DANGLING   Upon entering the doctor's office, a skeleton caught my attention.

This sentence suggests — absurdly — that the skeleton entered the doctor's office.

To repair a dangling modifier, you can revise the sentence in one of two ways:

1. Name the actor in the subject of the sentence.
2. Name the actor in the modifier.

▶ Upon entering the doctor's office, a skeleton ~~caught my attention~~. *I noticed*

▶ ~~Upon entering~~ *As I entered* the doctor's office, a skeleton caught my attention.

You cannot repair a dangling modifier simply by moving it: *A skeleton caught my attention upon entering the doctor's office.* The sentence still suggests that the skeleton entered the doctor's office.

▶ Wanting to create checks and balances on power, *the framers of* the Constitution divided the government into three branches.

The framers (not the Constitution itself) wanted to create checks and balances.

▶ After completing seminary training, ~~women's~~ *women were often denied* access to the priesthood. ~~was often denied.~~

The women (not their access to the priesthood) completed the training. The writer has revised the sentence by making *women* (not *women's access*) the subject.

7d Split infinitives

An infinitive consists of *to* plus a verb: *to think, to dance.* When a modifier appears between its two parts, an infinitive is said to be "split": *to carefully balance.* If a split infinitive is awkward, move the modifier to another position in the sentence.

▶ Cardiologists encourage their patients to ~~more carefully~~ watch their cholesterol levels ⌃*more carefully*.

Attempts to avoid split infinitives sometimes result in awkward sentences. When alternative phrasing sounds unnatural, most experts allow — and even encourage — splitting the infinitive. *We decided to actually enforce the law* is a natural construction in English. *We decided actually to enforce the law* is not.

8 Provide sentence variety.

When a rough draft is filled with too many same-sounding sentences, try to inject some variety — as long as you can do so without sacrificing clarity or ease of reading.

8a Combining choppy sentences

If a series of short sentences sounds choppy, consider combining sentences. Look for opportunities to tuck some of your ideas into subordinate clauses. A subordinate clause, which contains a subject and a verb, begins with a word such as *after, although, because, before, if, since, that, unless, until, when, where, which,* or *who.* (See p. 276.)

▶ We keep our use of insecticides to a minimum⌃ *because we* ~~We~~ are concerned about the environment.

Also look for opportunities to tuck some of your ideas into phrases, word groups without subjects or verbs (or both).

▶ The Chesapeake and Ohio Canal⌃, ~~is~~ a 184-mile waterway constructed in the 1800s⌃, ~~It~~ was a major source of transportation for goods during the Civil War.

PRACTICE hackerhandbooks.com/pocket
> Clarity > 8–1 to 8–3

> ~~Sister Consilio was enveloped~~ *Enveloped* in a black robe with only her face and hands visible~~.~~*,* ~~She~~ *Sister Consilio* was an imposing figure.

When short sentences contain ideas of equal importance, it is often effective to combine them with *and*, *but*, or *or*.

> Shore houses were flooded up to the first floor~~.~~*, and* Brant's Lighthouse was swallowed by the sea.

8b Varying sentence openings

Most sentences in English begin with the subject, move to the verb, and continue to an object, with modifiers tucked in along the way or put at the end. For the most part, such sentences are fine. Put too many of them in a row, however, and they become monotonous.

Words, phrases, or clauses modifying the verb can often be inserted ahead of the subject.

> ~~A~~ *Eventually a* few drops of sap ~~eventually~~ began to trickle into the pail.

> ~~A~~ *Just as the sun was coming up, a* pair of black ducks flew over the pond~~.~~ ~~just as the sun was coming up.~~

Participial phrases (beginning with verb forms such as *driving* or *exhausted*) can frequently be moved to the beginning of a sentence without loss of clarity.

> ~~The committee,~~ *D*iscouraged by the researchers' apparent lack of progress, *the committee* nearly withdrew funding for the prize-winning experiments.

NOTE: In a sentence that begins with a participial phrase, the subject of the sentence must name the person or thing being described. If it doesn't, the phrase dangles. (See 7c.)

sentence openings • same-sounding sentences • plain language • avoiding jargon

9 Find an appropriate voice.

An appropriate voice is one that suits your subject, engages your audience, and conforms to the conventions of the genre in which you are writing, such as lab reports, informal essays, research papers, business memos, and so on.

In academic and professional writing, certain language is generally considered inappropriate: jargon, clichés, slang, and sexist or biased language.

9a Jargon

Jargon is specialized language used among members of a trade, profession, or group. Use jargon only when readers will be familiar with it; even then, use it only when plain English will not do as well.

JARGON We outsourced the work to an outfit in Ohio because we didn't have the bandwidth to tackle it in-house.

REVISED We hired a company in Ohio because we had too few employees to do the work.

Broadly defined, jargon includes puffed-up language designed more to impress readers than to inform them. The following are common examples from business, government, higher education, and the military, with plain English translations in parentheses.

commence (begin)	indicator (sign)
components (parts)	optimal (best)
endeavor (try)	parameters (boundaries, limits)
facilitate (help)	prior to (before)
finalize (finish)	utilize (use)
impact (v.) (affect)	viable (workable)

Sentences filled with jargon are hard to read and often wordy.

▶ The CEO should ~~dialogue~~ *talk* with investors about ~~partnering~~ *working* with clients to buy land in ~~economically deprived zones.~~ *poor neighborhoods.*

PRACTICE hackerhandbooks.com/pocket
> Clarity > 9–1 to 9–4

▶ All ~~employees functioning in the capacity of~~ work-study students ~~are required to give evidence of current enrollment.~~ *must prove that they are currently enrolled.*

9b Clichés

The pioneer who first announced that he had "slept like a log" no doubt amused his companions with a fresh and unlikely comparison. Today, however, that comparison is a cliché, a saying that can no longer add emphasis or surprise. To see just how predictable clichés are, put your hand over the right-hand column below and then finish the phrases given on the left.

cool as a	cucumber
beat around the	bush
busy as a	bee, beaver
crystal	clear
light as a	feather
like a bull	in a china shop
playing with	fire
nutty as a	fruitcake
selling like	hotcakes
water under the	bridge
white as a	sheet, ghost
avoid clichés like the	plague

The solution for clichés is simple: Just delete them. Sometimes you can write around a cliché by adding an element of surprise. One student who had written that she had butterflies in her stomach revised her cliché like this:

> If all of the action in my stomach is caused by butterflies, there must be a horde of them, with horseshoes on.

The image of butterflies wearing horseshoes is fresh and unlikely, not predictable like the original cliché.

9c Slang

Slang is an informal and sometimes private vocabulary that expresses the solidarity of a group such as teenagers, rock musicians, or sports fans. Although it does have a certain vitality, slang is a code that not everyone understands, and it is too informal for most written work.

> When the server crashed, three hours of unsaved data ~~went down the tubes.~~ *we lost*

9d Sexist language

Sexist language excludes, stereotypes, or demeans women or men and should be avoided.

In your writing, avoid referring to any one profession as exclusively male or exclusively female (teachers as women or engineers as men, for example). Also avoid using different conventions when identifying women and men.

> All executives' ~~wives~~ *spouses* are invited to the picnic.

> Boris Stotsky, attorney, and ~~Mrs.~~ Cynthia Jones, *graphic designer,* ~~mother of three,~~ are running for city council.

Traditionally, *he*, *him*, and *his* were used to refer generically to persons of either sex: *A journalist is motivated by his deadline.* You can avoid such sexist usage in one of three ways: substitute a pair of pronouns (*he or she*, *his or her*); reword in the plural; or revise the sentence to avoid the problem.

> A journalist is motivated by his *or her* deadline.

> *Journalists are* ~~A journalist is~~ motivated by ~~his deadline.~~ *their deadlines.*

> A journalist is motivated by ~~his~~ *a* deadline.

Like *he* and *his*, the nouns *man* and *men* and related words were once used generically to refer to persons of either sex. Use gender-neutral terms instead.

INAPPROPRIATE	APPROPRIATE
chairman	chairperson, chair
congressman	representative, legislator
fireman	firefighter
mailman	mail carrier, postal worker
mankind	people, humans
to man	to operate, to staff
weatherman	meteorologist, forecaster

9e Offensive language

Obviously it is impolite to use offensive terms such as *Polack* or *redneck*, but offensive language can take more subtle forms. When describing groups of people, choose names that the groups currently use to describe themselves.

▶ North Dakota takes its name from the ~~Indian~~ *Lakota* word meaning "friend" or "ally."

▶ Many ~~Oriental~~ *Asian* immigrants have recently settled in our small town.

Avoid stereotyping a person or a group even if you believe your generalization to be positive.

▶ It was no surprise that Greer, ~~a Chinese American,~~ *an excellent math and science student,* was selected for the honors chemistry program.

Grammar

10 Subject-verb agreement 20
11 Other problems with verbs 24
12 Pronouns 30
13 Adjectives and adverbs 38
14 Sentence fragments 40
15 Run-on sentences 42
16 Grammar concerns for multilingual writers 45

10 Make subjects and verbs agree.

In the present tense, verbs agree with their subjects in number (singular or plural) and in person (first, second, or third). The present-tense ending *-s* is used on a verb if its subject is third-person singular; otherwise the verb takes no ending. Consider, for example, the present-tense forms of the verb *give*:

	SINGULAR	PLURAL
FIRST PERSON	I give	we give
SECOND PERSON	you give	you give
THIRD PERSON	he/she/it gives	they give
	Yolanda gives	parents give

The verb *be* varies from this pattern; it has special forms in *both* the present and the past tense.

PRESENT-TENSE FORMS OF *BE*		PAST-TENSE FORMS OF *BE*	
I am	we are	I was	we were
you are	you are	you were	you were
he/she/it is	they are	he/she/it was	they were

This section describes particular situations that can cause problems with subject-verb agreement.

10a Words between subject and verb

Word groups often come between the subject and the verb. Such word groups, usually modifying the subject, may contain a noun that at first appears to be the subject. By mentally stripping away such modifiers, you can isolate the noun that is in fact the subject.

The *samples* on the tray in the lab *need* testing.

▶ High levels of air pollution damages̸ the respiratory tract.

The subject is *levels*, not *pollution*.

▶ The slaughter of pandas for their pelts ~~have~~ *has* caused the panda population to decline drastically.

The subject is *slaughter*, not *pandas* or *pelts*.

PRACTICE hackerhandbooks.com/pocket
> Grammar > 10–1 to 10–3

NOTE: Phrases beginning with the prepositions *as well as, in addition to, accompanied by, together with,* and *along with* do not make a singular subject plural: *The governor as well as his aide was* [not *were*] *on the plane.*

10b Subjects joined with *and*

Compound subjects joined with *and* are nearly always plural.

▶ Bleach and ammonia create~~s~~ a toxic gas when mixed.

EXCEPTION: If the parts of the subject form a single unit, you may treat the subject as singular: *Bacon and eggs is always on the menu.*

10c Subjects joined with *or* or *nor*

With compound subjects joined with *or* or *nor*, make the verb agree with the part of the subject nearer to the verb.

▶ If an infant or a child ~~are~~ *is* having difficulty breathing, seek medical attention immediately.

▶ Neither the lab assistant nor the students ~~was~~ *were* able to download the program.

10d Indefinite pronouns such as *someone*

Indefinite pronouns refer to nonspecific persons or things. The following indefinite pronouns are singular: *anybody, anyone, anything, each, either, everybody, everyone, everything, neither, nobody, no one, somebody, someone, something.*

▶ Nobody who participated in the taste tests ~~were~~ *was* paid.

▶ Each of the essays ~~have~~ *has* been graded.

A few indefinite pronouns (*all, any, none, some*) may be singular or plural depending on the noun or pronoun they refer to: *Some of our luggage was lost. Some of the rocks were slippery. None of his advice makes sense. None of the eggs were broken.*

10e Collective nouns such as *jury*

Collective nouns such as *jury*, *committee*, *audience*, *crowd*, *class*, *family*, and *couple* name a class or a group. In American English, collective nouns are usually treated as singular: They emphasize the group as a unit.

▶ The board of trustees ~~meet~~ *meets* in Denver twice a year.

Occasionally, to draw attention to the individual members of the group, a collective noun may be treated as plural: *The class are debating among themselves.* Many writers prefer to add a clearly plural noun such as *members*: *The class members are debating among themselves.*

NOTE: In general, when fractions or units of measurement are used with a singular noun, treat them as singular; when they are used with a plural noun, treat them as plural: *Three-fourths of the pie has been eaten. One-fourth of the drivers were texting.*

10f Subject after verb

Verbs ordinarily follow subjects. When this normal order is reversed, it is easy to be confused.

▶ Of particular concern ~~is~~ *are* penicillin and tetracycline, antibiotics used to make animals more resistant to disease.

The subject, *penicillin and tetracycline*, is plural.

The subject always follows the verb in sentences beginning with *there is* or *there are* (or *there was* or *there were*).

▶ There ~~was~~ *were* a turtle and a snake in the tank.

The subject, *turtle and snake*, is plural, so the verb must be *were*.

10g *Who*, *which*, and *that*

Like most pronouns, the relative pronouns *who*, *which*, and *that* have antecedents, nouns or pronouns to which they refer. Relative pronouns used as subjects of subordinate clauses take verbs that agree with their antecedents.

Take a *train that arrives* before 6:00.

Constructions such as *one of the students who* (or *one of the things that*) may cause problems for writers. Do not assume that the antecedent must be *one*. Instead, consider the logic of the sentence.

▶ Our ability to use language is one of the things that ~~sets~~ *set* us apart from animals.

The antecedent of *that* is *things*, not *one*. Several things set us apart from animals.

When the phrase *the only* comes before *one*, you are safe in assuming that *one* is the antecedent of the relative pronoun.

▶ Carmen is the only one of my friends who ~~live~~ *lives* in my building.

The antecedent of *who* is *one*, not *friends*. Only one friend lives in the building.

10h Plural form, singular meaning

Words such as *athletics, economics, mathematics, physics, politics, statistics, measles,* and *news* are usually singular, despite their plural form.

▶ Politics ~~are~~ *is* among my mother's favorite pastimes.

EXCEPTION: Occasionally some of these words, especially *economics, mathematics, politics,* and *statistics,* have plural meanings: *Office politics often affect decisions about hiring and promotion. The economics of the building plan are prohibitive.*

10i Titles, company names, and words mentioned as words

Titles, company names, and words mentioned as words are singular.

▶ *Lost Cities* ~~describe~~ *describes* the discoveries of fifty ancient civilizations.

▶ Delmonico Brothers ~~specialize~~ *specializes* in organic produce and additive-free meats.

▶ *Controlled substances* ~~are~~ *is* a euphemism for illegal drugs.

11 Be alert to other problems with verbs.

Section 10 deals with subject-verb agreement. This section describes a few other potential problems with verbs.

11a Irregular verbs

For all regular verbs, the past-tense and past-participle forms are the same, ending in *-ed* or *-d*, so there is no danger of confusion. This is not true, however, for irregular verbs, such as the following.

BASE FORM	PAST TENSE	PAST PARTICIPLE
begin	began	begun
fly	flew	flown
ride	rode	ridden

The past-tense form, which never has a helping verb, expresses action that occurred entirely in the past. The past participle is used with a helping verb—either with *has, have,* or *had* to form one of the perfect tenses or with *be, am, is, are, was, were, being,* or *been* to form the passive voice.

| PAST TENSE | Last July, we *went* to Paris. |
| PAST PARTICIPLE | We have *gone* to Paris twice. |

When you aren't sure which verb form to choose (*went* or *gone, began* or *begun,* and so on), consult the list

---

PRACTICE hackerhandbooks.com/pocket
> Grammar > 11–1 to 11–6

that begins at the bottom of this page. Choose the past-tense form if your sentence doesn't have a helping verb; choose the past-participle form if it does.

▶ Yesterday we ~~seen~~ *saw* a film about rain forests.

Because there is no helping verb, the past-tense form *saw* is required.

▶ By the end of the day, the stock market had ~~fell~~ *fallen* two hundred points.

Because of the helping verb *had*, the past-participle form *fallen* is required.

Distinguishing between *lie* and *lay* Writers often confuse the forms of *lie* (meaning "to recline or rest on a surface") and *lay* (meaning "to put or place something"). The intransitive verb *lie* does not take a direct object: *The tax forms lie on the table*. The transitive verb *lay* takes a direct object: *Please lay the tax forms on the table*.

In addition to confusing the meanings of *lie* and *lay*, writers are often unfamiliar with the standard English forms of these verbs.

BASE FORM	PAST TENSE	PAST PARTICIPLE	PRESENT PARTICIPLE
lie	lay	lain	lying
lay	laid	laid	laying

Elizabeth was so exhausted that she *lay* down for a nap. [Past tense of *lie*, meaning "to recline"]

The prosecutor *laid* the photograph on a table close to the jurors. [Past tense of *lay*, meaning "to place"]

Letters dating from the Civil War were *lying* in the corner of the chest. [Present participle of *lie*]

The patient had *lain* in an uncomfortable position all night. [Past participle of *lie*]

Common irregular verbs

BASE FORM	PAST TENSE	PAST PARTICIPLE
arise	arose	arisen
awake	awoke, awaked	awaked, awoke
be	was, were	been

BASE FORM	PAST TENSE	PAST PARTICIPLE
beat	beat	beaten, beat
become	became	become
begin	began	begun
bend	bent	bent
bite	bit	bitten, bit
blow	blew	blown
break	broke	broken
bring	brought	brought
build	built	built
burst	burst	burst
buy	bought	bought
catch	caught	caught
choose	chose	chosen
cling	clung	clung
come	came	come
cost	cost	cost
deal	dealt	dealt
dig	dug	dug
dive	dived, dove	dived
do	did	done
draw	drew	drawn
dream	dreamed, dreamt	dreamed, dreamt
drink	drank	drunk
drive	drove	driven
eat	ate	eaten
fall	fell	fallen
fight	fought	fought
find	found	found
fly	flew	flown
forget	forgot	forgotten, forgot
freeze	froze	frozen
get	got	gotten, got
give	gave	given
go	went	gone
grow	grew	grown
hang (suspend)	hung	hung
hang (execute)	hanged	hanged
have	had	had
hear	heard	heard
hide	hid	hidden
hurt	hurt	hurt
keep	kept	kept
know	knew	known
lay (put)	laid	laid
lead	led	led
lend	lent	lent
let (allow)	let	let
lie (recline)	lay	lain

BASE FORM	PAST TENSE	PAST PARTICIPLE
lose	lost	lost
make	made	made
prove	proved	proved, proven
read	read	read
ride	rode	ridden
ring	rang	rung
rise (get up)	rose	risen
run	ran	run
say	said	said
see	saw	seen
send	sent	sent
set (place)	set	set
shake	shook	shaken
shoot	shot	shot
shrink	shrank	shrunk, shrunken
sing	sang	sung
sink	sank	sunk
sit (be seated)	sat	sat
slay	slew	slain
sleep	slept	slept
speak	spoke	spoken
spin	spun	spun
spring	sprang	sprung
stand	stood	stood
steal	stole	stolen
sting	stung	stung
strike	struck	struck, stricken
swear	swore	sworn
swim	swam	swum
swing	swung	swung
take	took	taken
teach	taught	taught
throw	threw	thrown
wake	woke, waked	waked, woken
wear	wore	worn
wring	wrung	wrung
write	wrote	written

11b Tense

Tenses indicate the time of an action in relation to the time of the speaking or writing about that action. The most common problem with tenses—shifting from one tense to another—is discussed in 5b. Other problems with tenses are detailed in this section, after the following survey of tenses.

Survey of tenses   Tenses are classified as present, past, and future, with simple, perfect, and progressive forms for each.

The simple tenses indicate relatively simple time relations. The *simple present* tense is used primarily for actions occurring at the time they are being discussed or for actions occurring regularly. The *simple past* tense is used for actions completed in the past. The *simple future* tense is used for actions that will occur in the future. In the following table, the simple tenses are given for the regular verb *walk*, the irregular verb *ride*, and the highly irregular verb *be*.

SIMPLE PRESENT

SINGULAR		PLURAL	
I	walk, ride, am	we	walk, ride, are
you	walk, ride, are	you	walk, ride, are
he/she/it	walks, rides, is	they	walk, ride, are

SIMPLE PAST

SINGULAR		PLURAL	
I	walked, rode, was	we	walked, rode, were
you	walked, rode, were	you	walked, rode, were
he/she/it	walked, rode, was	they	walked, rode, were

SIMPLE FUTURE

I, you, he/she/it, we, they	will walk, ride, be

A verb in one of the perfect tenses (a form of *have* plus the past participle) expresses an action that was or will be completed at the time of another action.

PRESENT PERFECT

I, you, we, they	have walked, ridden, been
he/she/it	has walked, ridden, been

PAST PERFECT

I, you, he/she/it, we, they	had walked, ridden, been

FUTURE PERFECT

I, you, he/she/it, we, they	will have walked, ridden, been

Each of the six tenses has a progressive form used to describe actions in progress. A progressive verb consists of a form of *be* followed by the present participle.

PRESENT PROGRESSIVE

I	am walking, riding, being
he/she/it	is walking, riding, being
you, we, they	are walking, riding, being

PAST PROGRESSIVE

I, he/she/it	was walking, riding, being
you, we, they	were walking, riding, being

FUTURE PROGRESSIVE

I, you, he/she/it, we, they	will be walking, riding, being

PRESENT PERFECT PROGRESSIVE

I, you, we, they	have been walking, riding, being
he/she/it	has been walking, riding, being

PAST PERFECT PROGRESSIVE

I, you, he/she/it, we, they	had been walking, riding, being

FUTURE PERFECT PROGRESSIVE

I, you, he/she/it, we, they	will have been walking, riding, being

Special uses of the present tense Use the present tense when writing about literature or when expressing general truths.

▶ The scarlet letter ~~was~~ *is* a punishment placed on Hester's breast by the community, and yet it ~~was~~ *is* an imaginative product of Hester's own needlework.

▶ Galileo taught that the earth ~~revolved~~ *revolves* around the sun.

The past perfect tense The past perfect tense is used for an action already completed by the time of another past action. This tense consists of a past participle preceded by *had* (*had worked, had gone*).

▶ We built our cabin forty feet above an abandoned quarry that ~~was~~ *had been* flooded in 1920 to create a lake.

▶ By the time dinner was served, the guest of honor *had* left.

11c Mood

There are three moods in English: the *indicative*, used for facts, opinions, and questions; the *imperative*, used for orders or advice; and the *subjunctive*, used to express wishes, requests, or conditions contrary to fact. For many writers, the subjunctive is especially challenging.

For wishes and in *if* clauses expressing conditions contrary to fact, the subjunctive is the past-tense form of the verb; in the case of *be*, it is always *were* (not *was*), even if the subject is singular.

> I wish that Jamal *drove* more slowly late at night.
>
> If I *were* a member of Congress, I would vote for the bill.

TIP: Do not use the subjunctive mood in *if* clauses expressing conditions that exist or may exist: *If Danielle passes* [not *passed*] *the test, she will become a lifeguard.*

Use the subjunctive mood in *that* clauses following verbs such as *ask, insist, recommend,* and *request*. The subjunctive in such cases is the base form of the verb.

> Dr. Chung insists that her students *be* on time.
>
> We recommend that Dawson *file* form 1050 soon.

12 Use pronouns with care.

Pronouns are words that substitute for nouns: *he, it, them, her, me,* and so on. Pronoun errors are typically related to the four topics discussed in this section:

a. pronoun-antecedent agreement (singular vs. plural)
b. pronoun reference (clarity)
c. pronoun case (personal pronouns such as *I* vs. *me*)
d. pronoun case (*who* vs. *whom*)

12a Pronoun-antecedent agreement

The antecedent of a pronoun is the word the pronoun refers to. A pronoun and its antecedent agree when they are both singular or both plural.

PRACTICE hackerhandbooks.com/pocket
> Grammar > 12–1 to 12–3

SINGULAR The *doctor* finished *her* rounds.

PLURAL The *doctors* finished *their* rounds.

Indefinite pronouns

Indefinite pronouns refer to non-specific persons or things. Even though some of the following indefinite pronouns may seem to have plural meanings, treat them as singular in formal English: *anybody, anyone, anything, each, either, everybody, everyone, everything, neither, nobody, no one, nothing, somebody, someone, something*.

> In this class *everyone* performs at *his or her* [not *their*] own fitness level.

When *they* or *their* refers mistakenly to a singular antecedent such as *everyone*, you will usually have three options for revision:

1. Replace *they* with *he or she* (or *their* with *his or her*).
2. Make the antecedent plural.
3. Rewrite the sentence to avoid the problem.

Because the *he or she* construction is wordy, often the second or third revision strategy is more effective.

▶ If anyone wants to audition, ~~they~~ *he or she* should sign up.

▶ If ~~anyone wants~~ *singers want* to audition, they should sign up.

▶ ~~If~~ *Anyone who* anyone wants to audition/ ~~they~~ should sign up.

NOTE: The traditional use of *he* (or *his*) to refer to persons of either sex is now widely considered sexist. (See p. 17.)

Generic nouns

A generic noun represents a typical member of a group, such as *a student*, or any member of a group, such as *any lawyer*. Although generic nouns may seem to have plural meanings, they are singular.

> Every *runner* must train rigorously if *he or she wants* [not *they want*] to excel.

When a plural pronoun refers mistakenly to a generic noun, you will usually have the same revision options as for indefinite pronouns.

> A medical student must study hard if ~~they want~~ *he or she wants* to succeed.

> ~~A medical student~~ *Medical students* must study hard if they want to succeed.

> A medical student must study hard ~~if they want~~ to succeed.

Collective nouns   Collective nouns such as *jury, committee, audience, crowd, family,* and *team* name a group. In American English, collective nouns are usually singular because they emphasize the group functioning as a unit.

> The planning *committee* granted *its* [not *their*] permission to build.

If the members of the group function individually, however, you may treat the noun as plural: *The family put their signatures on the document.* Or you might add a plural antecedent such as *members* to the sentence: *The family members put their signatures on the document.*

12b Pronoun reference

In the sentence *When Andrew got home, he went straight to bed,* the noun *Andrew* is the antecedent of the pronoun *he.* A pronoun should refer clearly to its antecedent.

Ambiguous reference   Ambiguous reference occurs when the pronoun could refer to two possible antecedents.

> *The cake collapsed when Aunt Harriet put it*
> ~~When Aunt Harriet put the cake~~ on the table~~.~~ *, it* ~~collapsed.~~

> *"You have*
> Tom told James, ~~that he had~~ won the lottery*."*

What collapsed—the cake or the table? Who won the lottery—Tom or James? The revisions eliminate the ambiguity.

PRACTICE   hackerhandbooks.com/pocket
> Grammar > 12–4 to 12–6

Implied reference A pronoun must refer to a specific antecedent, not to a word that is implied but not actually stated.

▶ After braiding Ann's hair, Sue decorated ~~them~~ *the braids* with ribbons.

Vague reference of *this*, *that*, or *which* The pronouns *this*, *that*, and *which* should ordinarily refer to specific antecedents rather than to whole ideas or sentences. When a pronoun's reference is too vague, either replace the pronoun with a noun or supply an antecedent to which the pronoun clearly refers.

▶ Television advertising has created new demands for prescription drugs. People respond to ~~this~~ *the ads* by asking for drugs they may not need.

▶ Romeo and Juliet were both too young to have acquired much wisdom, ~~and~~ *a fact* that accounts for their rash actions.

Indefinite reference of *they*, *it*, or *you* The pronoun *they* should refer to a specific antecedent. Do not use *they* to refer indefinitely to persons who have not been specifically mentioned.

▶ ~~They~~ *The board* announced an increase in sports fees for all student athletes.

The word *it* should not be used indefinitely in constructions such as *In the article, it says that. . . .*

▶ ~~In the~~ *The* encyclopedia ~~it~~ states that male moths can smell female moths from several miles away.

The pronoun *you* is appropriate only when the writer is addressing the reader directly: *Once you have kneaded the dough, let it rise in a warm place.* Except in informal contexts, however, *you* should not be used to mean "anyone in general." (See the example on p. 34.)

> Ms. Pickersgill's *Guide to Etiquette* stipulates that ~~you~~ *a guest* should not arrive at a party too early or leave too late.

12c Case of personal pronouns (*I* vs. *me* etc.)

The personal pronouns in the following list change what is known as *case form* according to their grammatical function in a sentence. Pronouns functioning as subjects or subject complements appear in the *subjective* case; those functioning as objects appear in the *objective* case; and those showing ownership appear in the *possessive* case.

SUBJECTIVE CASE	OBJECTIVE CASE	POSSESSIVE CASE
I	me	my
we	us	our
you	you	your
he/she/it	him/her/it	his/her/its
they	them	their

For the most part, you know how to use these forms correctly. The structures discussed in this section may tempt you to choose the wrong pronoun.

Compound word groups   You may sometimes be confused when a subject or an object appears as part of a compound structure. To test for the correct pronoun, mentally strip away all of the compound structure except the pronoun in question.

> While diving for pearls, Ikiko and ~~her~~ *she* found a sunken boat.

> *Ikiko and she* is the subject of the verb *found*. Strip away the words *Ikiko and* to test for the correct pronoun: *she found* [not *her found*].

> The most traumatic experience for her father and ~~I~~ *me* occurred long after her operation.

> *Her father and me* is the object of the preposition *for*. Strip away the words *her father and* to test for the correct pronoun: *for me* [not *for I*].

PRACTICE   hackerhandbooks.com/pocket
> Grammar > 12–7 and 12–8
>   > 12–10 and 12–11 (pronoun case review)

When in doubt about the correct pronoun, some writers try to evade the choice by using a reflexive pronoun such as *myself*. Using a reflexive pronoun in such situations is nonstandard.

▶ The Indian cab driver gave my husband and ~~myself~~ **me** some good tips on traveling in New Delhi.

My husband and me is the indirect object of the verb *gave*.

Appositives

Appositives are noun phrases that rename nouns or pronouns. A pronoun used as an appositive has the same function (usually subject or object) as the word(s) it renames.

▶ The chief strategists, Dr. Bell and ~~me,~~ **I,** could not agree on a plan.

The appositive *Dr. Bell and I* renames the subject, *strategists*. Test: *I could not agree on a plan* [not *me could not agree on a plan*].

▶ The reporter interviewed only two witnesses, the shopkeeper and ~~I~~ **me.**

The appositive *the shopkeeper and me* renames the direct object, *witnesses*. Test: *interviewed me* [not *interviewed I*].

Subject complements

Use subjective-case pronouns for subject complements, which rename or describe the subject and usually follow *be, am, is, are, was, were, being,* or *been*.

▶ During the Lindbergh trial, Bruno Hauptmann repeatedly denied that the kidnapper was ~~him.~~ **he.**

If *kidnapper was he* seems too stilted, rewrite the sentence: *During the Lindbergh trial, Bruno Hauptmann repeatedly denied that he was the kidnapper.*

We or us before a noun

When deciding whether *we* or *us* should precede a noun, choose the pronoun that would be appropriate if the noun were omitted.

▶ ~~Us~~ **We** tenants would rather fight than move.

Test: *We would rather fight* [not *Us would rather fight*].

▶ Management is shortchanging ~~we~~ *us* tenants.

Test: *Management is shortchanging us* [not *Management is shortchanging we*].

Pronoun after *than* or *as* When a comparison begins with *than* or *as*, your choice of pronoun will depend on your meaning. To test for the correct pronoun, finish the sentence.

▶ My brother is six years older than ~~me~~ *I*.

Test: *older than I* [*am*].

▶ We respected no other candidate for city council as much as ~~she~~ *her*.

Test: *as much as* [*we respected*] *her*.

Pronoun before or after an infinitive An infinitive is the word *to* followed by a verb. Both subjects and objects of infinitives take the objective case.

▶ Ms. Wilson asked John and ~~I~~ *me* to drive the senator and ~~she~~ *her* to the airport.

John and me is the subject and *senator and her* is the object of the infinitive *to drive*.

Pronoun or noun before a gerund If a pronoun modifies a gerund, use the possessive case: *my*, *our*, *your*, *his*, *her*, *its*, *their*. A gerund is a verb form ending in *-ing* that functions as a noun.

▶ The chances of ~~you~~ *your* being hit by lightning are about two million to one.

Nouns as well as pronouns may modify gerunds. To form the possessive case of a noun, use an apostrophe and *-s* (*victim's*) for a singular noun or just an apostrophe (*victims'*) for a plural noun. (See also 19a.)

▶ The old order in France paid a high price for the ~~aristocracy~~ *aristocracy's* exploiting the lower classes.

12d Who or whom

Who, a subjective-case pronoun, is used for subjects and subject complements. *Whom*, an objective-case pronoun, is used for objects. The words *who* and *whom* appear primarily in subordinate clauses or in questions.

In subordinate clauses When deciding whether to use *who* or *whom* in a subordinate clause, check for the word's function within the clause.

▶ He tells that story to ~~whomever~~ *whoever* will listen.

Whoever is the subject of *will listen*. The entire subordinate clause *whoever will listen* is the object of the preposition *to*.

▶ You will work with our senior engineers, ~~who~~ *whom* you will meet later.

Whom is the direct object of the verb *will meet*. This becomes clear if you restructure the clause: *you will meet whom later*.

In questions When deciding whether to use *who* or *whom* in a question, check for the word's function within the question.

▶ ~~Whom~~ *Who* was responsible for creating that computer virus?

Who is the subject of the verb *was*.

▶ ~~Who~~ *Whom* would you nominate for council president?

Whom is the direct object of the verb *would nominate*. This becomes clear if you restructure the question: *You would nominate whom?*

PRACTICE hackerhandbooks.com/pocket
> Grammar > 12–9
> > 12–10 and 12–11 (pronoun case review)

13 Use adjectives and adverbs appropriately.

Adjectives modify nouns or pronouns; adverbs modify verbs, adjectives, or other adverbs.

Many adverbs are formed by adding *-ly* to adjectives (*formal, formally*). But don't assume that all words ending in *-ly* are adverbs or that all adverbs end in *-ly*. Some adjectives end in *-ly* (*lovely, friendly*), and some adverbs don't (*always, here*). When in doubt, consult a dictionary.

13a Adjectives

Adjectives ordinarily precede the nouns they modify. But they can also function as subject complements following linking verbs (usually a form of *be: be, am, is, are, was, were, being, been*). When an adjective functions as a subject complement, it describes the subject.

Justice is *blind*.

Verbs such as *smell, taste, look, appear, grow,* and *feel* may also be linking. If the word following one of these verbs describes the subject, use an adjective; if the word modifies the verb, use an adverb.

ADJECTIVE The detective looked *cautious*.

ADVERB The detective looked *cautiously* for the fingerprints.

Linking verbs usually suggest states of being, not actions. For example, to look *cautious* suggests the state of being cautious, whereas to look *cautiously* is to perform an action in a cautious way.

▸ Lori looked ~~well~~ *good* in her new raincoat.

▸ All of us on the debate team felt ~~badly~~ *bad* about our performance.

> The verbs *looked* and *felt* suggest states of being, not actions, so they should be followed by adjectives.

PRACTICE hackerhandbooks.com/pocket
> Grammar > 13–1 and 13–2

describing nouns • describing verbs, adjectives, adverbs • *more* vs. *most* • *-er* vs. *-est* forms

adj/adv 13c

13b Adverbs

Use adverbs to modify verbs, adjectives, and other adverbs. Adverbs usually answer one of these questions: When? Where? How? Why? Under what conditions? How often? To what degree?

Adjectives are often used incorrectly in place of adverbs in casual or nonstandard speech.

▶ The manager must ensure that the office runs ~~smooth~~ *smoothly* and ~~efficient~~ *efficiently*.

▶ The chance of recovering any property lost in the fire looks ~~real~~ *really* slim.

The incorrect use of the adjective *good* in place of the adverb *well* is especially common in casual or nonstandard speech.

▶ We were delighted that Nomo had done so ~~good~~ *well* on the exam.

13c Comparatives and superlatives

Most adjectives and adverbs have three forms: the positive, the comparative, and the superlative.

POSITIVE	COMPARATIVE	SUPERLATIVE
soft	softer	softest
fast	faster	fastest
careful	more careful	most careful
bad	worse	worst
good	better	best

Comparative vs. superlative Use the comparative to compare two things, the superlative to compare three or more.

▶ Which of these two brands of toothpaste is ~~best?~~ *better?*

▶ Hermos is the ~~more~~ *most* qualified of the three applicants.

Form of comparatives and superlatives To form comparatives and superlatives of one-syllable adjectives, use the endings *-er* and *-est*: *smooth, smoother, smoothest*. For adjectives with three or more syllables, use *more* and *most* (or *less* and *least*): *exciting, more exciting, most exciting*. Two-syllable adjectives form comparatives and superlatives in both ways: *lovely, lovelier, loveliest; helpful, more helpful, most helpful*.

Some one-syllable adverbs take the endings *-er* and *-est* (*fast, faster, fastest*), but longer adverbs and all of those ending in *-ly* use *more* and *most* (or *less* and *least*).

Double comparatives or superlatives When you have added *-er* or *-est* to an adjective or an adverb, do not also use *more* or *most* (or *less* or *least*).

▶ All the polls indicated that Gore was more ~~likelier~~ *likely* to win than Bush.

Absolute concepts Do not use comparatives or superlatives with absolute concepts such as *unique* or *perfect*. Either something is unique or it isn't. It is illogical to suggest that absolute concepts come in degrees.

▶ That is the most ~~unique~~ *unusual* wedding gown I have ever seen.

14 Repair sentence fragments.

As a rule, do not treat a piece of a sentence as if it were a sentence. When you do, you create a fragment. To be a sentence, a word group must consist of at least one full independent clause. An independent clause has a subject and a verb, and it either stands alone as a sentence or could stand alone.

You can repair a fragment in one of two ways: Either pull the fragment into a nearby sentence, punctuating the new sentence correctly, or rewrite the fragment as a complete sentence.

PRACTICE hackerhandbooks.com/pocket
> Grammar > 14–1 to 14–4

14a Fragmented clauses

A subordinate clause is patterned like a sentence, with both a subject and a verb, but it begins with a word that tells readers it cannot stand alone—a word such as *after, although, because, before, if, so that, that, though, unless, until, when, where, who,* or *which*. (For a longer list, see p. 276.)

Most fragmented clauses beg to be pulled into a sentence nearby.

▶ We fear the West Nile virus~~.~~ ~~Because~~ *because* it is transmitted by the common mosquito.

If a fragmented clause cannot be combined gracefully with a nearby sentence, try rewriting it. The simplest way to turn a fragmented clause into a sentence is to delete the opening word or words that mark it as subordinate.

▶ Uncontrolled development is taking a deadly toll on the environment. ~~So that in~~ *In* many parts of the world, fragile ecosystems are collapsing.

14b Fragmented phrases

Like subordinate clauses, certain phrases are sometimes mistaken for sentences. They are fragments if they lack a subject, a verb, or both. Frequently a fragmented phrase may simply be pulled into a nearby sentence.

▶ The archaeologists worked slowly~~.~~, ~~Examining~~ *examining* and labeling hundreds of pottery shards.

> The word group beginning with *Examining* is a verbal phrase, not a sentence.

▶ Many adults suffer silently from agoraphobia~~.~~, ~~A~~ *a* fear of the outside world.

> *A fear of the outside world* is an appositive phrase, not a sentence.

▶ It has been said that there are only three indigenous American art forms /: ~~Jazz,~~ ^jazz,^ musical comedy, and soap operas.

> The list is not a sentence. Notice how easily a colon corrects the problem. (See 18b.)

If the fragmented phrase cannot be attached to a nearby sentence, turn the phrase into a sentence. You may need to add a subject, a verb, or both.

▶ Jamie explained how to access the database. ~~Also~~ ^She also taught us^ how to submit reports and request vendor payments.

> The revision turns the fragmented phrase into a sentence by adding a subject and a verb.

14c Acceptable fragments

Skilled writers occasionally use sentence fragments for emphasis. Although fragments are sometimes appropriate, writers and readers do not always agree on when they are appropriate. Therefore, you will find it safer to write in complete sentences.

15 Revise run-on sentences.

Run-on sentences are independent clauses that have not been joined correctly. An independent clause is a word group that stands alone or could stand alone as a sentence. When two or more independent clauses appear in one sentence, they must be joined in one of these ways:

- with a comma and a coordinating conjunction (*and, but, or, nor, for, so, yet*)
- with a semicolon (or occasionally a colon or a dash)

There are two types of run-on sentences. When a writer puts no mark of punctuation and no coordinating conjunction between independent clauses, the result is a *fused sentence*.

PRACTICE hackerhandbooks.com/pocket
> Grammar > 15–1 to 15–4

FUSED

Air pollution poses risks to all humans it can be deadly for people with asthma.

A far more common type of run-on sentence is the *comma splice*—two or more independent clauses joined with a comma and no coordinating conjunction. In some comma splices, the comma appears alone.

COMMA SPLICE

Air pollution poses risks to all humans, it can be deadly for people with asthma.

In other comma splices, the comma is accompanied by a joining word, such as *however*, that is *not* a coordinating conjunction. (See 15b.)

COMMA SPLICE

Air pollution poses risks to all humans, however, it can be deadly for people with asthma.

To correct a run-on sentence, you have four choices:

1. Use a comma and a coordinating conjunction.
2. Use a semicolon (or, if appropriate, a colon or a dash).
3. Make the clauses into separate sentences.
4. Restructure the sentence, perhaps by subordinating one of the clauses.

One of these revision techniques will usually work better than the others for a particular sentence. The fourth technique, the one requiring the most extensive revision, is often the most effective.

CORRECTED WITH COMMA AND COORDINATING CONJUNCTION

Air pollution poses risks to all humans, but it can be deadly for people with asthma.

CORRECTED WITH SEMICOLON

Air pollution poses risks to all humans; it can be deadly for people with asthma.

CORRECTED WITH SEPARATE SENTENCES

Air pollution poses risks to all humans. It can be deadly for people with asthma.

CORRECTED BY RESTRUCTURING

Although air pollution poses risks to all humans, it can be deadly for people with asthma.

15a Revision with a comma and a coordinating conjunction

When a coordinating conjunction (*and, but, or, nor, for, so, yet*) joins independent clauses, it is usually preceded by a comma.

▶ Most of his friends had made plans for their retirement, *but* Tom had not.

15b Revision with a semicolon (or a colon or a dash)

When the independent clauses are closely related and their relation is clear without a coordinating conjunction, a semicolon is an acceptable method of revision.

▶ Tragedy depicts the individual confronted with the fact of death; comedy depicts the adaptability of human society.

A semicolon is required between independent clauses that have been linked with a conjunctive adverb such as *however* or *therefore* or a transitional phrase such as *in fact* or *of course*. (See p. 62 for longer lists.)

▶ The timber wolf looks like a large German shepherd; however, the wolf has longer legs, larger feet, and a wider head.

If the first independent clause introduces a quoted sentence, use a colon.

▶ Scholar and crime writer Carolyn Heilbrun says this about the future: "Today's shocks are tomorrow's conventions."

Either a colon or a dash may be appropriate when the second clause summarizes or explains the first. (See 18b and 21d.)

fixing run-on sentences • verbs • basic forms

15c Revision by separating sentences

If both independent clauses are long—or if one is a question and the other is not—consider making them separate sentences.

▶ Why should we spend money on space exploration~~,~~**?** ~~we~~ **We** have enough underfunded programs here on Earth.

15d Revision by restructuring the sentence

For sentence variety, consider restructuring the run-on sentence, perhaps by turning one of the independent clauses into a subordinate clause or a phrase.

▶ One of the most famous advertising slogans is Wheaties cereal's "Breakfast of Champions," ~~it~~ **which** was penned in 1933.

▶ Mary McLeod Bethune**,** ~~was~~ the seventeenth child of former slaves, ~~she~~ founded the National Council of Negro Women in 1935.

16 Review grammar concerns for multilingual writers.

16a Verbs

This section offers a brief review of English verb forms and tenses and the passive voice.

Verb forms Every main verb in English has five forms (except *be*, which has eight). These forms are used to create all of the verb tenses in standard English. The following list shows these forms for the regular verb *help* and the irregular verbs *give* and *be*.

PRACTICE hackerhandbooks.com/pocket
> Grammar > 16–1 to 16–3

	REGULAR (*HELP*)	IRREGULAR (*GIVE*)	IRREGULAR (*BE*)*
BASE FORM	help	give	be
PAST TENSE	helped	gave	was, were
PAST PARTICIPLE	helped	given	been
PRESENT PARTICIPLE	helping	giving	being
-*S* FORM	helps	gives	is

Be also has the forms *am* and *are*, which are used in the present tense. (See also p. 28.)

Verb tense   Here are descriptions of the tenses and progressive forms in standard English. See also 11b.

The simple tenses show general facts, states of being, and actions that occur regularly.

Simple present tense (base form or -*s* form) expresses general facts, constant states, habitual or repetitive actions, or scheduled future events: *The sun rises in the east. The plane leaves tomorrow at 6:30.*

Simple past tense (base form + -*ed* or -*d* or irregular form) is used for actions that happened at a specific time or during a specific period in the past or for repetitive actions that have ended: *She drove to Montana three years ago. When I was young, I walked to school.*

Simple future tense (*will* + base form) expresses actions that will occur at some time in the future and promises or predictions of future events: *I will call you next week.*

The simple progressive forms show continuing action.

Present progressive (*am*, *is*, *are* + present participle) shows actions in progress that are not expected to remain constant or future actions (with verbs such as *go, come, move*): *We are building our house at the shore. They are moving tomorrow.*

Past progressive (*was*, *were* + present participle) shows actions in progress at a specific past time or a continuing action that was interrupted: *Roy was driving his new car yesterday. When she walked in, we were planning her party.*

Future progressive (*will* + *be* + present participle) expresses actions that will be in progress at a certain time in the future: *Nan will be flying home tomorrow.*

TIP: Certain verbs are not normally used in the progressive: *appear, believe, belong, contain, have, hear, know, like, need, see, seem, taste, think, understand,* and *want.* There are exceptions, however, that you must notice as you encounter them: *We are thinking of buying a summer home.*

The perfect tenses show actions that happened or will happen before another time.

Present perfect tense (*have, has* + past participle) expresses actions that began in the past and continue to the present or actions that happened at an unspecific time in the past: *She has not spoken of her grandfather in a long time. They have traveled to Africa twice.*

Past perfect tense (*had* + past participle) expresses an action that began or occurred before another time in the past: *By the time Hakan was fifteen, he had learned to drive. I had just finished my walk when my brother drove up.* (See also p. 29.)

Future perfect tense (*will* + *have* + past participle) expresses actions that will be completed before or at a specific future time: *By the time I graduate, I will have taken five film study classes.*

The perfect progressive forms show continuous past actions before another time.

Present perfect progressive (*have, has* + *been* + present participle) expresses continuous actions that began in the past and continue to the present: *My sister has been living in Oregon since 2001.*

Past perfect progressive (*had* + *been* + present participle) conveys actions that began and continued in the past until some other past action: *By the time I moved to Georgia, I had been supporting myself for five years.*

Future perfect progressive (*will* + *have* + *been* + present participle) expresses actions that are or will be in progress before another specified time in the future: *By the time we reach the cashier, we will have been waiting in line for an hour.*

Modal verbs The nine modal verbs—*can, could, may, might, must, shall, should, will,* and *would*—are used with the base form of verbs to show certainty, necessity, or possibility. Modals do not change form to indicate tense. (See the examples on p. 48.)

▶ The art museum will ~~launches~~ *launch* its fundraising campaign next month.

▶ We could ~~spoke~~ *speak* Portuguese when we were young.

Passive voice   When a sentence is written in the passive voice, the subject receives the action instead of doing it. To form the passive voice, use a form of *be*—*am, is, are, was, were, being, be,* or *been*—followed by the past participle of the main verb. (For appropriate uses of the passive voice, see 2b.)

▶ *Dreaming in Cuban* was ~~writing~~ *written* by Cristina García.

▶ Senator Dixon will *be* defeated.

NOTE: Verbs that do not take direct objects—such as *occur, happen, sleep, die,* and *fall*—do not form the passive voice.

16b Articles (*a, an, the*)

Articles and other noun markers   Articles (*a, an, the*) are part of a category of words known as *noun markers* or *determiners.* Noun markers identify the nouns that follow them. Besides articles, noun markers include possessive nouns (*Elena's, child's*); possessive pronoun/adjectives (*my, your, their*); demonstrative pronoun/adjectives (*this, that*); quantifiers (*all, few, neither, some*); and numbers (*one, twenty-six*).

               ART   N

Felix is reading a book about mythology.

           ART   ADJ   N

We took an exciting trip to Alaska last summer.

When to use *a* or *an*   Use *a* or *an* with singular count nouns that refer to one unspecific item (not a whole category). *Count nouns* refer to persons, places, things, or ideas that can be counted: *one girl, two girls; one city, three cities; one goose, four geese.*

▶ My professor asked me to bring *a* dictionary to class.

PRACTICE   hackerhandbooks.com/pocket
> Grammar > 16-4 to 16-6

▶ We want to rent **an** apartment close to the lake.

When to use *the* Use *the* with most nouns that the reader can identify specifically. Usually the identity will be clear to the reader for one of the following reasons:

1. The noun has been previously mentioned.

▶ **A truck cut in front of our van. When the truck skidded a few seconds later, we almost crashed into it.**

2. A phrase or clause following the noun restricts its identity.

▶ **Bryce warned me that the GPS in his car was not working.**

3. A superlative adjective such as *best* or *most intelligent* makes the noun's identity specific. (See also 13c.)

▶ **Brita had the best players on her team.**

4. The noun describes a unique person, place, or thing.

▶ **During an eclipse, one should not look directly at the sun.**

5. The context or situation makes the noun's identity clear.

▶ **Please don't slam the door when you leave.**

6. The noun is singular and refers to a class or category of items (most often animals, musical instruments, and inventions).

▶ **The tin whistle is common in traditional Irish music.**

When not to use articles Do not use *a* or *an* with non-count nouns. *Noncount nouns* refer to things or abstract ideas that cannot be counted or made plural: *salt, silver, air, furniture, patience, knowledge*. (See the chart at the bottom of this page.)

To express an approximate amount of a noncount noun, use a quantifier such as *some* or *more*: *some water, enough coffee, less violence*.

▶ Ava gave us ~~an~~ information about the Peace Corps.

▶ Claudia said she had ~~a~~ *some* news that would surprise her parents.

Do not use articles with nouns that refer to all of something or something in general.

▶ ~~The kindness~~ *Kindness* is a virtue.

▶ In some parts of the world, ~~the~~ rice is preferred to all other grains.

Commonly used noncount nouns

Food and drink

beef, bread, butter, candy, cereal, cheese, cream, meat, milk, pasta, rice, salt, sugar, wine

Nonfood substances

air, cement, coal, dirt, gasoline, gold, paper, petroleum, plastic, rain, silver, snow, soap, steel, wood, wool

Abstract nouns

advice, anger, beauty, confidence, courage, employment, fun, happiness, health, honesty, information, intelligence, knowledge, love, poverty, satisfaction, wealth

Other

biology (and other areas of study), clothing, equipment, furniture, homework, jewelry, luggage, machinery, mail, money, news, poetry, pollution, research, scenery, traffic, transportation, violence, weather, work

NOTE: A few noncount nouns can also be used as count nouns: *He had two loves: music and archery.*

When to use articles with proper nouns Do not use articles with most singular proper nouns: *Prime Minister Cameron, Jamaica, Lake Huron, Ivy Street, Mount Everest.* Use *the* with most plural proper nouns: *the McGregors, the Bahamas, the Finger Lakes, the United States.* Also use *the* with large regions, oceans, rivers, and mountain ranges: *the Sahara, the Indian Ocean, the Amazon River, the Rocky Mountains.*

There are, however, many exceptions, especially with geographic names. Note exceptions when you encounter them or consult a native speaker or an ESL dictionary.

16c Sentence structure

This section focuses on the major challenges that multilingual students face when writing sentences in English.

Omitted verbs Some languages do not use linking verbs (*am, is, are, was, were*) between subjects and complements (nouns or adjectives that rename or describe the subject). Every English sentence, however, must include a verb.

▶ Jim ^*is*^ intelligent.

▶ Many streets in San Francisco ^*are*^ very steep.

Omitted subjects Some languages do not require a subject in every sentence. Every English sentence, however, needs a subject.

▶ Your aunt is very energetic. ~~Seems~~ ^*She seems*^ young for her age.

EXCEPTION: In commands, the subject *you* is understood but not present in the sentence: *Give me the book.*

The word *it* is used as the subject of a sentence describing the weather or temperature, stating the time, indicating distance, or suggesting an environmental fact. Do not omit *it* in such sentences.

It is raining in the valley and snowing in the mountains.

It is 9:15 a.m.

PRACTICE hackerhandbooks.com/pocket
> Grammar > 16–7 and 16–8

It is three hundred miles to Chicago.

In July, *it* is very hot in Arizona.

In some English sentences, the subject comes after the verb, and a placeholder (called an expletive)—*there* or *it*—comes before the verb.

> EXP V ⌐ S ┐ ⌐ S ┐ V
> There are many people here today. (Many people are here today.)

> EXP V ⌐ S ┐ ⌐ S ┐ V
> It is important to study daily. (To study daily is important.)

▶ As you know, ^there are^ many religious sects in India.

Repeated subjects, objects, and adverbs English does not allow a subject to be repeated in its own clause.

▶ The doctor ~~she~~ advised me to cut down on salt.

Do not add a pronoun even when a word group comes between the subject and the verb.

▶ The car that had been stolen ~~it~~ was found.

Do not repeat an object or an adverb in an adjective clause. Adjective clauses begin with relative pronouns (*who*, *whom*, *whose*, *which*, *that*) or relative adverbs (*when*, *where*). Relative pronouns usually serve as subjects or objects in the clauses they introduce; another word in the clause cannot serve the same function. Relative adverbs should not be repeated by other adverbs later in the clause.

▶ The cat ran under the car that ~~it~~ was parked on the street.

The relative pronoun *that* is the subject of the adjective clause, so the pronoun *it* cannot be added as the subject.

If the clause begins with a relative adverb, do not use another adverb with the same meaning later in the clause.

▶ The office where I work ~~there~~ is close to home.

The adverb *there* cannot repeat the relative adverb *where*.

16d Prepositions showing time and place

The chart on this page is limited to three prepositions that show time and place: *at*, *on*, and *in*. Not every possible use is listed in the chart, so don't be surprised when you encounter exceptions and idiomatic uses that you must learn one at a time. For example, in English, we ride *in* a car but *on* a bus, plane, train, or subway.

At, *on*, and *in* to show time and place

Showing time

- **AT** *at* a specific time: *at* 7:20, *at* dawn, *at* dinner
- **ON** *on* a specific day or date: *on* Tuesday, *on* June 4
- **IN** *in* a part of a day: *in* the afternoon, *in* the daytime [but *at* night]

   in a year or month: *in* 1999, *in* July

   in a period of time: finished *in* three hours

Showing place

- **AT** *at* a meeting place or location: *at* home, *at* the club

   at a specific address: living *at* 10 Oak Street

   at the edge of something: sitting *at* the desk

   at the corner of something: turning *at* the intersection

   at a target: throwing the snowball *at* Lucy

- **ON** *on* a surface: placed *on* the table, hanging *on* the wall

   on a street: the house *on* Spring Street

   on an electronic medium: *on* television, *on* the Internet

- **IN** *in* an enclosed space: *in* the garage, *in* an envelope

   in a geographic location: *in* San Diego, *in* Texas

   in a print medium: *in* a book, *in* a magazine

PRACTICE hackerhandbooks.com/pocket
> Grammar > 16–9

Punctuation

17 The comma 55
18 The semicolon and the colon 62
19 The apostrophe 65
20 Quotation marks 67
21 Other marks 71

17 The comma

The comma was invented to help readers. Without it, sentence parts can collide into one another unexpectedly, causing misreadings.

CONFUSING If you cook Elmer will do the dishes.

CONFUSING While we were eating a rattlesnake approached our campsite.

Add commas in the logical places (after *cook* and *eating*), and suddenly all is clear. No longer is Elmer being cooked, the rattlesnake being eaten.

Various rules have evolved to prevent such misreadings and to guide readers through complex grammatical structures. According to most experts, you should use a comma in the following situations.

17a Before a coordinating conjunction joining independent clauses

When a coordinating conjunction connects two or more independent clauses—word groups that could stand alone as separate sentences—a comma must precede the conjunction. There are seven coordinating conjunctions in English: *and, but, or, nor, for, so,* and *yet*.

A comma tells readers that one independent clause has come to a close and that another is about to begin.

▶ Jake has no talent for numbers, so he hires someone to prepare his taxes.

EXCEPTION: If the two independent clauses are short and there is no danger of misreading, the comma may be omitted.

The plane took off and we were on our way.

TIP: Do *not* use a comma to separate compound word groups that are not independent clauses. See 17j.

17b After an introductory word group

Use a comma after an introductory clause or phrase. A comma tells readers that the introductory word group has come to a close and that the main part of the sentence

PRACTICE hackerhandbooks.com/pocket
> Punctuation > 17–1 to 17–5

is about to begin. The most common introductory word groups are adverb clauses, prepositional phrases, and participial phrases.

▶ When Arthur ran his first marathon, he was pleased to finish in under four hours.

▶ Near a stream at the bottom of the canyon, rangers discovered an abandoned mine.

▶ Buried under layers of younger rocks, the earth's oldest rocks contain no fossils.

EXCEPTION: The comma may be omitted after a short clause or phrase if there is no danger of misreading.

In no time we were at 2,800 feet.

17c Between items in a series

Use a comma between all items in a series, including the last two.

▶ Bubbles of air, leaves, ferns, bits of wood, and insects are often found trapped in amber.

Although some writers view the comma between the last two items as optional, most experts advise using it because its omission can result in ambiguity or misreading.

17d Between coordinate adjectives

Use a comma between coordinate adjectives, those that each modify a noun separately.

▶ Should patients with severe, irreversible brain damage be put on life support systems?

Adjectives are coordinate if they can be connected with *and*: *severe and irreversible*.

NOTE: Do not use a comma between cumulative adjectives, those that do not each modify the noun separately.

Three large gray shapes moved slowly toward us.

Cumulative adjectives cannot be joined with *and* (not *three and large and gray shapes*).

17e To set off a nonrestrictive element, but not a restrictive element

A *restrictive* element defines or limits the meaning of the word it modifies; it is therefore essential to the meaning of the sentence and is not set off with commas. A *nonrestrictive* element describes a word whose meaning already is clear. Because it is not essential to the meaning of the sentence, it is set off with commas.

RESTRICTIVE (NO COMMAS)

The campers need clothes *that are durable.*

NONRESTRICTIVE (WITH COMMAS)

The campers need sturdy shoes, *which are expensive.*

If you remove a restrictive element from a sentence, the meaning changes significantly, becoming more general than intended. The writer of the first sample sentence does not mean that the campers need clothes in general. The meaning is more restricted: The campers need *durable* clothes.

If you remove a nonrestrictive element from a sentence, the meaning does not change significantly. Some meaning may be lost, but the defining characteristics of the person or thing described remain the same: The campers need *sturdy shoes*, and these happen to be expensive.

Elements that may be restrictive or nonrestrictive include adjective clauses, adjective phrases, and appositives.

Adjective clauses Adjective clauses, which usually follow the noun or pronoun they describe, begin with a relative pronoun (*who, whom, whose, which, that*) or a relative adverb (*when, where*). When an adjective clause is nonrestrictive, set it off with commas; when it is restrictive, omit the commas.

NONRESTRICTIVE CLAUSE (WITH COMMAS)

▶ The Kyoto Protocol, which was adopted in 1997, aims to reduce greenhouse gases.

RESTRICTIVE CLAUSE (NO COMMAS)

▶ A corporation/that has government contracts/must maintain careful personnel records.

NOTE: Use *that* only with restrictive clauses. Many writers use *which* only with nonrestrictive clauses, but usage varies.

Adjective phrases   Prepositional or verbal phrases functioning as adjectives may be restrictive or nonrestrictive. Nonrestrictive phrases are set off with commas; restrictive phrases are not.

NONRESTRICTIVE PHRASE (WITH COMMAS)

▶ The helicopter, with its million-candlepower spotlight illuminating the area, circled above.

RESTRICTIVE PHRASE (NO COMMAS)

▶ One corner of the attic was filled with newspapers/dating from the 1920s.

Appositives   An appositive is a noun or pronoun that renames a nearby noun. Nonrestrictive appositives are set off with commas; restrictive appositives are not.

NONRESTRICTIVE APPOSITIVE (WITH COMMAS)

▶ Darwin's most important book, *On the Origin of Species,* was the result of many years of research.

RESTRICTIVE APPOSITIVE (NO COMMAS)

▶ The song/"Firework/" was blasted out of amplifiers.

17f To set off transitional and parenthetical expressions, absolute phrases, and contrasted elements

Transitional expressions   Transitional expressions serve as bridges between sentences or parts of sentences. They include conjunctive adverbs such as *however, therefore,* and *moreover* and transitional phrases such as *for example* and *as a matter of fact.* For a longer list, see page 62.

When a transitional expression appears between independent clauses in a compound sentence, it is preceded by a semicolon and usually followed by a comma.

▶ Minh did not understand our language; moreover, he was unfamiliar with our customs.

When a transitional expression appears at the beginning of a sentence or in the middle of an independent clause, it is usually set off with commas.

▶ In fact, stock values rose after the company's press release.

▶ Natural foods are not always salt-free; celery, for example, is high in sodium.

Parenthetical expressions Expressions that are distinctly parenthetical, interrupting the flow of a sentence, should be set off with commas.

▶ Evolution, so far as we know, doesn't work this way.

Absolute phrases An absolute phrase consists of a noun followed by a participle or participial phrase. It modifies the whole sentence and should be set off with commas.

```
   ┌───── ABSOLUTE PHRASE ─────┐
   N     ┌──── PARTICIPLE ────┐
```
Our grant having been approved, we were at last able to begin the archaeological dig.

Contrasted elements Sharp contrasts beginning with words such as *not* and *unlike* are set off with commas.

▶ The Epicurean philosophers sought mental, not bodily, pleasures.

17g To set off nouns of direct address, the words *yes* and *no*, interrogative tags, and mild interjections

▶ Forgive me, Angela, for forgetting our date.

▶ Yes, the loan will probably be approved.

- The film was faithful to the book, wasn't it?

- Well, cases like this are difficult to decide.

17h To set off direct quotations introduced with expressions such as *he said*

- "Happiness in marriage is entirely a matter of chance," says Charlotte Lucas in *Pride and Prejudice* (69; ch. 6).

17i With dates, addresses, and titles

Dates In dates, the year is set off from the rest of the sentence with commas.

- On December 12, 1890, orders were sent out for the arrest of Sitting Bull.

EXCEPTIONS: Commas are not needed if the date is inverted or if only the month and year are given: *The 15 April 2011 deadline is approaching. May 2006 was a surprisingly cold month.*

Addresses The elements of an address or a place name are separated by commas. A zip code, however, is not preceded by a comma.

- Greg lived at 708 Spring Street, Washington, Illinois 61571.

Titles If a title follows a name, set off the title with a pair of commas.

- Sandra Barnes, MD, was appointed to the board.

17j Misuses of the comma

Do not use commas unless you have good reasons for using them. In particular, avoid using commas in the following situations.

BETWEEN COMPOUND ELEMENTS THAT ARE NOT INDEPENDENT CLAUSES

- Marie Curie discovered radium/and later applied her work on radioactivity to medicine.

with *he said* • with dates • with addresses • with titles • misuses **17j**

TO SEPARATE A VERB FROM ITS SUBJECT

▶ Zoos large enough to give the animals freedom to roam/are becoming more popular.

BETWEEN CUMULATIVE ADJECTIVES (See p. 56.)

▶ We found an old/maroon hatbox.

TO SET OFF RESTRICTIVE ELEMENTS (See pp. 57–58.)

▶ Drivers/who think they own the road/make cycling a dangerous sport.

▶ Margaret Mead's book/*Coming of Age in Samoa*/caused controversy when it was published.

AFTER A COORDINATING CONJUNCTION

▶ Occasionally TV talk shows are performed live, but/more often they are taped.

AFTER *SUCH AS* OR *LIKE*

▶ Plants such as/begonias and impatiens add color to a shady garden.

BEFORE *THAN*

▶ Touring Crete was more thrilling for us/than visiting the Greek islands frequented by the rich.

BEFORE A PARENTHESIS

▶ At InterComm, Sylvia began at the bottom/(with only a cubicle and a swivel chair), but within three years she had been promoted to supervisor.

TO SET OFF AN INDIRECT (REPORTED) QUOTATION

▶ Samuel Goldwyn once said/that a verbal contract isn't worth the paper it's written on.

WITH A QUESTION MARK OR AN EXCLAMATION POINT

▶ "Why don't you try it?/" she coaxed.

18 The semicolon and the colon

18a The semicolon

The semicolon is used between independent clauses not joined with a coordinating conjunction. It can also be used between items in a series containing internal punctuation.

The semicolon is never used between elements of unequal grammatical rank.

Between independent clauses When two independent clauses appear in one sentence, they are usually linked with a comma and a coordinating conjunction (*and*, *but*, *or*, *nor*, *for*, *so*, *yet*). The coordinating conjunction signals the relation between the clauses. If the relation is clear without a conjunction, a writer may choose to connect the clauses with a semicolon instead.

> In film, a low-angle shot makes the subject look powerful; a high-angle shot does just the opposite.

A writer may also connect the clauses with a semicolon and a conjunctive adverb such as *however* or a transitional phrase such as *for example*.

> Many corals grow very gradually; in fact, the creation of a coral reef can take centuries.

CONJUNCTIVE ADVERBS

accordingly, also, anyway, besides, certainly, consequently, conversely, finally, furthermore, hence, however, incidentally, indeed, instead, likewise, meanwhile, moreover, nevertheless, next, nonetheless, now, otherwise, similarly, specifically, still, subsequently, then, therefore, thus

TRANSITIONAL PHRASES

after all, as a matter of fact, as a result, at any rate, at the same time, even so, for example, for instance, in addition, in conclusion, in fact, in other words, in the first place, on the contrary

NOTE: A semicolon must be used whenever a coordinating conjunction does not appear between independent clauses. To use merely a comma—or to use a comma and a

PRACTICE hackerhandbooks.com/pocket
> Punctuation > 18–1 to 18–3

conjunctive adverb or transitional expression—creates an error known as a *comma splice*. (See 15.)

Between items in a series containing internal punctuation   Items in a series are usually separated by commas. If one or more of the items contain internal punctuation, however, a writer may use semicolons for clarity.

> Classic science fiction sagas include *Star Trek*, with Captain Kirk, Dr. McCoy, and Mr. Spock; *Battlestar Galactica*, with its Cylons; and *Star Wars*, with Han Solo, Luke Skywalker, and Darth Vader.

Misuses of the semicolon   Do not use a semicolon in the following situations.

BETWEEN AN INDEPENDENT CLAUSE AND A SUBORDINATE CLAUSE

▶ The media like to portray my generation as lazy*;*/, although polls show that we work as hard as the twentysomethings before us.

BETWEEN AN APPOSITIVE AND THE WORD IT REFERS TO

▶ We were fascinated by the species *Argyroneta aquatica*;/, a spider that lives underwater.

TO INTRODUCE A LIST

▶ Some birds are flightless*;*/: emus, penguins, and ostriches.

BETWEEN INDEPENDENT CLAUSES JOINED BY *AND, BUT, OR, NOR, FOR, SO,* OR *YET*

▶ Five of the applicants had worked with spreadsheets*;*/, but only one was familiar with database management.

18b The colon

Main uses of the colon   A colon can be used after an independent clause to direct readers' attention to a list, an appositive, or a quotation.

A LIST

The routine includes the following: twenty knee bends, fifty leg lifts, and five minutes of running in place.

AN APPOSITIVE

My roommate is guilty of two of the seven deadly sins: gluttony and sloth.

A QUOTATION

Consider the words of Benjamin Franklin: "There never was a good war or a bad peace."

For other ways of introducing quotations, see pages 69–70.

A colon may also be used between independent clauses if the second summarizes or explains the first.

> Faith is like love: It cannot be forced.

The second clause may begin with a capital or a lowercase letter: *Minds are like parachutes: They* [or *they*] *function only when open.* (See 22e.)

Conventional uses Use a colon after the salutation in a formal letter, to indicate hours and minutes, to show proportions, between a title and a subtitle, and to separate city and publisher in bibliographic entries.

> Dear Sir or Madam:
>
> 5:30 p.m.
>
> The ratio of women to men was 2:1.
>
> *Alvin Ailey: A Life in Dance*
>
> Boston: Bedford, 2012

NOTE: In biblical references, a colon is ordinarily used between chapter and verse (Luke 2:14). MLA recommends a period (Luke 2.14).

Misuses of the colon A colon must be preceded by an independent clause. Therefore, avoid using it in the following situations.

BETWEEN A VERB AND ITS OBJECT OR COMPLEMENT

▶ Some important vitamins found in vegetables are: vitamin A, thiamine, niacin, and vitamin C.

BETWEEN A PREPOSITION AND ITS OBJECT

▶ The heart's two pumps each consist of ~~,~~ an upper chamber, or atrium, and a lower chamber, or ventricle.

AFTER *SUCH AS*, *INCLUDING*, OR *FOR EXAMPLE*

▶ The NCAA regulates college athletic teams, including ~~,~~ basketball, baseball, softball, and football.

19 The apostrophe

The apostrophe indicates possession and marks contractions. In addition, it has a few conventional uses.

19a To indicate possession

The apostrophe is used to indicate that a noun or an indefinite pronoun is possessive. Possessives usually indicate ownership, as in *Tim's hat*, *the editor's desk*, or *someone's gloves*. Frequently, however, ownership is only loosely implied: *the tree's roots*, *a day's work*. If you are not sure whether a word is possessive, try turning it into an *of* phrase: *the roots of the tree*, *the work of a day*.

When to add -'s   Add *-'s* if the noun does not end in *-s* or if the noun is singular and ends in *-s* or an *s* sound.

> Luck often propels a rock musician's career.
>
> Thank you for refunding the children's money.
>
> Lois's sister spent last year in India.
>
> Her article presents an overview of Marx's teachings.

EXCEPTION: If pronunciation would be awkward with an apostrophe and an *-s*, some writers use only the apostrophe: *Sophocles'*.

PRACTICE hackerhandbooks.com/pocket
> Punctuation > 19–1 and 19–2

When to add only an apostrophe If the noun is plural and ends in *-s*, add only an apostrophe.

> Both diplomats' briefcases were searched by guards.

Joint possession To show joint possession, use *-'s* (or *-s'*) with the last noun only; to show individual possession, make all nouns possessive.

> Have you seen Joyce and Greg's new camper?

> Hernando's and Maria's expectations were quite different.

Compound nouns If a noun is compound, use *-'s* (or *-s'*) with the last element.

> Her father-in-law's sculpture won first place.

Indefinite pronouns such as *someone* Use *-'s* to indicate that an indefinite pronoun is possessive. Indefinite pronouns refer to no specific person or thing: *anyone, everyone, someone, no one*, and so on.

> This diet will improve almost anyone's health.

NOTE: Possessive pronouns (*its, his,* and so on) do not use an apostrophe. (See 19d.)

19b To mark contractions

In a contraction, an apostrophe takes the place of missing letters.

> It's a shame that Frank can't go on the tour.

It's stands for *it is, can't* for *cannot.*
The apostrophe is also used to mark the omission of the first two digits of a year (*the class of '13*) or years (*the '60s generation*).

19c Conventional uses

An apostrophe typically is not used to pluralize numbers, abbreviations, letters, or words mentioned as words. Note the few exceptions and be consistent in your writing.

Plural numbers and abbreviations Do not use an apostrophe in the plural of any numbers (including decades) or of any abbreviations.

Peggy skated nearly perfect figure 8s.

We've paid only four IOUs out of six.

Plural letters   Italicize the letter and use roman (regular) font style for the -*s* ending. Use of an apostrophe is usually optional; MLA recommends the apostrophe.

Two large *J*s [or *J*'s] were painted on the door.

Plural of words mentioned as words   Italicize the word and use roman (regular) font style for the -*s* ending.

We've heard enough *maybe*s.

Words mentioned as words may also appear in quotation marks. When you choose this option, use the apostrophe: *We've heard enough "maybe's."*

19d Misuses of the apostrophe

Do not use an apostrophe in the following situations.

WITH NOUNS THAT ARE PLURAL BUT NOT POSSESSIVE

▶ Some ~~outpatient's~~ outpatients have special parking permits.

IN THE POSSESSIVE PRONOUNS *ITS*, *WHOSE*, *HIS*, *HERS*, *OURS*, *YOURS*, AND *THEIRS*

▶ Each area has ~~it's~~ its own conference room.

It's means "it is." The possessive pronoun *its* contains no apostrophe despite the fact that it is possessive.

20 Quotation marks

Quotation marks are used to enclose direct quotations. They are also used around some titles and to set off words used as words.

20a To enclose direct quotations

Direct quotations of a person's words, whether spoken or written, must be in quotation marks (see p. 68).

PRACTICE   hackerhandbooks.com/pocket
  > Punctuation > 20–1 and 20–2

"The contract negotiations are stalled," the executive told reporters, "but I'll bring both sides together."

EXCEPTION: When a long quotation has been set off from the text by indenting, quotation marks are not needed. (See pp. 112–13, 170–71, and 214.)

Use single quotation marks to enclose a quotation within a quotation.

> According to Paul Eliott, Eskimo hunters "chant an ancient magic song to the seal they are after: 'Beast of the sea! Come and place yourself before me in the early morning!'"

NOTE: Do not use quotation marks around indirect quotations, which report what a person said without using the person's exact words: *The executive pledged to find a compromise even though negotiations had broken down.*

20b Around titles of short works

Use quotation marks around titles of newspaper and magazine articles, poems, short stories, songs, episodes of television and radio programs, and chapters or subdivisions of books.

> The poem "Mother to Son" is by Langston Hughes.

NOTE: Titles of books, plays, Web sites, television and radio programs, films, magazines, and newspapers are put in italics. (See pp. 81–82.)

20c To set off words used as words

Although words used as words are ordinarily italicized (see p. 82), quotation marks are also acceptable.

> The words "affect" and "effect" are frequently confused.

20d Other punctuation with quotation marks

This section describes the conventions to observe in placing various marks of punctuation inside or outside quotation marks. It also explains how to punctuate when introducing quoted material.

Periods and commas Place periods and commas inside quotation marks.

> "I'm here for my service-learning project," I told the teacher. "I'd like to become a reading specialist."

This rule applies to single and double quotation marks, and it applies to all uses of quotation marks.

EXCEPTION: In MLA and APA parenthetical in-text citations, the period follows the citation in parentheses. MLA: *According to Cole, "The instruments of science have vastly extended our senses" (53).* APA: *According to Cole (1999), "The instruments of science have vastly extended our senses" (p. 53).*

Colons and semicolons Put colons and semicolons outside quotation marks.

> Harold wrote, "I regret that I cannot attend the fundraiser for AIDS research"; his letter, however, contained a contribution.

Question marks and exclamation points Put question marks and exclamation points inside quotation marks unless they apply to the whole sentence.

> Contrary to tradition, bedtime at my house is marked by "Mommy, can I tell you a story now?"

> Have you heard the old proverb "Do not climb the hill until you reach it"?

In the first sentence, the question mark applies only to the quoted question. In the second sentence, the question mark applies to the whole sentence.

Introducing quoted material After a word group introducing a quotation, use a colon, a comma, or no punctuation at all, whichever is appropriate in context.

If a quotation has been formally introduced, a colon is appropriate. A formal introduction is a full independent clause, not just an expression such as *he said* or *she writes*.

> Lance Morrow views personal ads as an art form: "The personal ad is like a haiku of self-celebration, a brief solo played on one's own horn."

If a quotation is introduced or followed by an expression such as *he said* or *she writes*, use a comma.

Stephen Leacock once said, "I am a great believer in luck, and I find the harder I work the more I have of it."

"You can be a little ungrammatical if you come from the right part of the country," writes Robert Frost.

When you blend a quotation into your own sentence, use either a comma or no punctuation, depending on the way the quotation fits into your sentence structure.

The champion could, as he put it, "float like a butterfly and sting like a bee."

Virginia Woolf wrote in 1928 that "a woman must have money and a room of her own if she is to write fiction" (4).

If a quotation appears at the beginning of a sentence, use a comma after it unless the quotation ends with a question mark or an exclamation point.

"I've always thought of myself as a reporter," claimed American poet Gwendolyn Brooks (162).

"What is it?" I asked, bracing myself.

If a quoted sentence is interrupted by explanatory words, use commas to set off the explanatory words.

"With regard to air travel," Stephen Ambrose notes, "Jefferson was a full century ahead of the curve" (53).

If two successive quoted sentences from the same source are interrupted by explanatory words, use a comma before the explanatory words and a period after them.

"It's considered unseemly to discuss one's personal finances in public," Lionel Shriver writes. "But I'm not very polite" (28).

20e Misuses of quotation marks

Avoid using quotation marks in the following situations.

FAMILIAR SLANG, TRITE EXPRESSIONS, OR HUMOR

▶ The economist emphasized that 5 percent was a ~~"~~ballpark figure.~~"~~

INDIRECT QUOTATIONS

▶ After finishing the exam, Chuck said that ~~"~~ he was due for a coffee break. ~~"~~

NOTE: Do not use quotation marks around the title of your own essay.

21 Other marks

21a The period

Use a period to end all sentences except direct questions or genuine exclamations.

> Celia asked whether the picnic would be canceled.

A period is conventionally used with personal titles, Latin abbreviations, and designations for time.

Mr.	i.e.	a.m. (or AM)
Ms.	e.g.	p.m. (or PM)
Dr.	etc.	

NOTE: If a sentence ends with a period marking an abbreviation, do not add a second period.

A period is not used for the following: US Postal Service abbreviations for states, abbreviations for organization and country names, academic degrees, and designations for eras.

| CA | UNESCO | FCC | NATO | BS | BC |
| NY | AFL-CIO | IRS | USA | PhD | BCE |

21b The question mark

Use a question mark after a direct question.

> What is the horsepower of a 747 engine?

NOTE: Use a period, not a question mark, after an indirect question, one that is reported rather than asked directly.

> He asked me who was teaching the mythology course.

PRACTICE hackerhandbooks.com/pocket
> Punctuation > 21–1

21c The exclamation point

Use an exclamation point after a sentence that expresses exceptional feeling or deserves special emphasis.

> We yelled to the police officer, "He's not drunk! He's in diabetic shock!"

Do not overuse the exclamation point.

▶ In the fisherman's memory, the fish lives on, increasing in length and weight each year, until it is big enough to shade a fishing boat!.

This sentence doesn't need to be pumped up with an exclamation point. It is emphatic enough without it.

21d The dash

The dash may be used to set off parenthetical material that deserves special emphasis. When typing, use two hyphens to form a dash (--), with no spaces before or after the dash. (If your word processing program has what is known as an "em-dash" (—), you may use it instead, with no space before or after it.)

Use a dash to introduce a list, a restatement, an amplification, or a striking shift in tone or thought.

> Along the wall are the bulk liquids—sesame seed oil, honey, safflower oil, and half-liquid peanut butter.

> Peter decided to focus on his priorities—applying to graduate school, getting financial aid, and finding a roommate.

> Kiere took a few steps back, came running full speed, kicked a mighty kick—and missed the ball.

In the first two examples, the writer could also use a colon. (See 18b.) The colon is more formal than the dash and not quite as dramatic.

Use a pair of dashes to set off parenthetical material that deserves special emphasis or to set off an appositive that contains commas.

> Everything that went wrong—from the peeping Tom at her window to my head-on collision—was blamed on our move.

In my hometown, people's basic needs—food, clothing, and shelter—are less costly than in Denver.

TIP: Unless you have a specific reason for using the dash, avoid it. Unnecessary dashes create a choppy effect.

21e Parentheses

Use parentheses to enclose supplemental material, minor digressions, and afterthoughts.

Nurses record patients' vital signs (temperature, pulse, and blood pressure) several times a day.

Use parentheses to enclose letters or numbers labeling items in a series.

There are three points of etiquette in poker: (1) allow someone to cut the cards, (2) don't forget to ante up, and (3) never stack your chips.

TIP: Do not overuse parentheses. Often a sentence reads more gracefully without them.

▶ Research shows that seventeen million ~~(estimates~~ *from* ~~run as high as~~ *to* twenty-three million*)* Americans have diabetes.

21f Brackets

Use brackets to enclose any words or phrases you have inserted into an otherwise word-for-word quotation.

Audubon reports that "if there are not enough young to balance deaths, the end of the species [California condor] is inevitable" (4).

The *Audubon* article did not contain the words *California condor* in the sentence quoted.

The Latin word "sic" in brackets indicates that an error in a quoted sentence appears in the original source.

According to the review, Nelly Furtado's performance was brilliant, "exceding [sic] the expectations of even her most loyal fans."

21g The ellipsis mark

Use an ellipsis mark, three spaced periods, to indicate that you have deleted material from an otherwise word-for-word quotation.

> Harmon (2011) noted, "During hibernation, heart rate would drop to nine beats per minute between breaths . . . and then speed up with each inhale."

If you delete a full sentence or more in the middle of a quoted passage, use a period before the three ellipsis dots.

NOTE: Do not use the ellipsis mark at the beginning or end of a quotation unless it is important, for clarity, to indicate that the passage quoted is from the middle of a sentence.

21h The slash

Use the slash to separate two or three lines of poetry that have been run into your text. Add a space both before and after the slash.

> In the opening lines of "Jordan," George Herbert pokes fun at popular poems of his time: "Who says that fictions only and false hair / Become a verse? Is there in truth no beauty?"

Use the slash sparingly, if at all, to separate options: *pass/fail*, *producer/director*. Put no space around the slash. Avoid using expressions such as *he/she* and *his/her* and the awkward construction *and/or*.

Mechanics

22 Capitalization 76
23 Abbreviations, numbers, and italics 78
24 Spelling and the hyphen 82

22 Capitalization

In addition to the following guidelines, a good dictionary can tell you when to use capital letters.

22a Proper vs. common nouns

Proper nouns and words derived from them are capitalized; common nouns are not. Proper nouns name specific persons, places, and things. All other nouns are common nouns.

The following types of words are usually capitalized: names of deities, religions, religious followers, and sacred books; words of family relationships used as names; particular places; nationalities and their languages, races, and tribes; educational institutions, departments, degrees, particular courses; government departments, organizations, political parties; historical movements, periods, events, documents; specific electronic sources; and trade names.

PROPER NOUNS	COMMON NOUNS
God (used as a name)	a god
Book of Common Prayer	a sacred book
Uncle Pedro	my uncle
Father (used as a name)	my father
Lake Superior	a picturesque lake
the Capital Center	a center for the arts
the South	a southern state
Wrigley Field	a baseball stadium
University of Wisconsin	a good university
Geology 101	a geology course
Veterans Administration	a federal agency
Phi Kappa Psi	a fraternity
the Democratic Party	a political party
the Enlightenment	the eighteenth century
the Great Depression	a recession
the Treaty of Versailles	a treaty
the World Wide Web, the Web	a home page
the Internet, the Net	a computer network
Advil	a painkiller

Months, holidays, and days of the week are capitalized: *May*, *Labor Day*, *Monday*. The seasons and numbers of the days of the month are not: *summer*, *the fifth of June*.

Names of school subjects are capitalized only if they are names of languages: *geology*, *history*, *English*, *French*.

PRACTICE hackerhandbooks.com/pocket
> Mechanics > 22–1

Names of particular courses are capitalized: *Geology 101*, *Principles of Economics*.

NOTE: Do not capitalize common nouns to make them seem important: *Our company is currently hiring technical support staff* [not *Company, Technical Support Staff*].

22b Titles with proper names

Capitalize a title when used as part of a proper name but usually not when used alone.

> Prof. Margaret Burnes; Dr. Sinyee Sein; John Scott Williams Jr.; Anne Tilton, LLD
>
> District Attorney Mill was ruled out of order.
>
> The district attorney was elected for a two-year term.

Usage varies when the title of an important public figure is used alone: *The president* [or *President*] *vetoed the bill*.

22c Titles of works

Major words should be capitalized in both titles and subtitles of works such as books, articles, and songs. Minor words—articles, prepositions, and coordinating conjunctions—are not capitalized unless they are the first or last word of a title or subtitle.

> *The Impossible Theater: A Manifesto*
>
> "Man in the Middle"
>
> "I Want to Hold Your Hand"

22d First word of a sentence or quoted sentence

The first word of a sentence should be capitalized. Capitalize the first word of a quoted sentence but not a quoted phrase.

> In *Time* magazine, Robert Hughes writes, "There are only about sixty Watteau paintings on whose authenticity all experts agree" (102).
>
> Russell Baker has written that sports are "the opiate of the masses" (46).

If a quoted sentence is interrupted by explanatory words, do not capitalize the first word after the interruption.

"When we all think alike," he said, "no one is thinking."

22e First word following a colon

Capitalize the first word after a colon if it begins an independent clause.

I came to a startling conclusion: The house must be haunted.

NOTE: MLA and *Chicago* styles use a lowercase letter to begin an independent clause following a colon. APA style uses a capital letter. CSE style uses a lowercase letter except for a direct quotation that is a complete sentence.

22f Abbreviations

Capitalize abbreviations for departments and agencies of government, other organizations, and corporations; capitalize trade names and the call letters of radio and television stations.

EPA, FBI, DKNY, IBM, Xerox, WCRB, KNBC-TV

23 Abbreviations, numbers, and italics

23a Abbreviations

Use abbreviations only when they are clearly appropriate.

Appropriate abbreviations   Use standard abbreviations for titles immediately before and after proper names.

TITLES BEFORE PROPER NAMES	TITLES AFTER PROPER NAMES
Ms. Nancy Linehan	Thomas Hines Jr.
Dr. Margaret Simmons	Anita Lor, PhD
Rev. John Stone	Robert Simkowski, MD
St. Joan of Arc	William Lyons, MA
Prof. James Russo	Polly Stern, DDS

PRACTICE hackerhandbooks.com/pocket
> Mechanics > 23–1 to 23–3

Do not abbreviate a title if it is not used with a proper name: *My history professor* [not *prof.*] *was an expert on naval warfare.*

Familiar abbreviations for the names of organizations, corporations, and countries are also acceptable: *CIA, FBI, NAACP, EPA, YMCA, NBC, USA.*

> The CIA was established in 1947 by the National Security Act.

When using an unfamiliar abbreviation (such as NAB for National Association of Broadcasters) throughout a paper, write the full name followed by the abbreviation in parentheses at the first mention of the name. You may use the abbreviation in the rest of the paper.

Other commonly accepted abbreviations include *BC, AD, a.m., p.m., No.,* and *$*. The abbreviation *BC* ("before Christ") follows a date, and *AD* ("*anno Domini*") precedes a date. Acceptable alternatives are *BCE* ("before the common era") and *CE* ("common era").

40 BC (or 40 BCE)	4:00 a.m. (or AM)	No. 12 (or no. 12)
AD 44 (or 44 CE)	6:00 p.m. (or PM)	$150

Avoid using *a.m., p.m., No.,* or *$* when not accompanied by a specific figure: *We set off for the lake early in the morning* [not *a.m.*].

Inappropriate abbreviations In formal writing, abbreviations for the following are not commonly accepted.

PERSONAL NAME Charles (*not* Chas.)

UNITS OF MEASUREMENT pound (*not* lb.)

DAYS OF THE WEEK Monday (*not* Mon.)

HOLIDAYS Christmas (*not* Xmas)

MONTHS January, February (*not* Jan., Feb.)

COURSES OF STUDY political science (*not* poli. sci.)

DIVISIONS OF WRITTEN WORKS chapter, page (*not* ch., p.)

STATES AND COUNTRIES Florida (*not* FL or Fla.)

PARTS OF A BUSINESS NAME Adams Lighting Company (*not* Adams Lighting Co.); Kim and Brothers, Inc. (*not* Kim and Bros., Inc.)

Although Latin abbreviations are appropriate in footnotes and bibliographies and in informal writing, use the appropriate English phrases in formal writing.

cf. (Latin *confer*, "compare")

e.g. (Latin *exempli gratia*, "for example")

et al. (Latin *et alii*, "and others")

etc. (Latin *et cetera*, "and so forth")

i.e. (Latin *id est*, "that is")

N.B. (Latin *nota bene*, "note well")

23b Numbers

Spell out numbers of one or two words. Use figures for numbers that require more than two words to spell out.

▶ The 1980 eruption of Mount St. Helens blasted ash ~~16~~ *sixteen* miles into the sky and devastated ~~two hundred thirty~~ *230* square miles of land.

If a sentence begins with a number, spell out the number or rewrite the sentence.

▶ *One hundred fifty* ~~150~~ children in our program need expensive dental treatment.

Generally, figures are acceptable for the following.

DATES   July 4, 1776; 56 BC; AD 30

ADDRESSES   77 Latches Lane, 519 West 42nd Street

PERCENTAGES   55 percent (or 55%)

FRACTIONS, DECIMALS   1/2, 0.047

SCORES   7 to 3, 21–18

STATISTICS   average age 37

SURVEYS   4 out of 5

EXACT AMOUNTS OF MONEY $105.37, $0.05

DIVISIONS OF BOOKS   volume 3, chapter 4, page 189

DIVISIONS OF PLAYS   act 3, scene 3 (or act III, scene iii)

IDENTIFICATION NUMBERS   serial no. 1098

TIME OF DAY   4:00 p.m., 1:30 a.m.

NOTE: Academic styles vary for handling numbers in the text of a paper. In the humanities, MLA and *Chicago* spell out numbers below 101 and round numbers (*forty million*); they use numerals for specific numbers above one hundred (*234*). In the social sciences and the sciences, APA and CSE spell out the numbers one through nine and use numerals for all other numbers.

23c Italics

This section describes conventional uses for italics: for titles of works; names of ships, aircraft, and spacecraft; foreign words; and words as words.

NOTE: If your instructor prefers underlining, simply substitute underlining for italics in the examples in this section.

Titles of works   Titles of the following types of works are italicized.

TITLES OF BOOKS   *The Known World, Middlesex, Encarta*

MAGAZINES   *Time, Scientific American, Salon.com*

NEWSPAPERS   the *Baltimore Sun,* the *Orlando Sentinel*

PAMPHLETS   *Common Sense, Facts about Marijuana*

LONG POEMS   *The Waste Land, Paradise Lost*

PLAYS   *King Lear, Wicked*

FILMS   *Casablanca, The Hurt Locker*

TELEVISION PROGRAMS   *American Idol, Frontline*

RADIO PROGRAMS   *All Things Considered*

MUSICAL COMPOSITIONS   *Porgy and Bess*

CHOREOGRAPHIC WORKS   *Brief Fling*

WORKS OF VISUAL ART   *American Gothic*

COMIC STRIPS   *Dilbert*

ELECTRONIC DATABASES   *ProQuest*

WEB SITES   *ZDNet, Google*

ELECTRONIC GAMES   *Dragon Age, Call of Duty*

The titles of other works, such as short stories, essays, songs, and short poems, are enclosed in quotation marks. (See 20b.)

NOTE: Do not use italics when referring to the Bible; titles of books in the Bible (Genesis, not *Genesis*); the titles of legal documents (the Constitution, not the *Constitution*); or the titles of your own papers.

Names of ships, aircraft, spacecraft Italicize names of specific ships, aircraft, and spacecraft.

> *Queen Mary 2*, *Spirit of St. Louis*, *Challenger*

Foreign words Italicize foreign words used in an English sentence.

> Caroline's *joie de vivre* should be a model for all of us.

EXCEPTION: Do not italicize foreign words that have become part of the English language—"laissez-faire," "fait accompli," "modus operandi," and "per diem," for example.

Words as words, etc. Italicize words used as words, letters mentioned as letters, and numbers mentioned as numbers.

> Tomás assured us that the chemicals could probably be safely mixed, but his *probably* stuck in our minds.

> Some toddlers have trouble pronouncing the letters *f* and *s*.

> A big *3* was painted on the stage door.

NOTE: Quotation marks may be used instead of italics to set off words mentioned as words. (See 20c.)

Inappropriate italics Italicizing to emphasize words or ideas is distracting and should be used sparingly.

24 Spelling and the hyphen

24a Spelling

A word processing program equipped with a spell checker is a useful tool, but be aware of its limitations. A spell checker will not tell you how to spell words not listed in its dictionary; nor will it help you catch words commonly

PRACTICE hackerhandbooks.com/pocket
> Mechanics > 24–1

confused, such as *accept* and *except*, or common typographical errors, such as *own* for *won*. You will still need to proofread, and for some words you may need to turn to the dictionary.

NOTE: To check for correct use of commonly confused words (*accept* and *except*, *its* and *it's*, and so on), consult section 46, the glossary of usage.

Major spelling rules   If you need to improve your spelling, review the following rules and exceptions.

1. In general, use *i* before *e* except after *c* and except when sounded like "ay," as in *neighbor* and *weigh*.

I BEFORE *E*	relieve, believe, sieve, niece, fierce, frieze
E BEFORE *I*	receive, deceive, sleigh, freight, eight
EXCEPTIONS	seize, either, weird, height, foreign, leisure

2. Generally, drop a final silent *-e* when adding a suffix that begins with a vowel. Keep the final *-e* if the suffix begins with a consonant.

desire, desiring	achieve, achievement
remove, removable	care, careful

Words such as *changeable*, *judgment*, *argument*, and *truly* are exceptions.

3. When adding *-s* or *-ed* to words ending in *-y*, ordinarily change *-y* to *-i* when the *-y* is preceded by a consonant but not when it is preceded by a vowel.

comedy, comedies	monkey, monkeys
dry, dried	play, played

With proper names ending in *-y*, however, do not change the *-y* to *-i* even if it is preceded by a consonant: *the Dougherty family*, *the Doughertys*.

4. If a final consonant is preceded by a single vowel *and* the consonant ends a one-syllable word or a stressed syllable, double the consonant when adding a suffix beginning with a vowel.

bet, betting	occur, occurrence
commit, committed	

5. Add -s to form the plural of most nouns; add -es to singular nouns ending in -s, -sh, -ch, and -x.

table, tables
paper, papers
agenda, agendas

church, churches
dish, dishes
fox, foxes

Ordinarily add -s to nouns ending in -o when the -o is preceded by a vowel. Add -es when the -o is preceded by a consonant.

radio, radios
video, videos

hero, heroes
tomato, tomatoes

To form the plural of a hyphenated compound word, add the -s to the chief word even if it does not appear at the end.

mother-in-law, mothers-in-law

NOTE: English words derived from other languages such as Latin, Greek, or French sometimes form the plural as they would in their original language.

medium, media
criterion, criteria

chateau, chateaux

Spelling variations Following is a list of some common words spelled differently in American and British English. Consult a dictionary for others.

AMERICAN	BRITISH
canceled, traveled	cancelled, travelled
color, humor	colour, humour
judgment	judgement
check	cheque
realize, apologize	realise, apologise
defense	defence
program	programme
anemia, anesthetic	anaemia, anaesthetic
theater, center	theatre, centre
fetus	foetus
mold, smolder	mould, smoulder
civilization	civilisation
connection, inflection	connexion, inflexion
licorice	liquorice

24b The hyphen

In addition to the following guidelines, a dictionary will help you make decisions about hyphenation.

Compound words The dictionary will tell you whether to treat a compound word as a hyphenated compound (*water-repellent*), as one word (*waterproof*), or as two words (*water table*). If the compound word is not in the dictionary, treat it as two words.

▶ The prosecutor did not cross-examine any witnesses.

▶ Imogen kept her sketches in a small notebook.

▶ Alice walked through the looking-glass into a backward world.

Words functioning together as an adjective When two or more words function together as an adjective before a noun, connect them with a hyphen. Generally, do not use a hyphen when such compounds follow the noun.

▶ Pat Hobbs is not yet a well-known candidate.

▶ After our television campaign, Pat Hobbs will be well known.

Do not use a hyphen to connect *-ly* adverbs to the words they modify.

▶ A slowly moving truck tied up traffic.

NOTE: In a series, hyphens are suspended: *Do you prefer first-, second-, or third-class tickets?*

Conventional uses Hyphenate the written form of fractions and of compound numbers from twenty-one to ninety-nine. Also use the hyphen with the prefixes *all-*, *ex-*, and *self-* and with the suffix *-elect*.

▶ One-fourth of my income goes for rent.

▶ The charity is funding more self-help projects.

Hyphenation at ends of lines Set your word processing program to not hyphenate words at the end of a line of text. This setting ensures that only words that already contain a hyphen may be broken at the end of a line.

E-mail addresses, URLs, and other electronic addresses need special attention when they occur at the end of a line of text. Do not insert a hyphen to divide electronic addresses. Instead, break an e-mail address after the @ symbol or before a period. Break a URL after a slash or a double slash or before any other mark of punctuation. (For specific documentation styles, see 34a, 39a, 44a, and 45b.)

Research

25 Posing a research question 88
26 Finding appropriate sources 89
27 Evaluating sources 94
28 Managing information; avoiding plagiarism 100

College research assignments ask you to pose a question worth exploring, to read widely in search of possible answers, to interpret what you read, to draw reasoned conclusions, and to support those conclusions with valid and well-documented evidence.

This section and the color-coded sections that follow—MLA (red), APA (green), *Chicago* (blue), and CSE (orange)—will help you write your paper and properly document your sources in the style your instructor requires.

25 Posing a research question

Working within the guidelines of your assignment, pose a few questions that seem worth researching—questions that you want to explore, that you feel would interest your audience, and about which there is a substantial debate. As you formulate possible questions, make sure that they are appropriate lines of inquiry for a research paper. Choose questions that are narrow (not too broad), challenging (not too bland), and grounded (not too speculative).

25a Choosing a narrow question

If your initial question is too broad, given the length of the paper you plan to write, look for ways to restrict your focus. Here, for example, is how two students narrowed their initial questions.

TOO BROAD	NARROWER
What are the hazards of fad diets?	What are the hazards of low-carbohydrate diets?
What are the benefits of stricter auto emissions standards?	How will stricter auto emissions standards create new, more competitive auto industry jobs?

25b Choosing a challenging question

Your research paper will be more interesting to both you and your audience if you base it on an intellectually challenging line of inquiry. Try to draft questions that provoke thought or engage readers in a debate.

PRACTICE hackerhandbooks.com/pocket
> Research > 25–1

TOO BLAND

What is obsessive-compulsive disorder?

How does DNA testing work?

CHALLENGING

Why is obsessive-compulsive disorder so difficult to treat?

How reliable is DNA testing?

You may need to address a bland question in the course of answering a more challenging one, but it would be a mistake to use the bland question as the focus for the whole paper.

25c Choosing a grounded question

Finally, you will want to make sure that your research question is grounded, not too speculative. Although speculative questions—such as those that address morality or beliefs—are worth asking and may receive some attention in a research paper, they are inappropriate central questions. The central argument of a research paper should be grounded in facts.

TOO SPECULATIVE

Is it wrong to share pornographic personal photos by cell phone?

Do scientists have the right to conduct medical experiments on animals?

GROUNDED

What role should the US government play in regulating mobile content?

How have breakthroughs in technology made medical experiments on animals increasingly unnecessary?

26 Finding appropriate sources

Depending on your research question, some sources will prove more useful than others. For example, if your research question addresses a historical issue, you might look at reference works, books, scholarly articles, and primary sources such as speeches. If your research question addresses a current political issue, however, you might turn to magazine and newspaper articles, Web sites, and government documents.

26a Locating reference works

For some topics, you may want to begin your search by consulting general or specialized reference works. General reference works include encyclopedias, almanacs, atlases, and biographical references. Many specialized reference works are available: *Encyclopedia of Bioethics*, *Almanac of American Politics*, *The Historical and Cultural Atlas of African Americans*, and *The New Grove Dictionary of Music and Musicians*, to name a few. Reference works can help you learn about a topic, but you will need to consult more in-depth sources as you write.

26b Locating articles

Libraries subscribe to a variety of databases (sometimes called *periodical* or *article databases*) that give students access to articles and other materials without charge. Older works that have not been digitized will not be available in databases; you may need to consult a print index as well.

What databases offer Your library's databases can lead you to articles in newspapers, magazines, and scholarly or technical journals. General databases cover several subject areas; subject-specific databases cover one subject area in depth. Your library might subscribe to some of the following databases.

GENERAL DATABASES

Academic Search Premier. A database that indexes popular and scholarly journals.

Expanded Academic ASAP. A database that indexes the contents of magazines, newspapers, and scholarly journals.

JSTOR. A full-text archive of scholarly journals from many disciplines.

LexisNexis. A set of databases particularly strong in news, business, legal, and political topics.

ProQuest. A database of periodical articles.

SUBJECT-SPECIFIC DATABASES

ERIC. An education database.

MLA Bibliography. A database of literary criticism.

PsycINFO. A database of psychology research.

PubMed. A database with abstracts of medical studies.

Many databases include the full text of at least some articles; others list only citations or citations with short summaries called *abstracts*. When the full text is not available, a citation will give you enough information to track down an article.

> **Refining keyword searches in databases and search engines**
>
> Although command terms and characters vary among databases and Web search engines, some of the most common functions are listed here.
>
> - Use quotation marks around words that are part of a phrase: "gateway drug".
> - Use AND to connect words that must appear in a document: hyperactivity AND children. Some search engines require a plus sign instead: hyperactivity+children.
> - Use NOT in front of words that must not appear in a document: Persian Gulf NOT war. Some search engines require a minus sign (hyphen) instead: Persian Gulf -war.
> - Use OR if only one of the terms must appear in a document: "mountain lion" OR cougar.
> - Use an asterisk as a substitute for letters that might vary: "marine biolog*" (to find *marine biology* or *marine biologist*).
> - Use parentheses to group a search expression and combine it with another: (standard OR student OR test*) AND reform.
>
> **NOTE:** Many search engines and databases offer an advanced search option for refining your search with filters for phrases that should or should not appear, date restrictions, and so on.

How to search a database To find articles on your topic in a database, start by searching with keywords, terms related to the information you need. If the first keyword you try results in no matches, experiment with synonyms. If your keyword search results in too many matches, narrow it by using one of the strategies in the chart above.

26c Locating books

The books your library owns are listed along with other resources in its catalog. You can search the catalog by author, title, or subject.

If your search calls up too few results, try different keywords or search for books on broader topics. If your search gives you too many results, try the strategies in the chart at the top of this page.

Use a book's call number to find the book on the shelf. When you're retrieving the book, take time to scan other books in the area since they are likely to cover the same topic.

26d Locating other sources online

You can find a variety of reliable resources using online tools beyond those offered by your library. For example, government agencies post information on their Web sites, and the sites of many organizations are filled with information about current issues. Museums and libraries often post digital versions of primary sources, such as photographs, political speeches, and classic literary texts.

Although the Internet can be a rich source of information, it lacks quality control. Anyone can publish to the Web, so you'll need to evaluate online sources with special care (see 27c).

This section describes the following Internet resources: search engines, directories, digital archives, government and news sites, blogs, and wikis.

Search engines When using a search engine, such as *Google* or *Yahoo!*, focus your search as narrowly as possible. You can sharpen your search by using the tips listed in the chart on page 91 or by using a search engine's advanced search form.

Directories Unlike search engines, which hunt for Web pages automatically, directories are put together by information specialists who arrange reputable sites by topic: education, health, politics, and so on.

Try the following directories for scholarly research:

Internet Scout Project: http://scout.wisc.edu/Archives

Librarian's Internet Index: http://lii.org

Open Directory Project: http://dmoz.org

WWW Virtual Library: http://vlib.org

Digital archives Archives like the following can help you find primary resources: the texts of poems, books, speeches, and historically significant documents; photographs; and political cartoons.

American Memory: http://memory.loc.gov

Avalon Project: http://yale.edu/lawweb/avalon/avalon.htm

Eurodocs: http://eudocs.lib.byu.edu

Google Books: http://books.google.com

Google Scholar: http://scholar.google.com

Making of America: http://moa.umdl.umich.edu

Online Books Page: http://onlinebooks.library.upenn.edu

Government and news sites For current topics, both government and news sites can prove useful. Many government agencies at every level provide online information. Government-maintained sites include resources such as facts and statistics, legal texts, government reports, and searchable reference databases. Here are just a few government sites:

Census Bureau: http://www.census.gov

Fedstats: http://www.fedstats.gov

GPO Access: http://www.gpoaccess.gov

United Nations: http://www.un.org

University of Michigan Documents Center: http://www.lib.umich.edu/m/moagrp

Many news organizations offer up-to-date information online. Some require registration and may charge fees for some articles. (Find out if your library subscribes to news sites that you can access at no charge.) The following news sites offer many free resources:

BBC: http://www.bbc.co.uk

Google News: http://news.google.com

Kidon Media-Link: http://www.kidon.com/media-link

New York Times: http://nytimes.com

Reuters: http://www.reuters.com

Blogs A blog (short for *Weblog*) is a site that contains text or multimedia entries usually written and maintained by one person, with comments contributed by readers. Though some blogs are personal or devoted to partisan politics, many journalists and academics maintain blogs that cover topics of interest to researchers. The following Web sites can lead you to a wide range of blogs:

Academic Blog Portal: http://academicblogs.org

Google Blog Search: http://www.google.com/blogsearch

Science Blogs: http://scienceblogs.com
Technorati: http://technorati.com

Wikis A wiki is a collaborative Web site with many contributors and with content that may change frequently. *Wikipedia*, the collaborative online encyclopedia, is one of the most frequently consulted wikis.

In general, *Wikipedia* may be helpful if you're checking for something that is common knowledge or looking for current information about a topic in contemporary culture. (For a discussion of common knowledge in various disciplines, see pp. 108, 166–67, and 210.) However, many scholars do not consider *Wikipedia* and wikis in general to be appropriate sources for college research. Authorship is not limited to experts; articles may be written or changed by anyone. When possible, locate and cite another, more reliable source for any useful information you find in a wiki.

27 Evaluating sources

You can often locate dozens or even hundreds of potential sources for your topic—far more than you will have time to read. Your challenge will be to determine what kinds of sources you need and to find a reasonable number of quality sources.

Later, once you have decided on sources worth consulting, your challenge will be to read them with an open mind and a critical eye.

27a Selecting sources

Determining how sources contribute to your writing
How you plan to use sources affects how you evaluate them. Sources can have various functions in a paper. You can use them to

- provide background information or context for your topic
- explain terms or concepts that your readers might not understand
- provide evidence for your argument
- lend authority to your argument
- offer counterevidence and alternative interpretations

> ### Determining if a source is scholarly
>
> Many college assignments require you to use scholarly sources. Written by experts for a knowledgeable audience, these sources often go into more depth than books and articles written for a general audience. To determine if a source is scholarly, look for the following:
>
> - Formal language and presentation
> - Authors with academic or scientific credentials
> - Footnotes or a bibliography documenting the works cited by the author in the source
> - Original research and interpretation (rather than a summary of other people's work)
> - Quotations from and analysis of primary sources
> - A description of research methods or a review of related research
>
> See pages 96–97 for a sample scholarly source and popular source.

For examples of how student writers use sources for a variety of purposes, see 31, 37, and 42.

Scanning search results The chart on page 91 shows how to refine your searches. This section explains how to scan through the results for the most useful and reliable sources.

Databases Most article databases (see p. 90) provide at least the following information to help you decide if a source is relevant, current, scholarly enough, and a suitable length.

>   Title and brief description (How relevant?)
>   Date (How current?)
>   Name of periodical (How scholarly?)
>   Length (How extensive in coverage?)

Book catalogs A book's title and date of publication are often your first clues as to whether the book is worth consulting. If a title looks interesting, you can click on it for further information.

Search engines Because anyone can publish a Web site, legitimate sources and unreliable sources live side-by-side online. Look for the following clues about the probable

Common features of a scholarly source

1. Formal presentation with abstract and research methods
2. Includes review of previous research studies
3. Reports original research
4. Includes references
5. Multiple authors with academic credentials

FIRST PAGE OF ARTICLE

Cyberbullying: Using Virtual Scenarios to Educate and Raise Awareness

Vivian H. Wright, Joy J. Burnham, Christopher T. Inman, and Heather N. Ogorchock

Abstract

This study examined cyberbullying in three distinct phases to facilitate a multifaceted understanding of cyberbullying. The phases included (a) a quantitative survey, (b) a qualitative focus group, and (c) development of educational scenarios/simulations (within the Second Life virtual environment). Phase III was based on adolescent feedback from Phases I and II of this study. In all three phases, adolescent reactions to cyberbullying were examined and reported to raise awareness and to educate others about cyberbullying. Results from scenario development indicate that simulations created in a virtual environment are engaging and have the potential to be powerful tools in helping schools address problems such as cyberbullying education and prevention. (Keyword: cyberbullying, virtual worlds, Second Life, teacher education, counselor education)

Introduction

Cyberbullying has gained attention and recognition in recent years (Beale & Hall, 2007; Carney, 2008; Casey-Canon, Hayward, & Gowen, 2001; Kowalski & Limber, 2007; Li, 2007; Shariff, 2005). The increased interest and awareness of cyberbullying relates to such factors as the national media attention after several publicized cyberbullying tragedies (Maag, 2007; Stelter, 2008; Zifcak, 2006), the attenuation of communication boundaries with advances in technology use among youth, presently there remains a critical need for more descriptions of the worst cyberbullying incidences (Maag, 2007; Stelter, 2008; Zifcak, 2006), are becoming more prevalent (Beale & Hall, 2007; Carney, 2008; Kowalski & Limber, 2007; Li, 2007). At this time, there is a need to raise awareness about the effects of cyberbullying and to create educational opportunities to serve multiple audiences (i.e., teachers, teacher educators, school administrators, school counselors, mental health professionals, students, parents) in the quest to identify and hopefully prevent cyberbullying in the future. Consequently, to facilitate a multifaceted understanding of cyberbullying, this study sought to examine cyberbullying through three phases: (a) a quantitative survey, (b) a qualitative focus group, and (c) development of the educational scenarios/simulations (i.e., using virtual world avatars similar to those used in Linden Lab's (1993) Second Life (SL; http://secondlife.com) based on adolescent feedback from Phases I and II of this study. Adolescent reactions to cyberbullying in all three phases of this study were examined and reported with two aims in mind: (a) to raise awareness of cyberbullying, and (b) to educate others about cyberbullying.

Defining Cyberbullying

Cyberbullying has been described as a traumatic experience that can lead to physical, cognitive, emotional, and social consequences (Carney, 2008; Casey-Canon et al., 2001; Patchin & Hinduja, 2006). Cyberbullying has been defined as "bullying through the e-mail, instant messaging, in a chat room, on a website, or through digital messages or images sent to a cell phone" (Kowalski & Limber, 2007, p. 822). There are numerous methods to engage in cyberbullying, including e-mail, instant messaging, online gaming, chat rooms, and text messaging (Beale & Hall, 2007; Li, 2007). In addition, cyberbullying appears in different forms than traditional bullying. For example, Beale and Hall (2007), Mason (2007), and Willard (2008) found that at least seven different types of cyberbullying exist, including:

- Exclusion: excluding someone purposefully

Research suggests that cyberbullying has distinct gender and age differences. According to the literature, girls are more likely to be online and to cyberbully (Beale & Hall, 2007; Kowalski & Limber, 2007; Li, 2006, 2007). This finding is "opposite of what happens off-line," where boys are more likely to bully than girls (Beale & Hall, p. 8). Age also appears to be a factor in cyberbullying. Cyberbullying increases in the elementary years, peaks during the middle school years, and declines in the high school years (Beale & Hall). Based on the literature, cyberbullying is a growing concern among middle school-aged children (Beale & Hall; Hinduja & Patchin, 2008; Kowalski & Limber, 2007; Li, 2007; Pellegrini & Bartini, 2000; Smith, Mahdavi, Carvalho, & Tippett, 2006; Williams & Guerra, 2007). Of the middle school grades, 6th grade students are usually the

EXCERPTS FROM OTHER PAGES

Table 2: Percentage of Students Who Experienced Cyberbullying through Various Methods

	E-mail	Facebook	MySpace	Cell Phone	Online Video	Chat Rooms
Victim	35.3%	11.8%	52.9%	50%	14.7%	11.8%
Bully	17.6%	0%	70.6%	47.1%	11.8%	5.9%

References

Bainbridge, W. S. (2007, July). The scientific research potential of virtual worlds. *Science, 317,* 472–476.

Beale, A., & Hall, K. (2007, September/October). Cyberbullying: What

Vivian H. Wright is an associate professor of instructional technology at the University of Alabama. In addition to teaching in the graduate program, Dr. Wright works with teacher educators on innovative ways to infuse technology in the curriculum

Wright, Vivian H., et al. "Cyberbullying: Using Virtual Scenarios to Educate and Raise Awareness." *Journal of Computing in Teacher Education* 26.1 (2009): 35–42.

Common features of a popular source

1. Provocative title
2. Written by a staff reporter, not an expert
3. Presents anecdotes about the topic
4. Presents a summary of research but no original research
5. No consistent citation of sources

FIRST PAGE OF ARTICLE

EXCERPT FROM ANOTHER PAGE

"The lack of face-to-face contact might tempt bullies to new levels of cruelty"

communication. "There is a distancing of the self and immediacy in response that we don't have in any other form of communication," she says. "On the computer, it's like it's not really you."

So what can be done? Led by Ruth Aylett of Heriot-Watt University in Edinburgh, UK,

Meanwhile, some governments have taken legislative action. In January 2006, the US Congress passed a law making it a federal crime to "annoy, abuse, threaten or harass" another person over the internet. Approximately 36 states have enacted similar legislation. And in South Korea, the "internet real-

McKenna, Phil. "The Cyber-Bullies Are Always with You. . . ." *New Scientist* July 2007: 26-27.

relevance, currency, and reliability of a site—but be aware that the clues are by no means foolproof.

Title, keywords, and lead-in text (How relevant?)

A date (How current?)

An indication of the site's sponsor or purpose (How reliable?)

The URL, especially the domain name extension: for example, .com, .edu, .gov, or .org (How relevant? How reliable?)

27b Reading with an open mind and a critical eye

As you begin reading the sources you have chosen, keep an open mind. Do not let your personal beliefs prevent you from listening to new ideas and opposing viewpoints. Your research question—not a snap judgment about the question—should guide your reading.

When you read critically, you are not necessarily judging an author's work harshly; you are simply examining its

---

Evaluating all sources

Checking for signs of bias

- Does the author or publisher endorse political or religious views that could affect objectivity?
- Is the author or publisher associated with a special-interest group, such as Greenpeace or the National Rifle Association, that might present a narrow view of an issue?
- How fairly does the author treat opposing views?
- Does the author's language show signs of bias?

Assessing an argument

- What is the author's central claim or thesis?
- How does the author support this claim—with relevant and sufficient evidence or with anecdotes or emotional examples?
- Are statistics accurate and used fairly? Does the author explain where the statistics come from?
- Are any of the author's assumptions questionable?
- Does the author consider opposing arguments and refute them persuasively?

assumptions, assessing its evidence, and weighing its conclusions. For a checklist on evaluating sources, see page 98.

27c Assessing Web sources with special care

Web sources can provide valuable information, but verifying their credibility may take time. Even sites that appear to be professional and fair-minded may contain questionable information. Before using a Web source in your paper, make sure you know who created the material and for what purpose. The following chart provides a checklist for evaluating Web sources.

Evaluating Web sources

Authorship

- Is there an author? You may need to do some clicking and scrolling to find the author's name. Check the home page or an "about this site" link.
- Can you tell whether an author is knowledgeable and credible? If the author's qualifications aren't listed on the site, look for links to the author's home page, which may provide evidence of his or her expertise.

Sponsorship

- Who, if anyone, sponsors the site? The sponsor of a site is often named and described on the home page.
- What does the URL tell you? The domain name extension often indicates the type of group hosting the site: commercial (.com), educational (.edu), nonprofit (.org), governmental (.gov), military (.mil), or network (.net). URLs may also indicate a country of origin: .uk (United Kingdom) or .jp (Japan), for instance.

Purpose and audience

- Why was the site created: To argue a position? To sell a product? To inform readers?
- Who is the site's intended audience?

Currency

- How current is the site? Check for the date of publication or the latest update.
- How current are the site's links? If many of the links no longer work, the site may be outdated for your purposes.

28 Managing information; avoiding plagiarism

Whether you decide to keep records on paper or on your computer—or both—you will need methods for managing information: maintaining a working bibliography, keeping track of source materials, and taking notes without plagiarizing your sources. (For more on avoiding plagiarism, see 30 for MLA style, 36 for APA style, and 41 for *Chicago* style.)

28a Maintaining a working bibliography

Keep a record of any sources you decide to consult. This record, called a *working bibliography*, will help you compile the list of sources that will appear at the end of your paper. The format of this list depends on the documentation style you are using. (For MLA style, see 33b; for APA style, see 38b; for *Chicago* style, see 43c; for CSE style, see 45b.)

Once you have created a working bibliography, you can annotate it. Writing several brief sentences summarizing key points of a source in your own words will help you identify how the source relates to your argument and to your other sources. Clarifying the source's ideas at this stage will help you separate them from your own ideas and avoid plagiarizing them later.

SAMPLE ANNOTATED BIBLIOGRAPHY ENTRY (MLA STYLE)

Gonsalves, Chris. "Wasting Away on the Web." *eWeek.com*. Ziff Davis Enterprise Holdings, 8 Aug. 2005. Web. 16 Feb. 2009.

> In this editorial, Gonsalves considers the implications [1] of several surveys, including one in which 61% of respondents said that their companies have the right to spy on them. The [2] author agrees with this majority, claiming that it's fine if his company chooses to monitor him as long as the company discloses its monitoring practices. He argues that "the days of [3] Internet freedom at work are justifiably finished," adding that he would prefer not to know the extent of the surveillance. Gonsalves writes for *eWeek.com*, a publication focused on technology products. He presents himself as an employee who [4] is comfortable with being monitored, but his job may be a

MODELS hackerhandbooks.com/pocket
> Model papers > MLA annotated bibliography: Orlov
> APA annotated bibliography: Haddad

source of bias. This editorial contradicts some of my other sources, which claim that employees want to know and should know all the details of their company's monitoring procedures. **[5]**

1. Summarize the source.
2. Annotations should be three to seven sentences long.
3. Use quotations sparingly. Put quotation marks around any words from the source.
4. Evaluate the source for bias and relevance.
5. Interpret the relationship between this source and others in the bibliography.

28b Keeping track of source materials

Save a copy of each source. Many databases will allow you to e-mail, save, or print citations or full texts of articles, and you can easily download, copy, or take screen shots of information from the Web.

Working with saved files or printouts—as opposed to relying on memory or hastily written notes—lets you highlight key passages and make notes in the margins of the source as you read. You also reduce the chances of unintentional plagiarism, since you will be able to compare your use of a source in your paper with the actual source, not just with your notes.

NOTE: It's especially important to keep print or electronic copies of Web sources, which may change or even become inaccessible over time. Make sure that your copy includes the site's URL and your date of access.

28c Avoiding unintentional plagiarism as you take notes

When you take notes, be very careful to identify borrowed words and phrases as quotations. Even if you half-copy the author's sentences—either by mixing the author's phrases with your own without using quotation marks or by plugging your synonyms into the author's sentence structure—you are committing plagiarism, a serious academic offense.

Summarizing and paraphrasing ideas and quoting exact language are three ways of taking notes. Be sure to include exact page references for all three types of notes, since you will need the page numbers later if you use the information in your paper. (See the following chart for advice about avoiding plagiarism.)

Integrating and citing sources to avoid plagiarism

Source text

> Our language is constantly changing. Like the Mississippi, it keeps forging new channels and abandoning old ones, picking up debris, depositing unwanted silt, and frequently bursting its banks. In every generation there are people who deplore changes in the language and many who wish to stop its flow. But if our language stopped changing it would mean that American society had ceased to be dynamic, innovative, pulsing with life — that the great river had frozen up.
> — Robert MacNeil and William Cran, *Do You Speak American?*, p. 1

NOTE: The examples in this chart follow MLA style (see 33). For information on APA, *Chicago*, and CSE styles, see 38, 43, and 45, respectively.

If you are using an exact sentence from a source, with no changes . . . →	. . . put quotation marks around the sentence. Use a signal phrase and include a page number in parentheses. *MacNeil and Cran write, "Our language is constantly changing" (1).*
If you are using a few exact words from the source but not an entire sentence . . . →	. . . put quotation marks around the exact words that you have used from the source. Use a signal phrase and include a page number in parentheses. *Some people, according to MacNeil and Cran, "deplore changes in the language" (1).*

If you are using near-exact words from the source but changing some word forms (*I* to *she*, *walk* to *walked*) or adding words to clarify and make the quotation flow with your own text . . .	→	. . . put quotation marks around the quoted words and put brackets around the changes you have introduced. Include a signal phrase and follow the quotation with the page number in parentheses. MacNeil and Cran compare the English language to the Mississippi River, which "forg[es] new channels and abandon[s] old ones" (1). MacNeil and Cran write, "In every generation there are people who deplore changes in the [English] language and many who wish to stop its flow" (1).
If you are paraphrasing or summarizing the source, using the author's ideas but not any of the author's exact words . . .	→	. . . introduce the ideas with a signal phrase and put the page number at the end of your sentence. Do not use quotation marks. (See 30, 36, and 41.) MacNeil and Cran argue that changes in the English language are natural and that they represent cultural progress (1).
If you have used the source's sentence structure but substituted a few synonyms for the author's words . . .	→	STOP! This is a form of plagiarism even if you use a signal phrase and a page number. Change your sentence by using one of the techniques given in this chart or in 31, 37, or 42. **PLAGIARIZED** MacNeil and Cran claim that, like a river, English creates new waterways and discards old ones. **INTEGRATED AND CITED CORRECTLY** MacNeil and Cran claim, "Like the Mississippi, [English] keeps forging new channels and abandoning old ones" (1).

MLA Papers

29 Supporting a thesis 105
30 Avoiding plagiarism 107
31 Integrating nonfiction sources 110
32 Integrating literary quotations 118
33 MLA documentation style 121

Directory to MLA in-text citation models 122

Directory to MLA works cited models 131

34 MLA manuscript format 155

SAMPLE PAGES 159

Most English and some humanities instructors will ask you to document your sources with the Modern Language Association (MLA) system of citations described in 33. When writing an MLA paper based on sources, you face three main challenges: (1) supporting a thesis, (2) citing your sources and avoiding plagiarism, and (3) integrating quotations and other source material.

29 Supporting a thesis

Most research assignments ask you to form a thesis, or main idea, and to support that thesis with well-organized evidence.

29a Forming a thesis

Once you have read a variety of sources and considered your issue from different perspectives, you are ready to form a working thesis—a one-sentence (or occasionally a two-sentence) statement of your central idea. The thesis expresses not just your opinion but also your informed, reasoned judgment. Usually your thesis will appear at the end of the first paragraph (see p. 159).

Your ideas may change as you learn more about your subject through reading and writing. You can revise your working thesis as you draft.

In a research paper, your thesis will answer the central question that you pose, as in the following examples.

PUBLIC POLICY QUESTION

Should employers monitor their employees' online activities in the workplace?

POSSIBLE THESIS

Employers should not monitor their employees' online activities because electronic surveillance can compromise workers' privacy.

LITERATURE QUESTION

What does Stephen Crane's short story "The Open Boat" reveal about the relationship between humans and nature?

PRACTICE hackerhandbooks.com/pocket
> MLA > 29–1 and 29–2

POSSIBLE THESIS

In Stephen Crane's gripping tale "The Open Boat," four men lost at sea discover not only that nature is indifferent to their fate but also that their own particular talents make little difference as they struggle for survival.

MEDIA STUDIES QUESTION

What statement does the television show *House* make about the patient's right to choose or decline medical treatment?

POSSIBLE THESIS

On the television show *House*, Dr. House frequently accuses his patients of ignorance or deceit and sometimes manipulates them into undergoing treatment they do not want. Despite these negative qualities, Dr. House usually emerges as the hero, demonstrating that medical expertise is more valuable than a patient's right to make decisions about treatment.

Notice that each of these thesis statements takes a stand on a debatable issue—an issue about which intelligent, well-meaning people might disagree. Each writer's job will be to convince such people that his or her view is worth taking seriously.

29b Organizing your ideas

The body of your paper will consist of evidence in support of your thesis. To get started, list your key points, as student writer Anna Orlov did in this rough outline.

- Employers monitor workers more efficiently with electronic surveillance.
- Companies may have financial and legal reasons to monitor employees' Internet usage.
- But monitoring employees' Internet usage may create distrust and lower worker productivity.
- Current laws do little to protect employees' privacy rights, so employees and employers must negotiate the risks and benefits of electronic surveillance.

After you have written a rough draft, a more formal outline can help you shape the complexities of your argument.

29c Using sources to inform and support your argument

Sources can play several different roles as you develop your points.

Providing background information or context You can use facts and statistics to support generalizations or to establish the importance of your topic.

Explaining terms or concepts Explain words, phrases, or ideas that might be unfamiliar to your readers. Quoting or paraphrasing a source can help you define terms and concepts in accessible language.

Supporting your claims Back up your assertions with facts, examples, and other evidence from your research.

Lending authority to your argument Expert opinion can give weight to your argument. But don't rely on experts to make your argument for you. Construct your argument in your own words and cite authorities in the field to support your position.

Anticipating and countering objections Do not ignore sources that seem to contradict your position or that offer arguments different from your own. Instead, use them to give voice to opposing ideas and interpretations before you counter them.

30 Avoiding plagiarism

Your research paper is a collaboration between you and your sources. To be fair and ethical, you must acknowledge your debt to the writers of those sources. When you acknowledge your sources, you avoid plagiarism, a serious academic offense.

Three different acts are considered plagiarism: (1) failing to cite quotations and borrowed ideas, (2) failing to enclose borrowed language in quotation marks, and (3) failing to put summaries and paraphrases in your own words.

PRACTICE hackerhandbooks.com/pocket
> MLA > 30-1 to 30-6

30a Citing quotations and borrowed ideas

When you cite sources, you give credit to writers from whom you've borrowed words and ideas. You also let your readers know where your information comes from so that they can evaluate the original source.

You must cite anything you borrow from a source, including direct quotations; statistics and other specific facts; visuals such as cartoons, graphs, and diagrams; and any ideas you present in a summary or a paraphrase.

The only exception is common knowledge—information your readers could easily find in general sources. For example, most encyclopedias will tell readers that Alfred Hitchcock directed *Notorious* in 1946 and that Emily Dickinson published only a handful of her many poems during her lifetime.

When you have seen information repeatedly in your reading, you don't need to cite it. However, when information has appeared in only one or two sources, when it is highly specific (as with statistics), or when it is controversial, you should cite the source.

MLA recommends a system of in-text citations. Here, briefly, is how the MLA citation system usually works:

1. The source is introduced by a signal phrase that names its author.
2. The material being cited is followed by a page number in parentheses.
3. At the end of the paper, a list of works cited, arranged alphabetically by authors' last names (or by titles for works with no authors), gives complete publication information about the source.

IN-TEXT CITATION

Legal scholar Jay Kesan points out that the law holds employers liable for employees' actions such as violations of copyright laws, the distribution of offensive or graphic sexual material, and illegal disclosure of confidential information (312).

ENTRY IN THE LIST OF WORKS CITED

Kesan, Jay P. "Cyber-Working or Cyber-Shirking? A First Principles Examination of Electronic Privacy in the Workplace." *Florida Law Review* 54.2 (2002): 289-332. Print.

This basic MLA format varies for different types of sources. For a detailed discussion of other models, see 33.

30b Enclosing borrowed language in quotation marks

To show that you are using a source's exact phrases or sentences, enclose them in quotation marks unless they have been set off from the text by indenting (see pp. 112–13). To omit the quotation marks is to claim—falsely—that the language is your own. Such an omission is plagiarism even if you have cited the source.

ORIGINAL SOURCE

> Without adequate discipline, the World Wide Web can be a tremendous time sink; no other medium comes close to matching the Internet's depth of materials, interactivity, and sheer distractive potential.
> —Frederick Lane, *The Naked Employee*, p. 142

PLAGIARISM

Frederick Lane points out that if people do not have adequate discipline, the World Wide Web can be a tremendous time sink; no other medium comes close to matching the Internet's depth of materials, interactivity, and sheer distractive potential (142).

BORROWED LANGUAGE IN QUOTATION MARKS

Frederick Lane points out that for those not exercising self-control, "the World Wide Web can be a tremendous time sink; no other medium comes close to matching the Internet's depth of materials, interactivity, and sheer distractive potential" (142).

30c Putting summaries and paraphrases in your own words

A summary condenses information from a source; a paraphrase conveys the information using about the same number of words as in the original source. When you summarize or paraphrase, you must name the source and restate the source's meaning in your own words. You commit plagiarism if you half-copy the author's sentences—either by mixing the author's phrases with your own without using quotation marks or by plugging your synonyms into the author's sentence structure.

The first paraphrase of the source on page 110 is plagiarized—even though the source is cited—because too much of its language is borrowed from the original. The underlined words have been copied exactly (without quotation marks). Also, the writer has echoed the sentence structure of the source, merely substituting some synonyms (*restricted* for *limited*, *modern era* for *computer age*, *monitoring* for *surveillance*, and *inexpensive* for *cheap*).

ORIGINAL SOURCE

> In earlier times, surveillance was limited to the information that a supervisor could observe and record firsthand and to primitive counting devices. In the computer age surveillance can be instantaneous, unblinking, cheap, and, maybe most importantly, easy.
> —Carl Botan and Mihaela Vorvoreanu, "What Do Employees Think about Electronic Surveillance at Work?," p. 126

PLAGIARISM: UNACCEPTABLE BORROWING

Scholars Carl Botan and Mihaela Vorvoreanu argue that <u>in earlier times</u> monitoring of employees was restricted to the <u>information that a supervisor could observe and record firsthand</u>. In the modern era, monitoring <u>can be instantaneous</u>, inexpensive, and, <u>most importantly, easy</u> (126).

To avoid plagiarizing an author's language, don't look at the source while you are summarizing or paraphrasing. After you've restated the author's idea in your own words, return to the source and check that you haven't used the author's language or sentence structure or misrepresented the author's ideas.

ACCEPTABLE PARAPHRASE

Scholars Carl Botan and Mihaela Vorvoreanu claim that the nature of workplace surveillance has changed over time. Before the arrival of computers, managers could collect only small amounts of information about their employees based on what they saw or heard. However, because computers are now standard workplace technology, employers can monitor employees efficiently (126).

31 Integrating nonfiction sources

Quotations, summaries, paraphrases, and facts will help you develop your argument, but they cannot speak for you. You can use several strategies to integrate information from research sources into your paper while maintaining your own voice.

PRACTICE hackerhandbooks.com/pocket
> MLA > 31–1 to 31–4

31a Using quotations appropriately

Limiting your use of quotations In your writing, keep the emphasis on your own ideas. Do not quote excessively. Except for the following legitimate uses of quotations, use your own words to summarize and paraphrase your sources and to explain your points.

WHEN TO USE QUOTATIONS

- When language is especially vivid or expressive
- When exact wording is needed for technical accuracy
- When it is important to let the debaters of an issue explain their positions in their own words
- When the words of an authority lend weight to an argument
- When the language of a source is the topic of your discussion (as in an analysis or interpretation)

It is not always necessary to quote full sentences from a source. Often you can integrate words or phrases from a source into your own sentence structure.

Kizza and Ssanyu observe that technology in the workplace has been accompanied by "an array of problems that needed quick answers," such as electronic monitoring to prevent security breaches (4).

Using the ellipsis mark To condense a quoted passage, you can use the ellipsis mark (three periods, with spaces between) to indicate that you have omitted words. What remains must be grammatically complete.

Lane acknowledges the legitimate reasons that many companies have for monitoring their employees' online activities, particularly management's concern about preventing "the theft of information that can be downloaded to a . . . disk, e-mailed to oneself . . . , or even posted to a Web page for the entire world to see" (12).

The writer has omitted from the source the words *floppy or Zip* before *disk* and *or a confederate* after *oneself*.

If you want to omit a full sentence or more, use a period before the three ellipsis dots.

Charles Lewis, director of the Center for Public Integrity, points out that "by 1987, employers were administering nearly 2,000,000 polygraph tests a year to job applicants and employees. . . . Millions of workers were required to produce urine samples under observation for drug testing . . ." (22).

Ordinarily, do not use an ellipsis mark at the beginning or at the end of a quotation. Your readers will understand that the quoted material is taken from a longer passage. The only exception occurs when you have dropped words at the end of the final quoted sentence. In such cases, put three ellipsis dots before the closing quotation mark and the parentheses, as in the previous example.

Using brackets Brackets allow you to insert your own words into quoted material—to clarify a confusing reference or to make the quoted words fit grammatically into the context of your writing.

Legal scholar Jay Kesan notes that "a decade ago, losses [from employees' computer crimes] were already mounting to five billion dollars annually" (311).

To indicate an error such as a misspelling, insert [sic], including the brackets, right after the error.

Setting off long quotations When you quote more than four typed lines of prose or more than three lines of poetry, set off the quotation by indenting it one inch from the left margin.

Long quotations should be introduced by an informative sentence, usually followed by a colon. Quotation marks are unnecessary because the indented format tells readers that the passage is taken word-for-word from the source.

Botan and Vorvoreanu examine the role of gender in company practices of electronic surveillance:

> By the middle 1990s, estimates of the proportion of surveilled employees that were women ranged from 75% to 85%. . . . Ironically, this gender imbalance in workplace surveillance may be evening out today because advances in surveillance technology are making surveillance of traditionally male dominated

fields, such as long-distance truck driving, cheap,

easy, and frequently unobtrusive. (127)

At the end of an indented quotation, the parenthetical citation goes outside the final punctuation mark.

31b Using signal phrases to integrate sources

When you include a paraphrase, summary, or direct quotation in your paper, introduce it with a *signal phrase* that names the author of the source and provides some context for the source material. (See the chart on page 114 for a list of verbs commonly used in signal phrases.)

Marking boundaries Readers need to move smoothly from your words to the words of a source. Avoid dropping quotations into the text without warning. Provide clear signal phrases, including at least the author's name, to indicate the boundary between your words and the source's words.

DROPPED QUOTATION
Some experts have argued that a range of legitimate concerns justifies employer monitoring of employee Internet usage. "Employees could accidentally (or deliberately) spill confidential corporate information . . . or allow worms to spread throughout a corporate network" (Tynan).

QUOTATION WITH SIGNAL PHRASE
Some experts have argued that a range of legitimate concerns justifies employer monitoring of employee Internet usage. As *PC World* columnist Daniel Tynan points out, companies that don't monitor network traffic can be penalized for their ignorance: "Employees could accidentally (or deliberately) spill confidential corporate information . . . or allow worms to spread throughout a corporate network."

Establishing authority The first time you mention a source, include in the signal phrase the author's title, credentials, or experience to help your readers recognize the source's authority and your own credibility as a responsible researcher who has located reliable sources.

SOURCE WITH NO CREDENTIALS

Jay Kesan points out that the law holds employers liable for employees' actions such as violations of copyright laws, the distribution of offensive or graphic sexual material, and illegal disclosure of confidential information (312).

SOURCE WITH CREDENTIALS

Legal scholar Jay Kesan points out that the law holds employers liable for employees' actions such as violations of copyright laws, the distribution of offensive or graphic sexual material, and illegal disclosure of confidential information (312).

Introducing summaries and paraphrases Introduce most summaries and paraphrases with a signal phrase that names the author and places the material in the context of your argument. Readers will then understand that everything between the signal phrase and the parenthetical citation summarizes or paraphrases the cited source.

Without the signal phrase (highlighted) in the following example, readers might think that only the quotation at the end is being cited, when in fact the whole paragraph is based on the source.

Frederick Lane believes that the personal computer has posed new challenges for employers worried about workplace productivity. Whereas early desktop computers were primitive enough to prevent employees from using them to waste time, the machines have become so sophisticated that they now make non-work-related computer activities easy and inviting. Perhaps most problematic from the employer's point of view, Lane asserts, is giving employees access to the Internet, "roughly the equivalent of installing a gazillion-channel television set for each employee" (15-16).

Sometimes a summary or a paraphrase does not require a signal phrase. When the context makes clear where the cited material begins, you may omit the signal phrase and include the author's last name in parentheses.

Integrating statistics and other facts When you are citing a statistic or another specific fact, a signal phrase is often not necessary. In most cases, readers will understand that the citation refers to the statistic or fact (not to the whole paragraph).

Using signal phrases in MLA papers

To avoid monotony, try to vary both the language and the placement of your signal phrases.

Model signal phrases

In the words of researchers Greenfield and Davis, ". . ."

As legal scholar Jay Kesan has noted, ". . ."

The ePolicy Institute, an organization that advises companies about reducing risks from technology, reports that ". . ."

". . .," writes Daniel Tynan, ". . ."

". . .," attorney Schmitt claims.

Kizza and Ssanyu offer a persuasive counterargument: ". . ."

Verbs in signal phrases

Are you providing background, explaining a concept, supporting a claim, lending authority, or refuting a belief? Choose a verb that is appropriate for the way you are using the source.

acknowledges	contends	insists
adds	declares	notes
admits	denies	observes
agrees	describes	points out
argues	disputes	refutes
asserts	emphasizes	rejects
believes	endorses	reports
claims	grants	responds
compares	illustrates	suggests
confirms	implies	writes

NOTE: In MLA style, use the present or present perfect tense (*argues* or *has argued*) to introduce source material unless you include a date that specifies the time of the original author's writing.

Roughly 60% of responding companies reported disciplining employees who had used the Internet in ways the companies deemed inappropriate; 30% had fired their employees for those transgressions (Greenfield and Davis 347).

There is nothing wrong, however, with using a signal phrase to introduce statistics and other facts.

Putting source material in context A signal phrase can help you connect your own ideas with those of another writer by clarifying how the source will contribute to your paper.

If you use another writer's words, you must explain how those words relate to your point; you must put the source in context. It's a good idea to embed a quotation between sentences of your own that interpret the source and link the quotation to your paper's argument. (See also 31c.)

QUOTATION WITH EFFECTIVE CONTEXT

The difference, Lane argues, between these old methods of data gathering and electronic surveillance involves quantity:

> Technology makes it possible for employers to gather enormous amounts of data about employees, often far beyond what is necessary to satisfy safety or productivity concerns. And the trends that drive technology—faster, smaller, cheaper—make it possible for larger and larger numbers of employers to gather ever-greater amounts of personal data. (3-4)

In an age when employers can collect data whenever employees use their computers—when they send e-mail, surf the Web, or even arrive at or depart from their workstations—the challenge for both employers and employees is to determine how much is too much.

31c Synthesizing sources

When you synthesize multiple sources in a research paper, you create a conversation about your research topic. You show readers how the ideas of one source relate to those of another by connecting and analyzing the ideas in the context of your argument. Keep the emphasis on your own writing. The thread of your argument should be easy to identify and to understand, with or without your sources.

In the following sample synthesis, Anna Orlov uses her own analyses to shape the conversation among her sources. She does not simply string quotations together or allow sources to overwhelm her writing. In her final sentence, she explains to readers how the various sources support her argument.

SAMPLE SYNTHESIS (DRAFT)

1 Productivity is not easily measured in the wired workplace. As a result, employers find it difficult to determine how much freedom to allow their employees. On the one hand, computers and Internet access give employees powerful tools to carry out their jobs; on the other hand, the same technology offers constant temptations to avoid work. As a 2005 study by *Salary.com* and *America Online* indicates, the Internet ranked as the top choice among employees for ways of wasting time on the job (Frauenheim).

2 Chris Gonsalves, an editor for *eWeek.com,* argues that technology has changed the terms between employers and employees: "While bosses can easily detect and interrupt water-cooler chatter," he writes, "the employee who is shopping at Lands' End or IMing with fellow fantasy baseball managers may actually appear to be working." The gap between observable behaviors and actual online activities has motivated some employers to invest in surveillance programs.

3 Many experts, however, disagree with employers' assumption that online monitoring can increase productivity. Employment law attorney Joseph Schmitt argues that, particularly for salaried employees, "a company shouldn't care whether employees spend one or 10 hours on the Internet as long as they are getting their jobs done—and provided that they are not accessing inappropriate sites" (qtd. in Verespej). Other experts even argue that time spent on personal Internet browsing can actually be productive for companies.

4 According to Bill Coleman, an executive at Salary.com, "Personal Internet use and casual office conversations often turn into new business ideas or suggestions for gaining operating efficiencies" (qtd. in Frauenheim). Employers, in other words, may benefit from showing more faith in their employees' ability to exercise their autonomy.

Student writer (¶1)
Source 1
Source 2
Student writer
Source 3
Student writer
Source 4
Student writer

1 Student writer Anna Orlov begins with a claim that needs support.

- **2** Signal phrases indicate how sources contribute to Orlov's paper and show that the ideas that follow are not her own.
- **3** Orlov presents a counterposition to extend her argument.
- **4** Orlov builds her case — each quoted passage offers a more detailed claim or example in support of her larger claim.

32 Integrating literary quotations

Smoothly integrating quotations from a literary work into your own text can present challenges. Do not be surprised to find yourself puzzling over the most graceful way to tuck in a short phrase or the clearest way to introduce a more extended passage from the work.

NOTE: The parenthetical citations at the ends of examples in this section tell readers where the quoted words can be found. They indicate the lines of a poem; the act, scene, and lines of a play; or the page number of a quotation from a short story or a novel. (For guidelines on citing literary works, see pp. 128–29.)

32a Introducing literary quotations

When writing about nonfiction articles and books, you will introduce every quotation with a signal phrase naming the author (see p. 115). When writing about a single work of fiction, however, you do not need to include the author's name each time you quote from the work. Mention the author's name in the introduction to your paper; in your discussion of the work, refer, as appropriate, to the narrator of a story, the speaker of a poem, or the characters in a play. Make sure, however, that you do not confuse the author of the work with the narrator, speaker, or characters.

INAPPROPRIATE

Poet Andrew Marvell describes his fear of death like this: "But at my back I always hear / Time's wingèd chariot hurrying near" (21-22).

APPROPRIATE

Addressing his beloved in an attempt to win her sexual favors, the speaker of the poem argues that death gives them no time to waste: "But at my back I always hear / Time's wingèd chariot hurrying near" (21-22).

When you quote the words of a narrator, speaker, or character in a literary work, you should name who is speaking and provide a context for the quoted words. In the following example, the quoted dialogue is from Tennessee Williams's play *The Glass Menagerie*.

> Laura is so completely under Amanda's spell that when urged to make a wish on the moon, she asks, "What shall I wish for, Mother?" (1.5.140).

For examples of quoted dialogue from a short story, see page 161.

32b Avoiding shifts in tense

Because it is conventional to write about literature in the present tense (see p. 29) and because literary works often use other tenses, you will need to exercise some care when weaving quotations into your own text. A first-draft attempt may result in an awkward shift, as it did for one student who was writing about Nadine Gordimer's short story "Friday's Footprint."

TENSE SHIFT

> When Rita sees Johnny's relaxed attitude, "she blushed, like a wave of illness" (159).

To avoid the distracting shift from present tense (*sees*) to past tense (*blushed*), the writer decided to paraphrase the reference to Rita's blushing and reduce the length of the quotation.

REVISED

> When Rita sees Johnny's relaxed attitude, she is overcome with embarrassment, "like a wave of illness" (159).

The writer could have changed the quotation to present tense, using brackets to indicate the change: *When Rita sees Johnny's relaxed attitude, "she blushe[s], like a wave of illness"* (159). (See also p. 112 for the use of brackets.)

32c Formatting and citing literary passages

MLA guidelines for formatting and citing quotations differ somewhat for short stories or novels, poems, and plays.

Short stories or novels If a quotation from a short story or a novel takes up four or fewer typed lines in your paper, put it in quotation marks and run it into the text of your essay. Include a page number in parentheses after the quotation.

The narrator of Eudora Welty's "Why I Live at the P.O.," known to us only as "Sister," makes many catty remarks about her enemies. For example, she calls Mr. Whitaker "this photographer with the pop-eyes" (46).

If a quotation from a short story or a novel is five typed lines or longer in your paper, set the quotation off from the text by indenting it one inch from the left margin; do not use quotation marks. (See also pp. 112–13.) Put the page number in parentheses after the final mark of punctuation.

Sister's tale begins with "I," and she makes every event revolve around herself, even her sister's marriage:

> I was getting along fine with Mama, Papa-Daddy, and Uncle Rondo until my sister Stella-Rondo just separated from her husband and came back home again. Mr. Whitaker! Of course I went with Mr. Whitaker first, when he first appeared here in China Grove, taking "Pose Yourself" photos, and Stella-Rondo broke us up. (46)

Poems Enclose quotations of three or fewer lines of poetry in quotation marks within your text, and indicate line breaks with a slash with a space on each side. Include line numbers in parentheses at the end of the quotation. For the first reference, use the word "lines." Thereafter, use just numbers.

The opening of Frost's "Fire and Ice" strikes a conversational tone: "Some say the world will end in fire, / Some say in ice" (lines 1-2).

When you quote four or more lines of poetry, set the quotation off from the text by indenting one inch and omit the quotation marks. Put the line numbers in parentheses after the final mark of punctuation.

The opening stanza of Louise Bogan's "Women" startles readers by presenting a negative stereotype of women:
> Women have no wilderness in them,
> They are provident instead,
> Content in the tight hot cell of their hearts
> To eat dusty bread. (lines 1-4)

Plays If a quotation from a play takes up four or fewer typed lines in your paper and is spoken by only one character, put quotation marks around it and run it into the text of your essay. Whenever possible, include the act number, scene number, and line numbers in parentheses at the end of the quotation. Separate the numbers with periods and use arabic numerals unless your instructor prefers roman numerals.

Two attendants silently watch as the sleepwalking Lady Macbeth subconsciously struggles with her guilt: "Here's the smell of blood still. All the perfumes of Arabia will not sweeten this little hand" (5.1.50-51).

33 MLA documentation style

In English and other humanities classes, you may be asked to use the MLA (Modern Language Association) system for documenting sources, which is set forth in the *MLA Handbook for Writers of Research Papers*, 7th ed. (New York: MLA, 2009).

To document sources, MLA recommends in-text citations that refer readers to a list of works cited at the end of the paper. The works cited list gives all the sources cited in the paper, arranged alphabetically by authors' last names (or by titles for works that have no authors). The author's name (or the work's title) is used in a signal phrase or in parentheses to cite the source in the text of the paper.

Directory to MLA in-text citation models

BASIC RULES FOR PRINT AND ELECTRONIC SOURCES
1. Author named in a signal phrase — 123
2. Author named in parentheses — 123
3. Author unknown — 124
4. Page number unknown — 124
5. One-page source — 124

VARIATIONS ON THE BASIC RULES
6. Two or three authors — 125
7. Four or more authors — 125
8. Organization as author — 125
9. Authors with the same last name — 126
10. Two or more works by the same author — 126
11. Two or more works in one citation — 126
12. Encyclopedia or dictionary entry — 126
13. Multivolume work — 127
14. Entire work — 127
15. Selection in an anthology — 127
16. Government document — 127
17. Historical document — 127
18. Legal source — 128
19. Indirect source (source quoted in another source) — 128

LITERARY WORKS AND SACRED TEXTS
20. Literary work without parts or line numbers — 128
21. Verse play or poem — 129
22. Novel with numbered divisions — 129
23. Sacred text — 129

33a MLA in-text citations

MLA in-text citations are made with a combination of signal phrases and parenthetical references. A signal phrase introduces information taken from a source (a quotation, summary, paraphrase, or fact); usually the signal phrase includes the author's name. The parenthetical reference comes after the cited material, often at the end of the sentence. It includes at least a page number (except for unpaginated sources, such as those found online). In the models in this section, the elements of the in-text citation are highlighted.

PRACTICE hackerhandbooks.com/pocket
> MLA > 33–1 to 33–3

IN-TEXT CITATION

Kwon points out that the Fourth Amendment does not give employees any protections from employers' "unreasonable searches and seizures" (6).

Readers can look up the author's last name in the alphabetized list of works cited, where they will learn the work's title and other publication information. If readers decide to consult the source, the page number will direct them to the passage that has been cited.

Basic rules for print and electronic sources The MLA system of in-text citations, which depends heavily on authors' names and page numbers, was created with print sources in mind. Although many online sources have unclear authorship and lack page numbers, the basic rules are the same for print and electronic sources.

The models in this section (items 1–5) show how the MLA system usually works and explain what to do if your source has no author or page numbers.

■ **1. Author named in a signal phrase** Ordinarily, introduce the material being cited with a signal phrase that includes the author's name. (See also 31b.)

Frederick Lane reports that employers can monitor their employees with "a hidden video camera pointed at an employee's monitor" and can even position a camera "so that a number of monitors [can] be viewed at the same time" (147).

The signal phrase—*Frederick Lane reports*—names the author; the parenthetical citation gives the page number of the book in which the quoted words may be found.

Notice that the period follows the parenthetical citation. When a quotation ends with a question mark or an exclamation point, leave the end punctuation inside the quotation mark and add a period at the end of your sentence.

O'Connor asks a critical question: "When does Internet surveillance cross the line between corporate responsibility and invasion of privacy?" (16).

■ **2. Author named in parentheses** If a signal phrase does not name the author, put the author's last name in parentheses along with the page number. Use no punctuation between the name and the page number.

> Companies can monitor employees' keystrokes without legal penalty, but they may have to combat low morale as a result (Lane 129).

■ **3. Author unknown** Either use the complete title in a signal phrase or use a short form of the title in parentheses. Titles of books are italicized; titles of articles are put in quotation marks.

> A popular keystroke logging program operates invisibly on workers' computers and provides supervisors with details of the workers' online activities ("Automatically").

If the author is an organization or a government agency, see item 8 on pages 125–26.

NOTE: See item 5 on page 134 for works cited entries for sources with unknown authors.

■ **4. Page number unknown** Do not include the page number if a work lacks page numbers, as is the case with many Web sources. Even if a printout from a Web site shows page numbers, treat the source as unpaginated because not all printouts give the same page numbers. (When the pages of a Web source are stable, as in PDF files, supply a page number in your in-text citation.)

> As a 2005 study by *Salary.com* and *America Online* indicates, the Internet ranked as the top choice among employees for ways of wasting time on the job; it beat talking with co-workers—the second most popular method—by a margin of nearly two to one (Frauenheim).

If a source has numbered paragraphs or sections, use "par." (or "pars.") or "sec." (or "secs.") in the parentheses: (Smith, par. 4). Notice that a comma follows the author's name.

■ **5. One-page source** If the source is one page long, MLA allows (but does not require) you to omit the page number. Even so, it's a good idea to supply the page number because without it readers may not know where your citation ends or, worse, may not realize that you have provided a citation at all.

Anush Yegyazarian reports that in 2000 the National Labor Relations Board's Office of the General Counsel helped win restitution for two workers who had been dismissed because their employers were displeased by the employees' e-mails about work-related issues (62). The case points to the ongoing struggle to define what constitutes protected speech in the workplace.

Variations on the basic rules This section describes the MLA guidelines for handling a variety of situations not covered by the basic rules in items 1–5. These rules for in-text citations are the same for both print and online sources.

■ **6. Two or three authors** Name the authors in a signal phrase, as in the following example, or include their last names in the parenthetical reference: (Kizza and Ssanyu 2).

Kizza and Ssanyu note that "employee monitoring is a dependable, capable, and very affordable process of electronically or otherwise recording all employee activities at work" and elsewhere (2).

When three authors are named in the parentheses, separate the names with commas: (Alton, Davies, and Rice 56).

■ **7. Four or more authors** Name all of the authors or include only the first author's name followed by "et al." (Latin for "and others"). The format you use should match the format in your works cited entry (see item 3 on p. 133).

The study was extended for two years, and only after results were reviewed by an independent panel did the researchers publish their findings (Blaine et al. 35).

■ **8. Organization as author** When the author is a corporation or an organization, name that author either in the signal phrase or in the parentheses. (For a government agency as author, see item 16 on p. 127.)

According to a 2001 survey of human resources managers by the American Management Association, more than three-quarters of the responding companies reported disciplining employees for "misuse or personal use of office telecommunications equipment" (2).

In the list of works cited, the American Management Association is treated as the author and alphabetized under *A*. When you give the organization name in parentheses, abbreviate common words in the name: "Assn.," "Dept.," "Natl.," "Soc.," and so on.

In a 2001 survey of human resources managers, more than three-quarters of the responding companies reported disciplining employees for "misuse or personal use of office telecommunications equipment" (Amer. Management Assn. 2).

■ **9. Authors with the same last name** If your list of works cited includes works by two or more authors with the same last name, include the author's first name in the signal phrase or first initial in the parentheses.

Estimates of the frequency with which employers monitor employees' use of the Internet each day vary widely (A. Jones 15).

■ **10. Two or more works by the same author** Mention the title of the work in the signal phrase or include a short version of the title in the parentheses.

The American Management Association and ePolicy Institute have tracked employers' practices in monitoring employees' e-mail use. The groups' 2003 survey found that one-third of companies had a policy of keeping and reviewing employees' e-mail messages ("2003 E-mail" 2); in 2005, more than 55% of companies engaged in e-mail monitoring ("2005 Electronic" 1).

Titles of articles and other short works are placed in quotation marks; titles of books are italicized.

■ **11. Two or more works in one citation** To cite more than one source in the parentheses, give the citations in alphabetical order and separate them with a semicolon.

Several researchers have analyzed the reasons that companies monitor employees' use of the Internet at work (Botan and Vorvoreanu 128-29; Kesan 317-19; Kizza and Ssanyu 3-7).

■ **12. Encyclopedia or dictionary entry** Unless an entry in an encyclopedia or a dictionary has an author, the source will be alphabetized in the list of works cited under the word or entry that you consulted (see item 24 on p. 140).

Either in your text or in the parenthetical citation, mention the word or entry. No page number is required, since readers can easily look up the word or entry.

The word *crocodile* has a surprisingly complex etymology ("Crocodile").

■ **13. Multivolume work** If your paper cites more than one volume of a multivolume work, indicate in the parentheses the volume you are referring to, followed by a colon and the page number.

In his studies of gifted children, Terman describes a pattern of accelerated language acquisition (2: 279).

■ **14. Entire work** Use the author's name in a signal phrase or in parentheses. There is no need to use a page number.

Lane explores the evolution of surveillance in the workplace.

■ **15. Selection in an anthology** Put the name of the author of the selection (not the editor of the anthology) in the signal phrase or the parentheses.

In "Love Is a Fallacy," the narrator's logical teachings disintegrate when Polly declares that she should date Petey because "[h]e's got a raccoon coat" (Shulman 379).

In the list of works cited, the work is alphabetized by the author's last name (Shulman), not by the name of the editor of the anthology. (See item 21 on pp. 139 and 140.)

■ **16. Government document** When a government agency is the author, you will alphabetize it in the list of works cited under the name of the government, such as United States or Great Britain (see item 66 on p. 153). For this reason, you must name the government as well as the agency in your in-text citation.

Online monitoring by the United States Department of the Interior over a one-week period found that employees' use of "sexually explicit and gambling websites . . . accounted for over 24 hours of Internet use" (3).

■ **17. Historical document** For a historical document, such as the United States Constitution, provide the document title, neither italicized nor in quotation marks, along with article and section numbers. In parenthetical citations, use common abbreviations such as "art." and "sec." and abbreviations of well-known titles (US Const., art. 1, sec. 2).

While the United States Constitution provides for the formation of new states (art. 4, sec. 3), it does not explicitly allow or prohibit the secession of states.

For other historical documents, cite as you would any other work, by the first element in the works cited entry (see item 67 on p. 153).

■ **18. Legal source** For legislative acts (laws) and court cases, name the act or case either in a signal phrase or in parentheses. Italicize the names of cases but not the names of acts.

The Jones Act of 1917 granted US citizenship to Puerto Ricans.

In 1857, Chief Justice Roger B. Taney declared in *Dred Scott v. Sandford* that blacks, whether enslaved or free, could not be citizens of the United States.

■ **19. Indirect source (source quoted in another source)** When a writer's or a speaker's quoted words appear in a source written by someone else, begin the parenthetical citation with the abbreviation "qtd. in."

According to Bill Coleman, an executive at *Salary.com*, "Personal Internet use and casual office conversations often turn into new business ideas or suggestions for gaining operating efficiencies" (qtd. in Frauenheim).

Literary works and sacred texts Literary works and sacred texts are usually available in a variety of editions. Your list of works cited will specify which edition you are using. When possible, give enough information—book parts, play divisions, line numbers—so that readers can locate the cited passage in any edition of the work.

■ **20. Literary work without parts or line numbers** When a work such as a short story, a novel, or a play has no parts or line numbers, cite the page number.

At the end of Kate Chopin's "The Story of an Hour," Mrs. Mallard drops dead upon learning that her husband is alive. In the final irony of the story, doctors report that she has died of a "joy that kills" (25).

■ **21. Verse play or poem** If possible, give act, scene, and line numbers for a verse play. Use arabic numerals and separate the numbers with periods.

In Shakespeare's *King Lear*, Gloucester, blinded for suspected treason, learns a profound lesson from his tragic experience: "A man may see how this world goes / with no eyes" (4.2.148-49).

For a poem, cite the part, stanza, and line numbers, if it has them, separated with periods.

The Green Knight claims to approach King Arthur's court "because the praise of you, prince, is puffed so high, / And your manor and your men are considered so magnificent" (1.12.258-59).

For a poem that is not divided into numbered parts or stanzas, use line numbers. For a first reference, use the word "lines": (lines 5-8). Thereafter use just the numbers: (12-13).

■ **22. Novel with numbered divisions** Give the page number followed by a semicolon, and then indicate the book, part, or chapter in which the passage may be found. Use abbreviations such as "bk.," "pt.," and "ch."

One of Kingsolver's narrators, teenager Rachel, pushes her vocabulary beyond its limits. For example, Rachel complains that being forced to live in the Congo with her missionary family is "a sheer tapestry of justice" because her chances of finding a boyfriend are "dull and void" (117; bk. 2, ch. 10).

■ **23. Sacred text** When citing a sacred text such as the Bible or the Qur'an, name the edition in your works cited entry (see item 25 on p. 140). In your parenthetical citation, give the book, chapter, and verse (or their equivalent), separated with periods. Common abbreviations for books of the Bible are acceptable.

Consider the words of Solomon: "If your enemy is hungry, give him bread to eat; and if he is thirsty, give him water to drink" (*Oxford Annotated Bible*, Prov. 25.21).

The title of a sacred work is italicized when it refers to a specific edition of the work, as in the preceding example. If you refer to the book in a general sense in your text, neither italicize it nor put it in quotation marks. (See also 23c.)

The Bible and the Qur'an provide allegories that help readers understand how to lead a moral life.

33b MLA list of works cited

An alphabetized list of works cited, which appears at the end of your research paper, gives publication information for each of the sources you have cited in the paper. Include only sources that you have quoted, summarized, or paraphrased. (For information about preparing the list, see pp. 157–58; for sample lists of works cited, see pp. 160 and 162.)

When a publisher is required in a works cited entry, give the city of publication without a state name. Shorten publishers' names, usually to the first principal word; abbreviate "University" and "Press" in the names of university publishers: UP of Florida. For the date of publication, use the date on the title page or the most recent date on the copyright page.

Include the medium in which a work was published, produced, or delivered. Usually put the medium at the end of the entry, capitalized but neither italicized nor in quotation marks. Typical designations for the medium are "Print," "Web," "Television," "CD," "Film," "DVD," "Photograph," "Performance," "Lecture," and "MP3 file."

Listing authors (print and online)   Alphabetize entries in the list of works cited by authors' last names (or by title if a work has no author).

NAME CITED IN TEXT
According to Nancy Flynn, . . .

BEGINNING OF WORKS CITED ENTRY
Flynn, Nancy.

PRACTICE   hackerhandbooks.com/pocket
> MLA > 33-4 to 33-8

Directory to MLA works cited models

LISTING AUTHORS (PRINT AND ONLINE)

1. Single author — 133
2. Two or three authors — 133
3. Four or more authors — 133
4. Organization as author — 133
5. Unknown author — 134
6. Two or more works by the same author — 134

ARTICLES IN PERIODICALS (PRINT)

7. Article in a journal (paginated by volume or by issue) — 135
   Citation at a glance 136
8. Article in a monthly magazine — 135
9. Article in a weekly magazine — 135
10. Article in a daily newspaper — 135
11. Article with a title in its title — 135
12. Editorial or other unsigned article — 137
13. Letter to the editor — 137
14. Review — 137

BOOKS (PRINT)

15. Basic format for a book — 137
    Citation at a glance 138
16. Book with an author and an editor — 137
17. Book with an author and a translator — 139
18. Book with an editor — 139
19. Graphic narrative or illustrated book — 139
20. Entire anthology — 139
21. One or more selections from an anthology — 139
    Citation at a glance 142
22. Edition other than the first — 140
23. Multivolume work — 140
24. Encyclopedia or dictionary entry — 140
25. Sacred text — 140
26. Foreword, introduction, preface, or afterword — 141
27. Book with a title in its title — 141
28. Book in a series — 141
29. Republished book — 141
30. Publisher's imprint — 141

ONLINE SOURCES

31. Entire Web site — 143
32. Short work from a Web site — 144
    Citation at a glance 145
33. Article in an online journal — 146
34. Article in an online magazine — 146
35. Article in an online newspaper — 146

ONLINE SOURCES (CONTINUED)

36. Article from a database — 146
    Citation at a glance 147
37. E-book (electronic book) — 146
38. Online book-length work — 148
39. Part of an online book — 148
40. Digital archives — 148
41. Online poem — 148
42. Entire blog (Weblog) — 149
43. Entry or comment in a blog (Weblog) — 149
44. Online video clip — 149
45. Online review — 149
46. E-mail message — 149
47. Posting to an online discussion list — 149
48. Entry in a wiki — 149

AUDIO AND VISUAL SOURCES (INCLUDING ONLINE VERSIONS)

49. Digital file — 150
50. Podcast — 150
51. Musical score — 150
52. Sound recording — 151
53. Film — 151
54. DVD or Blu-ray Disc (BD) — 151
55. Special feature on a DVD or Blu-ray Disc (BD) — 151
56. CD-ROM — 151
57. Computer software or video game — 151
58. Radio or television program — 151
59. Radio or television interview — 151
60. Live performance — 152
61. Lecture or public address — 152
62. Work of art — 152
63. Cartoon — 152
64. Advertisement — 152
65. Map or chart — 152

OTHER SOURCES (INCLUDING ONLINE VERSIONS)

66. Government document — 153
67. Historical document — 153
68. Legal source — 153
69. Pamphlet or brochure — 154
70. Unpublished dissertation — 154
71. Abstract of a dissertation — 154
72. Published proceedings of a conference — 154
73. Published interview — 154
74. Personal interview — 154
75. Personal letter — 154
76. Published letter — 154

1. Single author

Wood, James. *How Fiction Works.* New York: Farrar, 2008. Print.

2. Two or three authors

Gourevitch, Philip, and Errol Morris. *Standard Operating Procedure.* New York: Penguin, 2008. Print.

Farmer, John, John Azzarello, and Miles Kara. "Real Heroes, Fake Stories." *New York Times* 14 Sept. 2008: WK10. Print.

3. Four or more authors

Harris, Shon, Allen Harper, Chris Eagle, and Jonathan Ness. *Gray Hat Hacking.* 2nd ed. New York: McGraw, 2007. Print.

Name all the authors or name the first author followed by "et al." (Latin for "and others"). In an in-text citation, use the same form for the authors' names as you use in the works cited entry. See item 7 on page 125.

4. Organization as author

National Wildlife Federation. *Rain Check: Conservation Groups Monitor Mercury Levels in Milwaukee's Rain.* Ann Arbor: Natl. Wildlife Federation, 2001. Print.

Your in-text citation should also treat the organization as the author (see item 8 on pp. 125–26).

5. Unknown author

Article or other short work

"Poverty, by Outdated Numbers." [title (newspaper article)] Editorial. [label] *Boston Globe* [newspaper title] 20 Sept. 2008: [date of publication] A16. [page(s)] Print. [medium]

"Heat." [title (TV episode)] *Frontline*. [title (TV program)] Prod. Martin Smith. [producer] PBS. [network] KTWU, [station] Topeka, [city of broadcast] 21 Oct. 2008. [date of broadcast] Television. [medium]

For other examples of an article with no author and of a television program, see items 12 and 58, respectively.

Book, entire Web site, or other long work

New Concise World Atlas. [title (book)] New York: [city of publication] Oxford UP, [publisher] 2007. [date] Print. [medium]

Women of Protest: Photographs from the Records of the National Woman's Party. [title (Web site)] Lib. of Cong., [sponsor of site] n.d. [no date] Web. [medium] 29 Sept. 2008. [date of access]

Before concluding that the author of an online source is unknown, check carefully. The name of the author may appear at the end of the source, in tiny print, or on another page of the site, such as the home page. Also remember that an organization or a government agency may be the author (see items 4 and 66).

6. Two or more works by the same author

First alphabetize the works by title (ignoring the article *A*, *An*, or *The* at the beginning of a title). Use the author's name for the first entry only; for subsequent entries, use three hyphens followed by a period. The hyphens must stand for exactly the same name or names as in the first entry.

Knopp, Lisa. *Field of Vision.* Iowa City: U of Iowa P, 1996.
    Print.
---. *The Nature of Home: A Lexicon and Essays.* Lincoln: U of
    Nebraska P, 2002. Print.

Articles in periodicals (print) This section shows how to prepare works cited entries for articles in print journals, magazines, and newspapers. See "Listing authors" on page 130 and items 1–6 for how to handle basic parts of the entries. See also "Online sources" (pp. 141–50).

For articles appearing on consecutive pages, provide the range of pages (see items 7 and 8). When an article does not appear on consecutive pages, give the first page number followed by a plus sign: 32+. For dates requiring a month, abbreviate all but May, June, and July. For an illustrated citation of an article in a print periodical, see page 136.

■ 7. Article in a journal (paginated by volume or by issue)

Blackburn, Robin. "Economic Democracy: Meaningful, Desirable, Feasible?" *Daedalus* 136.3 (2007): 36-45. Print.

■ 8. Article in a monthly magazine

Lanting, Frans. "Life: A Journey through Time." *Audubon* Nov.-Dec. 2006: 48-52. Print.

■ 9. Article in a weekly magazine

von Drehle, David. "The Ghosts of Memphis." *Time* 7 Apr. 2008: 34-37. Print.

■ 10. Article in a daily newspaper

Page number with section letter

McKenna, Phil. "It Takes Just One Village." *New York Times* 23 Sept. 2008, New England ed.: D1. Print.

Page number with section number

Knox, David Blake. "Lord Archer, Storyteller." *Sunday Independent* [Dublin] 14 Sept. 2008, sec. 2: 9. Print.

■ 11. Article with a title in its title

Use single quotation marks around a title of a short work or a quoted term that appears in an article title. Italicize a title or term normally italicized.

Shen, Min. "'Quite a Moon!' The Archetypal Feminine in *Our Town*." *American Drama* 16.2 (2007): 1-14. Print.

Citation at a glance
Article in a periodical (MLA)

To cite an article in a print periodical in MLA style, include the following elements:

1. Author of article
2. Title and subtitle of article
3. Title of periodical
4. Volume and issue numbers (for journal)
5. Date or year of publication
6. Page number(s) of article
7. Medium

TITLE PAGE

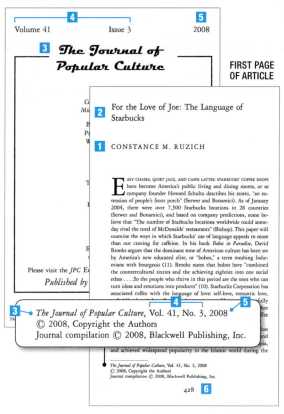

WORKS CITED ENTRY FOR AN ARTICLE IN A PRINT PERIODICAL

Ruzich, Constance M. "For the Love of Joe: The Language of Starbucks." *Journal of Popular Culture* 41.3 (2008): 428-42. Print.

For more on citing print periodical articles in MLA style, see pages 135 and 137.

■ 12. Editorial or other unsigned article

"Getting the Message: Communicating Electronically with Doctors
   Can Spur Honesty from Young Patients." Editorial. *Columbus
   [OH] Dispatch* 19 June 2008: 10A. Print.

■ 13. Letter to the editor

Morris, David. "Fiercely Proud." Letter. *Progressive* Feb. 2008:
   6. Print.

■ 14. Review
Begin with the name of the reviewer and the title of the review, if it has one. Add the words "Rev. of" and the title of the work reviewed, followed by the author, director, or other significant contributor. If the review has no author and no title, begin with "Rev. of" and alphabetize the entry by the first principal word in the title of the work reviewed.

Lane, Anthony. "Dream On." Rev. of *The Science of Sleep* and
   Renaissance, dir. Michel Gondry. *New Yorker* 25 Sept. 2006:
   155-57. Print.

Dodge, Chris. Rev. of *The Radical Jack London: Writings on War and
   Revolution,* ed. Jonah Raskni. *Utne Reader* Sept.-Oct. 2008:
   35. Print.

Books (print) Items 15–30 apply to print books. For electronic and online books, see items 37–39. For an illustrated citation of a print book, see page 138.

■ 15. Basic format for a book

Sacks, Oliver. *Musicophilia: Tales of Music and the Brain.* New York:
   Knopf, 2007. Print.

(author: last name first | book title | city of publication | publisher | date | medium)

■ 16. Book with an author and an editor
The abbreviation "Ed." means "Edited by," so it is the same for one or multiple editors.

Plath, Sylvia. *The Unabridged Journals of Sylvia Plath.* Ed. Karen V.
   Kukil. New York: Anchor-Doubleday, 2000. Print.

Citation at a glance
Book (MLA)

To cite a print book in MLA style, include the following elements:

1. Author
2. Title and subtitle
3. City of publication
4. Publisher
5. Date of publication
6. Medium

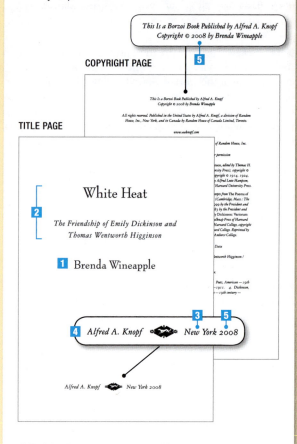

WORKS CITED ENTRY FOR A PRINT BOOK

Wineapple, Brenda. *White Heat: The Friendship of Emily Dickinson and Thomas Wentworth Higginson*. New York: Knopf, 2008. Print.

For more on citing print books in MLA style, see pages 137–41.

■ **17. Book with an author and a translator** "Trans." means "Translated by," so it is the same for one or multiple translators.

Scirocco, Alfonso. *Garibaldi: Citizen of the World*. Trans. Allan
 Cameron. Princeton: Princeton UP, 2007. Print.

■ **18. Book with an editor** Begin with the editor's name. For one editor, use "ed." after the name; for multiple editors, use "eds."

Lago, Mary, Linda K. Hughes, and Elizabeth MacLeod Walls, eds. *The
 BBC Talks of E. M. Forster, 1929-1960*. Columbia: U of Missouri
 P, 2008. Print.

■ **19. Graphic narrative or illustrated book** For a book that combines text and illustrations, begin your citation with the person you wish to emphasize (writer, illustrator, artist) and list any other contributors after the title of the book.

Weaver, Dustin, illus. *The Tenth Circle*. By Jodi Picoult. New York:
 Washington Square, 2006. Print.

Moore, Alan. *V for Vendetta*. Illus. David Lloyd. New York:
 Vertigo-DC Comics, 2008. Print.

■ **20. Entire anthology**

Dumanis, Michael, and Cate Marvin, eds. *Legitimate Dangers:
 American Poets of the New Century*. Louisville: Sarabande,
 2006. Print.

■ **21. One or more selections from an anthology**

One selection from anthology

| author of selection: last name first | title of selection | title of anthology |

Brouwer, Joel. "The Spots." *Legitimate Dangers: American Poets

| | editor(s) of anthology: in normal order |

 of the New Century*. Ed. Michael Dumanis and Cate Marvin.

| city of publication | publisher | date | page(s) of selection | medium |

 Louisville: Sarabande, 2006. 51-52. Print.

For two or more selections from an anthology, see page 140. For an illustrated citation of a selection from a print anthology, see pages 142–43.

Two or more selections, with separate anthology entry

Provide an entry for the entire anthology (see item 20) and give a shortened entry for each selection. Use the medium only in the entry for the complete anthology.

Brouwer, Joel. "The Spots." Dumanis and Marvin 51-52.
[author of selection | title of selection | editor(s) of anthology: last name(s) only | pages(s) of selection]

Dumanis, Michael, and Cate Marvin, eds. *Legitimate Dangers:*
[editor(s) of anthology | title of anthology]

American Poets of the New Century. Louisville: Sarabande,
[city of publication | publisher]

2006. Print.
[date | medium]

Keith, Sally. "Orphean Song." Dumanis and Marvin 195-96.
[author of selection | title of selection | editor(s) of anthology: last name(s) only | page(s) of selection]

■ **22. Edition other than the first** If the book has a translator or an editor in addition to the author, give the name of the translator or editor before the edition number, using the abbreviation "Trans." for "Translated by" (see item 17) or "Ed." for "Edited by" (see item 16).

Auletta, Ken. *The Underclass.* 2nd ed. Woodstock: Overlook, 2000.
    Print.

■ **23. Multivolume work** See item 13 on page 127 for an in-text citation of a multivolume work.

Stark, Freya. *Letters.* Ed. Lucy Moorehead. 8 vols. Salisbury:
    Compton, 1974-82. Print.

■ **24. Encyclopedia or dictionary entry**

Posner, Rebecca. "Romance Languages." *The Encyclopaedia
    Britannica: Macropaedia.* 15th ed. 1987. Print.

"Sonata." *The American Heritage Dictionary of the English Language.*
    4th ed. 2000. Print.

■ **25. Sacred text**

The Oxford Annotated Bible with the Apocrypha. Ed. Herbert G. May
    and Bruce M. Metzger. New York: Oxford UP, 1965. Print. Rev.
    Standard Vers.

The Qur'an: Translation. Trans. Abdullah Yusuf Ali. Elmhurst: Tahrike, 2000. Print.

■ 26. Foreword, introduction, preface, or afterword

Bennett, Hal Zina. Foreword. *Shimmering Images: A Handy Little Guide to Writing Memoir*. By Lisa Dale Norton. New York: Griffin-St. Martin's, 2008. xiii-xvi. Print.

Ozick, Cynthia. "Portrait of the Essay as a Warm Body." Introduction. *The Best American Essays 1998*. Ed. Ozick. Boston: Houghton, 1998. xv-xxi. Print.

■ 27. Book with a title in its title

Woodson, Jon. *A Study of Joseph Heller's* Catch-22*: Going Around Twice*. New York: Lang, 2001. Print.

■ 28. Book in a series
After the medium of publication, give the series name as it appears on the title page, followed by the series number, if any.

Douglas, Dan. *Assessing Languages for Specific Purposes*. Cambridge: Cambridge UP, 2000. Print. Cambridge Applied Linguistics Ser.

■ 29. Republished book

Trilling, Lionel. *The Liberal Imagination*. 1950. Introd. Louis Menand. New York: New York Review of Books, 2008. Print.

■ 30. Publisher's imprint
Give the name of the imprint (a division of a publishing company), a hyphen, and the name of the publisher.

Ackroyd, Peter. *The Fall of Troy*. New York: Talese-Doubleday, 2007. Print.

Online sources MLA guidelines assume that readers can locate most online sources by entering the author, title, or other identifying information in a search engine or a database. Consequently, the *MLA Handbook* does not require a Web address (URL) in citations for online sources. If your instructor requires one, see the note at the end of item 31 on page 144.

MLA style calls for a sponsor or a publisher in works cited entries for most online sources. If a source has no sponsor or publisher, use the abbreviation "N.p." (for "No publisher") in the sponsor position. If there is no

Citation at a glance
Selection from an anthology (MLA)

To cite a selection from a print anthology in MLA style, include the following elements:

1. Author of selection
2. Title of selection
3. Title and subtitle of anthology
4. Editor(s) of anthology
5. City of publication
6. Publisher
7. Date of publication
8. Page number(s) of selection
9. Medium

TITLE PAGE

ASIAN-AMERICAN LITERATURE

An Anthology

Shirley Geok-lin Lim
University of California, Santa Barbara

NTC Publishing Group
a division of NTC/Contemporary Publishing Company
Lincolnwood, Illinois USA

Lincolnwood, Illinois USA

FROM COPYRIGHT PAGE

Published by NTC/Contemporary Publishing Group, Inc.
4255 West Touhy Avenue, Lincolnwood (Chicago), Illinois 60646-1975 U.S.A.
©2000 NTC/Contemporary Publishing Group, Inc.

FIRST PAGE OF SELECTION

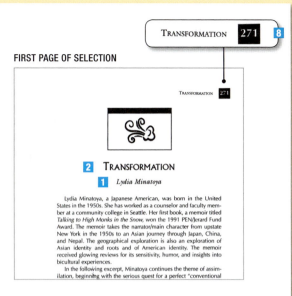

WORKS CITED ENTRY FOR A SELECTION FROM A PRINT ANTHOLOGY

For more on citing selections from print anthologies in MLA style, see pages 139 and 140.

---

date of publication or update, use "n.d." (for "no date") after the sponsor. For an article in an online journal or an article from a database, give page numbers if they are available; if they are not, use the abbreviation "n. pag." (See item 33 on p. 146.)

■ 31. Entire Web site

Web site with author

author: last name first | title of Web site | sponsor of site (personal page)

Peterson, Susan Lynn. *The Life of Martin Luther*. Susan Lynn Peterson,

update   medium   date of access: day + month + year

2005. Web. 24 Jan. 2009.

Web site with organization (group) as author

American Library Association. *American Library Association.* ALA, 2008. Web. 14 Jan. 2009.

- organization name: not abbreviated → American Library Association.
- title of Web site → *American Library Association.*
- sponsor: abbreviated → ALA,
- update → 2008.
- medium → Web.
- date of access: day + month + year → 14 Jan. 2009.

Web site with no author

Margaret Sanger Papers Project. History Dept., New York U, 18 Oct. 2000. Web. 6 Jan. 2009.

- title of Web site → *Margaret Sanger Papers Project.*
- sponsor of site → History Dept., New York U,
- update → 18 Oct. 2000.
- medium → Web.
- date of access: day + month + year → 6 Jan. 2009.

Web site with no title

Use the label "Home page" or another appropriate description in place of a title.

Yoon, Mina. Home page. Oak Ridge Natl. Laboratory, 28 Dec. 2006. Web. 12 Jan. 2009.

NOTE: If your instructor requires a URL for Web sources, include the URL, enclosed in angle brackets, at the end of the entry. When a URL in a works cited entry must be divided at the end of a line, break it after a double slash or a slash. Do not insert a hyphen.

Peterson, Susan Lynn. *The Life of Martin Luther.* Susan Lynn Peterson, 2005. Web. 24 Jan. 2009. <http://www.susanlynnpeterson.com/index_files/luther.htm>.

■ **32. Short work from a Web site** Short works include articles, poems, and other documents that are not book length or that appear as internal pages on a Web site. For an illustrated citation of a short work from a Web site, see page 145.

Short work with author

Shiva, Vandana. "Bioethics: A Third World Issue." *NativeWeb.* NativeWeb, n.d. Web. 22 Jan. 2010.

- author: last name first → Shiva, Vandana.
- title of short work → "Bioethics: A Third World Issue."
- title of Web site → *NativeWeb.*
- sponsor → NativeWeb,
- no update date → n.d.
- medium → Web.
- date of access: day + month + year → 22 Jan. 2010.

For a short work with no author, see page 146.

Citation at a glance
Short work from a Web site (MLA)

To cite a short work from a Web site in MLA style, include the following elements:

1 Author of short work (if any)
2 Title of short work
3 Title of Web site
4 Sponsor of Web site ("N.p." if none)
5 Update date ("n.d." if none)
6 Medium
7 Date you accessed the source

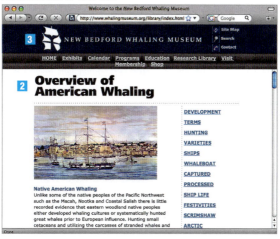

WORKS CITED ENTRY FOR A SHORT WORK FROM A WEB SITE

"Overview of American Whaling." *New Bedford Whaling Museum.* Old Dartmouth Hist. Soc./New Bedford Whaling Museum, 2009. Web. 27 Oct. 2009.

For more on citing sources from Web sites in MLA style, see pages 141–46.

Short work with no author

   title of   title of   sponsor
short work   Web site   of site   update

"Sister Aimee." *American Experience*. PBS Online, 2 Apr. 2007.

           date of access:
medium   day + month + year

  Web. 30 Oct. 2010.

■ 33. Article in an online journal
Use the abbreviation "n. pag." for an online journal that is not paginated.

Mason, John Edwin. "'Mannenberg': Notes on the Making of an Icon and Anthem." *African Studies Quarterly* 9.4 (2007): n. pag. Web. 23 Feb. 2010.

■ 34. Article in an online magazine

Burton, Robert. "The Certainty Epidemic." *Salon.com*. Salon Media Group, 29 Feb. 2008. Web. 18 Jan. 2010.

■ 35. Article in an online newspaper

Smith, Andrew D. "Poll: More than 70% of US Workers Use Internet on the Job." *Dallasnews.com*. Dallas Morning News, 25 Sept. 2008. Web. 29 Sept. 2010.

■ 36. Article from a database
For an illustrated citation of an article from a database, see page 147.

author of source: title of   volume,
last name first   article   journal title   issue   year   page(s)

Heyen, William. "Sunlight." *American Poetry Review* 36.2 (2007): 55-56.

                                    date of access:
     database name   medium day + month + year

Expanded Academic ASAP. Web. 24 Mar. 2010.

Barrera, Rebeca María. "A Case for Bilingual Education." *Scholastic Parent and Child* Nov.-Dec. 2004: 72-73. *Academic Search Premier*. Web. 1 Feb. 2009.

Williams, Jeffrey J. "Why Today's Publishing World Is Reprising the Past." *Chronicle of Higher Education* 13 June 2008: n. pag. *LexisNexis Academic*. Web. 29 Sept. 2009.

■ 37. E-book (electronic book)

Tolstoy, Leo. *War and Peace*. Trans. Richard Pevear and Larissa Volokhonsky. New York: Knopf, 2010. Nook file.

Citation at a glance
Article from a database (MLA)

To cite an article from a database in MLA style, include the following elements:

1. Author of article
2. Title of article
3. Title of periodical
4. Volume and issue numbers (for journal)
5. Date or year of publication
6. Page number(s) of article ("n. pag." if none)
7. Name of database
8. Medium
9. Date you accessed the source

ON-SCREEN VIEW OF DATABASE RECORD

WORKS CITED ENTRY FOR AN ARTICLE FROM A DATABASE

Kranz, David L. "Tracking the Sounds of Franco Zeffirelli's *The Taming of the Shrew*." *Literature-Film Quarterly* 36.2 (2008): 94-112. *Academic OneFile*. Web. 28 Oct. 2009.

For more on citing articles from a database in MLA style, see item 36.

38. Online book-length work

Cite as you would a short work from a Web site (see item 32), but italicize the title of the work.

Milton, John. *Paradise Lost: Book I*. *Poetryfoundation.org*. Poetry Foundation, 2008. Web. 14 Dec. 2009.

[author: last name first] [title of long poem] [title of Web site] [sponsor of site] [update] [medium] [date of access: day + month + year]

Give the print publication information for the work, if available (see items 15–30), followed by the title of the Web site, the medium, and your date of access.

Jacobs, Harriet A. *Incidents in the Life of a Slave Girl: Written by Herself*. Ed. L. Maria Child. Boston, 1861. *Documenting the American South*. Web. 3 Feb. 2010.

[author: last name first] [book title] [editor of original book] [city of publication] [year] [title of Web site] [medium] [date of access: day + month + year]

39. Part of an online book

Adams, Henry. "Diplomacy." *The Education of Henry Adams*. Boston: Houghton, 1918. N. pag. *Bartleby.com: Great Books Online*. Web. 8 Jan. 2010.

40. Digital archives

Digital archives are online collections of documents or records—books, letters, photographs, data—that have been converted to digital form. Cite publication information for the original document, if available. Then give the location of the document, if any, neither italicized nor in quotation marks; the name of the archive, italicized; the medium ("Web"); and your date of access.

Fiore, Mark. *Shockwaves*. 18 Oct. 2001. *September 11 Digital Archive*. Web. 3 Apr. 2009.

Oblinger, Maggie. Letter to Charlie Thomas. 31 Mar. 1895. Nebraska State Hist. Soc. *Prairie Settlement: Nebraska Photographs and Family Letters, 1862-1912*. Web. 3 Nov. 2009.

41. Online poem

Cite as you would a short work from a Web site (item 32) or part of an online book (item 39).

Bell, Acton [Anne Brontë]. "Mementos." *Poems by Currer, Ellis, and Acton Bell*. London, 1846. N. pag. *A Celebration of Women Writers*. Web. 18 Sept. 2009.

■ 42. Entire blog (Weblog)

Cite as you would an entire Web site (see item 31).

Gristmill. Grist Magazine, 2008. Web. 19 Jan. 2009.

■ 43. Entry or comment in a blog (Weblog)

Cite as you would a short work from a Web site (see item 32).

"Social Media: Facebook and MySpace as University Curricula." *Open Education*. Open Education.net, n.d. Web. 19 Sept. 2008.

Cynthia. Weblog comment. *Open Education*. Open Education.net, 8 Jan. 2010. Web. 14 Feb. 2010.

■ 44. Online video clip

Cite as you would a short work from a Web site (see item 32).

Murphy, Beth. "Tips for a Good Profile Piece." *YouTube*. YouTube, 7 Sept. 2008. Web. 19 Apr. 2010.

■ 45. Online review

Greer, W. R. "Who's the Fairest One of All?" Rev. of *Mirror, Mirror*, by Gregory Maguire. *Reviewsofbooks.com*. Reviewsofbooks.com, 2003. Web. 26 Oct. 2009.

■ 46. E-mail message

Lowe, Walter. "Review Questions." Message to the author. 15 Mar. 2010. E-mail.

■ 47. Posting to an online discussion list

Fainton, Peter. "Re: Backlash against New Labour." *Media Lens Message Board*. Media Lens, 7 May 2008. Web. 2 June 2008.

■ 48. Entry in a wiki

A wiki is an online reference that is openly edited by its users. Treat an entry in a wiki as you would a short work from a Web site (see item 32). Because wiki content is collectively edited and can be updated frequently, do not include an author.

"Hip Hop Music." *Wikipedia*. Wikimedia Foundation, 2 Mar. 2010. Web. 18 Mar. 2010.

"Negation in Languages." *UniLang Wiki*. UniLang, 12 Jan. 2009.
Web. 9 Mar. 2010.

Audio and visual sources (including online versions)

■ **49. Digital file** A digital file is any document or image that exists in digital form, independent of a Web site. To cite a digital file, begin with information required for the source (such as a photograph, a report, a sound recording, or a radio program), following the guidelines throughout 33b. Then for the medium, indicate the type of file: "JPEG file," "PDF file," "MP3 file," and so on.

Hine, Lewis W. *Girl in Cherryville Mill*. 1908. Prints and Photographs
Div., Lib. of Cong. JPEG file.

"Scenes from a Recession." *This American Life*. Narr. Ira Glass. NPR,
30 Mar. 2009. MP3 file.

National Institute of Mental Health. *What Rescue Workers Can Do*.
Washington: US Dept. of Health and Human Services, 2006.
PDF file.

■ **50. Podcast** If you view or listen to a podcast online, cite it as you would a short work from a Web site (see item 32). If you download the podcast and view or listen to it on a computer or portable player, cite it as a digital file (see item 49).

Podcast online

"Calculating the Demand for Charter Schools." Narr. David
Guenthner. *Texas PolicyCast*. Texas Public Policy Foundation,
28 Aug. 2008. Web. 10 Jan. 2009.

Podcast downloaded as digital file

"Calculating the Demand for Charter Schools." Narr. David
Guenthner. *Texas PolicyCast*. Texas Public Policy Foundation,
28 Aug. 2008. MP3 file.

■ **51. Musical score**

Handel, G. F. *Messiah: An Oratorio*. N.d. *CCARH Publications: Scores
and Parts*. Center for Computer Assisted Research in the
Humanities, 2003. Web. 5 Jan. 2009.

■ 52. Sound recording

Bizet, Georges. *Carmen*. Perf. Jennifer Laramore, Thomas Moser, Angela Gheorghiu, and Samuel Ramey. Bavarian State Orch. and Chorus. Cond. Giuseppe Sinopoli. Warner, 1996. CD.

Blige, Mary J. "Be without You." *The Breakthrough*. Geffen, 2005. CD.

■ 53. Film

Frozen River. Dir. Courtney Hunt. Perf. Melissa Leo, Charlie McDermott, and Misty Upham. Sony, 2008. Film.

■ 54. DVD or Blu-ray Disc (BD)

Forster, Marc, dir. *Finding Neverland*. Perf. Johnny Depp, Kate Winslet, Julie Christie, Radha Mitchell, and Dustin Hoffman. Miramax, 2004. DVD.

■ 55. Special feature on a DVD or Blu-ray Disc (BD)

"Sweeney's London." Prod. Eric Young. *Sweeney Todd: The Demon Barber of Fleet Street*. Dir. Tim Burton. DreamWorks, 2007. DVD. Disc 2.

■ 56. CD-ROM

"Pimpernel." *The American Heritage Dictionary of the English Language*. 4th ed. Boston: Houghton, 2006. CD-ROM.

■ 57. Computer software or video game

Firaxis Games. *Sid Meier's Civilization Revolution*. Take-Two Interactive, 2008. Xbox 360.

■ 58. Radio or television program

"Machines of the Gods." *Ancient Discoveries*. History Channel. 14 Oct. 2008. Television.

"Elif Shafak: Writing under a Watchful Eye." *Fresh Air*. Narr. Terry Gross. Natl. Public Radio, 6 Feb. 2007. *NPR.org*. Web. 22 Feb. 2009.

■ 59. Radio or television interview

De Niro, Robert, Barry Levinson, and Art Linson. Interview by Charlie Rose. *Charlie Rose*. PBS. WGBH, Boston, 13 Oct. 2008. Television.

60. Live performance

The Brothers Size. By Tarell Alvin McCraney. Dir. Bijan Sheibani.
Young Vic Theatre, London. 15 Oct. 2008. Performance.

Symphony no. 4 in G. By Gustav Mahler. Cond. Mark Wigglesworth.
Perf. Juliane Banse and Boston Symphony Orch. Symphony
Hall, Boston. 17 Apr. 2009. Performance.

61. Lecture or public address

Wellbery, David E. "On a Sentence of Franz Kafka." Franke Inst.
for the Humanities. Gleacher Center, Chicago. 1 Feb. 2006.
Lecture.

62. Work of art

For artworks found online, omit the medium of composition and include the title of the Web site, the medium ("Web"), and your date of access.

Constable, John. *Dedham Vale*. 1802. Oil on canvas. Victoria and
Albert Museum, London.

Hessing, Valjean. *Caddo Myth*. 1976. Joslyn Art Museum, Omaha.
Joslyn Art Museum. Web. 19 Apr. 2009.

63. Cartoon

Keefe, Mike. "Veterans Affairs Overruns." Cartoon. *Denverpost.com*.
Denver Post, 11 Oct. 2009. Web. 12 Dec. 2009.

64. Advertisement

Truth by Calvin Klein. Advertisement. *Vogue* Dec. 2000: 95-98.
Print.

Arbella Insurance. Advertisement. *Boston.com*. NY Times, n.d. Web.
3 Sept. 2009.

65. Map or chart

Joseph, Lori, and Bob Laird. "Driving While Phoning Is Dangerous."
Chart. *USA Today* 16 Feb. 2001: 1A. Print.

"Serbia." Map. *Syrena Maps*. Syrena, 2 Feb. 2001. Web. 17 Mar. 2009.

Other sources (including online versions) This section includes a variety of sources not covered elsewhere. For online sources, consult the appropriate model in this section and also see items 31–48.

■ 66. Government document

United States. Dept. of the Interior. Office of Inspector General.
[government] [department] [agency]

"Excessive Indulgences: Personal Use of the Internet at the
[document title]

Department of the Interior." *Office of Inspector General*.
[Web site title]

Dept. of the Interior, Sept. 1999. Web. 20 May 2010.
[publisher/sponsor] [publication date] [medium] [date of access: day + month + year]

Canada. Minister of Indian Affairs and Northern Dev. *Gathering Strength: Canada's Aboriginal Action Plan*. Ottawa: Minister of Public Works and Govt. Services Can., 2000. Print.

■ 67. Historical document

Jefferson, Thomas. First Inaugural Address. 1801. *The American Reader*. Ed. Diane Ravitch. New York: Harper, 1990. 42-44. Print.

The Virginia Declaration of Rights. 1776. *A Chronology of US Historical Documents*. U of Oklahoma Coll. of Law, 2008. Web. 23 Feb. 2009.

■ 68. Legal source

Legislative act (law)

Begin with the name of the act, neither italicized nor in quotation marks. Then provide the act's Public Law number; its Statutes at Large volume and page numbers; its date of enactment; and the medium of publication.

Electronic Freedom of Information Act Amendments of 1996. Pub. L. 104-231. 110 Stat. 3048. 2 Oct. 1996. Print.

Court case

Name the first plaintiff and the first defendant. Then give the volume, name, and page numbers of the law report; the court name; the year of the decision; and publication information. Do not italicize the name of the case. (In the text of the paper, the name of the case is italicized; see item 18 on p. 128.)

Utah v. Evans. 536 US 452. Supreme Court of the US. 2002. *Supreme Court Collection*. Legal Information Inst., Cornell U Law School, n.d. Web. 30 Apr. 2008.

■ 69. Pamphlet or brochure

Commonwealth of Massachusetts. Dept. of Jury Commissioner. *A Few Facts about Jury Duty*. Boston: Commonwealth of Massachusetts, 2004. Print.

■ 70. Unpublished dissertation

Jackson, Shelley. "Writing Whiteness: Contemporary Southern Literature in Black and White." Diss. U of Maryland, 2000. Print.

■ 71. Abstract of a dissertation

Chen, Shu-Ling. "Mothers and Daughters in Morrison, Tan, Marshall, and Kincaid." Diss. U of Washington, 2000. *DAI* 61.6 (2000): AAT 9975963. *ProQuest Dissertations and Theses*. Web. 22 Feb. 2009.

■ 72. Published proceedings of a conference

Urgo, Joseph R., and Ann J. Abadie, eds. *Faulkner and Material Culture*. Proc. of Faulkner and Yoknapatawpha Conf., 25-29 July 2004, U of Mississippi. Jackson: UP of Mississippi, 2007. Print.

■ 73. Published interview

Simon, David. "Beyond the Choir: An Interview with David Simon." *Film Quarterly* 62.2 (2008/2009): 44-49.

Florida, Richard. "The Great Reset." Interview by Conor Clarke. *Atlantic*. Atlantic Monthly Group, Feb. 2009. Web. 28 Feb. 2010.

■ 74. Personal interview

Akufo, Dautey. Personal interview. 11 Apr. 2010.

■ 75. Personal letter
For the medium, use "MS" for "manuscript," or a handwritten letter; use "TS" for "typescript," or a typed letter.

Primak, Shoshana. Letter to the author. 6 May 2010. TS.

■ 76. Published letter

Wharton, Edith. Letter to Henry James. 28 Feb. 1915. *Henry James and Edith Wharton: Letters, 1900-1915*. Ed. Lyall H. Powers. New York: Scribner's, 1990. 323-26. Print.

33c MLA information notes (optional)

Researchers who use the MLA system of parenthetical documentation may also use information notes for one of two purposes:

1. to provide additional material that is important but might interrupt the flow of the paper
2. to refer to several sources that support a single point or to provide comments on sources

Information notes may be either footnotes or endnotes. Footnotes appear at the foot of the page; endnotes appear on a separate page at the end of the paper, just before the list of works cited. For either style, the notes are numbered consecutively throughout the paper. The text of the paper contains a raised arabic numeral that corresponds to the number of the note.

TEXT

In the past several years, employees have filed a number of lawsuits against employers because of online monitoring practices.[1]

NOTE

1. For a discussion of federal law applicable to electronic surveillance in the workplace, see Kesan 293.

34 MLA manuscript format; sample pages

The following guidelines are consistent with advice given in the *MLA Handbook for Writers of Research Papers*, 7th ed. (New York: MLA, 2009), and with typical requirements for student papers. For sample pages from MLA papers, see pages 159–62.

34a MLA manuscript format

Formatting the paper Papers written in MLA style should be formatted as follows.

Materials and font Use good-quality 8½" × 11" white paper. If your instructor does not require a specific font, choose one that is standard and easy to read (such as Times New Roman).

Title and identification MLA does not require a title page. On the first page of your paper, place your name, your instructor's name, the course title, and the date on separate lines against the left margin. Then center your title. (See pp. 159 and 161 for sample first pages.)

If your instructor requires a title page, ask for formatting guidelines. A format similar to the one on page 239 may be acceptable.

Pagination Put the page number preceded by your last name in the upper right corner of each page, one-half inch below the top edge. Use arabic numerals (1, 2, 3, and so on).

Margins, line spacing, and paragraph indents Leave margins of one inch on all sides of the page. Left-align the text.

Double-space throughout the paper. Do not add extra space above or below the title of the paper or between paragraphs.

Indent the first line of each paragraph one-half inch from the left margin.

Capitalization and italics In titles of works, capitalize all words except articles (*a*, *an*, *the*), prepositions (*to*, *from*, *between*, and so on), coordinating conjunctions (*and*, *but*, *or*, *nor*, *for*, *so*, *yet*), and the *to* in infinitives—unless they are the first or last word of the title or subtitle.

In the text of an MLA paper, when a complete sentence follows a colon, lowercase the first word following the colon unless the sentence is a direct quotation or a well-known expression or principle.

Italicize the titles of books, periodicals, and other long works, such as Web sites. Use quotation marks around the titles of periodical articles, short stories, poems, and other short works.

Long quotations When a quotation is longer than four typed lines of prose or three lines of verse, set it off from the text by indenting the entire quotation one inch from the left margin. Double-space the indented quotation and do not add extra space above or below it.

Do not use quotation marks when a quotation has been set off from the text by indenting. See page 159 for an example.

URLs (Web addresses) When you need to break a URL at the end of a line in the text of your paper, break it only after a double slash or a slash and do not insert a hyphen. For MLA rules on dividing and formatting URLs in your list of works cited, see page 158.

Headings MLA neither encourages nor discourages the use of headings and provides no guidelines for their use. If you would like to insert headings in a long essay or research paper, check first with your instructor.

Visuals MLA classifies visuals as tables and figures (figures include graphs, charts, maps, photographs, and drawings). Label each table with an arabic numeral ("Table 1," "Table 2," and so on) and provide a clear caption that identifies the subject. The label and caption should appear on separate lines above the table, flush with the left margin.

For a table that you have borrowed or adapted, give the source below the table in a note like the following:

> Source: David N. Greenfield and Richard A. Davis; "Lost in Cyberspace: The Web @ Work"; *CyberPsychology and Behavior* 5.4 (2002): 349; print.

For each figure, place the figure number (using the abbreviation "Fig.") and a caption below the figure, flush left.

Place visuals in the text, as close as possible to the sentences that relate to them, unless your instructor prefers that visuals appear in an appendix.

Preparing the list of works cited

Begin the list of works cited on a new page at the end of the paper. Center the title "Works Cited" about one inch from the top of the page. Double-space throughout. See pages 160 and 162 for sample lists of works cited.

Alphabetizing the list Alphabetize the list by the last names of the authors (or editors); if a work has no author or editor, alphabetize by the first word of the title other than *A*, *An*, or *The*.

If your list includes two or more works by the same author, see item 6 on page 134.

Indenting Do not indent the first line of each works cited entry, but indent any additional lines one-half inch. See pages 160 and 162.

URLs (Web addresses) If you need to include a URL in a works cited entry and it must be divided across lines, break the URL only after a double slash or a slash. Do not insert a hyphen at the end of the line. Insert angle brackets around the URL. (See the note on p. 144.) If your word processing program automatically turns URLs into links (by underlining them and changing the color), turn off this feature.

34b Pages from two MLA papers

Following are excerpts from two MLA papers: a research paper written for a composition course and an analysis of a short story written for a literature class.

MODELS hackerhandbooks.com/pocket
> Model papers > MLA papers: Orlov; Houston; Daly; Levi
> MLA literature papers: Peel; Larson
> MLA annotated bibliography: Orlov

Sample MLA page: Research paper

Orlov 1

Anna Orlov
Professor Willis
English 101
17 March 2009

Online Monitoring:
A Threat to Employee Privacy in the Wired Workplace

Company policies on Internet usage have become as common as policies regarding vacation days or sexual harassment. A 2005 study by the American Management Association and ePolicy Institute found that **[1]** 76% of companies monitor employees' use of the Web, and the number of companies that block employees' access to certain Web sites has increased 27% since 2001 (1). Unlike other company rules, however, Internet usage policies raise questions about rights in the workplace. Although companies often have legitimate concerns that lead them **[2]** to monitor employees' Internet usage, the benefits of electronic surveillance are outweighed by its costs to employees' privacy and autonomy.

While surveillance of employees is not new, electronic surveillance allows employers to monitor workers with unprecedented efficiency. In *The Naked Employee*, Frederick Lane describes offline ways in which **[3]** employers have been permitted to intrude on employees' privacy for decades. The difference, Lane argues, between the old methods and electronic surveillance involves quantity:

> **[4]** Technology makes it possible for employers to gather enormous amounts of data about employees. . . . And the trends that drive technology—faster, smaller, cheaper—make it possible for larger and larger numbers of employers to gather ever-greater amounts of personal data. (3-4) **[5]**

---

[1] Source provides background information. **[2]** Debatable thesis. **[3]** Signal phrase introduces quotation. **[4]** Long quotation indented 1"; quotation marks omitted. **[5]** Page numbers in parentheses after the final period.

(Annotations indicate MLA-style formatting and effective writing.)

Sample MLA list of works cited

Orlov 5

[1] Works Cited

[2] Adams, Scott. *Dilbert and the Way of the Weasel*. New York: Harper, 2002. Print.

American Management Association and ePolicy Institute. "2005 Electronic Monitoring and Surveillance Survey." *American Management Association*. Amer. Management Assn., 2005. Web. 15 Feb. 2009.

[3] "Automatically Record Everything They Do Online! Spector Pro 5.0 FAQ's." *Netbus.org*. Netbus.Org, n.d. Web. 17 Feb. 2009. [4]

[5] Flynn, Nancy. "Internet Policies." *ePolicy Institute*. ePolicy Inst., n.d. Web. 15 Feb. 2009.

Frauenheim, Ed. "Stop Reading This Headline and Get Back to Work." *CNET News.com*. CNET Networks, 11 July 2005. Web. 17 Feb. 2009. [6]

[7] Gonsalves, Chris. "Wasting Away on the Web." *eWeek.com*. Ziff Davis Enterprise Holdings, 8 Aug. 2005. Web. 16 Feb. 2009.

Kesan, Jay P. "Cyber-Working or Cyber-Shirking? A First Principles Examination of Electronic Privacy in the Workplace." *Florida Law Review* 54.2 (2002): 289-332. Print. [8]

Lane, Frederick S., III. *The Naked Employee: How Technology Is Compromising Workplace Privacy*. New York: Amer. Management Assn., 2003. Print.

[9] Tam, Pui-Wing, et al. "Snooping E-Mail by Software Is Now a Workplace Norm." *Wall Street Journal* 9 Mar. 2005: B1+. Print.

---

[1] Heading, centered. [2] Authors' names inverted; works alphabetized by last names. [3] Work without author listed by title. [4] Abbreviation "n.d." for online source with no update date. [5] Short work from Web site. [6] First line of entry at left margin; extra lines indented ½". [7] Article from online periodical. [8] Double-spacing throughout. [9] Four authors listed by first author's name and the abbreviation "et al."

Larson 1

Dan Larson
Professor Duncan
English 102
19 April 2010

The Transformation of Mrs. Peters:
An Analysis of "A Jury of Her Peers"

In Susan Glaspell's 1917 short story "A Jury of Her Peers," two women accompany their husbands and a county attorney to an isolated house where a farmer named John Wright has been choked to death. The chief suspect is Wright's wife, Minnie, who is in jail awaiting trial. The sheriff's wife, Mrs. Peters, has come along to gather some items for Minnie, and Mrs. Hale has joined her. Initially, Mrs. Hale sympathizes with Minnie and objects to the male investigators "snoopin' round and criticizin' " her kitchen (191). But Mrs. Peters shows respect for the law, saying that the men are doing "no more than their duty" (191). By the end of the story, however, Mrs. Peters has joined Mrs. Hale in lying to the men and committing a crime—hiding key evidence. What causes this dramatic change?

One critic, Leonard Mustazza, argues that Mrs. Hale recruits Mrs. Peters "as a fellow 'juror' in the case, moving the sheriff's wife . . . towards identification with the accused wom[a]n" (494). However, Mrs. Peters also reaches insights on her own. Her observations in the kitchen lead her to understand Minnie's plight:

> The sheriff's wife had looked from the stove to the sink—to the pail of water which had been carried in from outside. . . . That look of seeing into things, of seeing through a thing to something else, was in the eyes of the sheriff's wife now. (194)

Sample MLA list of works cited

Larson 7

Works Cited

Ben-Zvi, Linda. " 'Murder, She Wrote': The Genesis of Susan Glaspell's *Trifles*." *Theatre Journal* 44.2 (1992): 141-62. Rpt. in *Susan Glaspell: Essays on Her Theater and Fiction*. Ed. Ben-Zvi. Ann Arbor: U of Michigan P, 1995. 19-48. Print.

Glaspell, Susan. "A Jury of Her Peers." *Literature and Its Writers: A Compact Introduction to Fiction, Poetry, and Drama*. Ed. Ann Charters and Samuel Charters. 5th ed. Boston: Bedford, 2010. 185-201. Print.

Hedges, Elaine. "Small Things Reconsidered: 'A Jury of Her Peers.' " *Women's Studies* 12.1 (1986): 89-110. Rpt. in *Susan Glaspell: Essays on Her Theater and Fiction*. Ed. Linda Ben-Zvi. Ann Arbor: U of Michigan P, 1995. 49-69. Print.

Mustazza, Leonard. "Generic Translation and Thematic Shift in Susan Glaspell's *Trifles* and 'A Jury of Her Peers.' " *Studies in Short Fiction* 26.4 (1989): 489-96. Print.

---

[1] List alphabetized by last names. [2] Article reprinted in anthology. [3] Article in journal.

APA Papers

35 Supporting a thesis 164
36 Avoiding plagiarism 166
37 Integrating sources 169
38 APA documentation style 173

Directory to APA in-text citation models 174

Directory to APA reference list models 179

39 APA manuscript format 195

SAMPLE PAGES 199

Many writing assignments in the social sciences are either reports of original research or reviews of the literature (previously published research) on a particular topic. Often an original research report contains a "review of the literature" section that places the writer's project in the context of other researchers' findings.

Many social science instructors will ask you to document your sources with the American Psychological Association (APA) system of in-text citations and references described in 38. You face three main challenges when writing a social science paper that draws on sources: (1) supporting a thesis, (2) citing your sources and avoiding plagiarism, and (3) integrating quotations and other source material.

35 Supporting a thesis

Most assignments ask you to form a thesis and to support it with well-organized evidence. A thesis, which usually appears at the end of the introduction, is a one-sentence (or occasionally a two-sentence) statement of your central idea. In a paper reviewing the literature on a topic, the thesis analyzes the often competing conclusions drawn by a variety of researchers.

35a Forming a thesis

You will be reading articles and other sources that are related to your central research question. Your thesis will express your reasoned and informed answer to that question, given the current state of research in the field. Here are some examples.

RESEARCH QUESTION

Is medication the right treatment for the escalating problem of childhood obesity?

POSSIBLE THESIS

Understanding the limitations of medical treatments for children highlights the complexity of the childhood obesity problem in the United States and underscores the need for physicians, advocacy groups, and policymakers to search for other solutions.

PRACTICE hackerhandbooks.com/pocket
> APA > 35–1 and 35–2

RESEARCH QUESTION

How can a business improve employee motivation?

POSSIBLE THESIS

Setting clear expectations, sharing information in a timely fashion, and publicly offering appreciation to specific employees can help align individual motivation with corporate goals.

RESEARCH QUESTION

Why are boys diagnosed with ADHD more often than girls?

POSSIBLE THESIS

Recent studies have suggested that ADHD is diagnosed more often in boys than in girls because of personality differences between boys and girls as well as gender bias in referring adults, but an overlooked cause is that ADHD often coexists with other behavior disorders that exaggerate or mask gender differences.

Each of these thesis statements expresses a view on a debatable issue—an issue about which informed people might disagree. The writers will need to persuade readers to take their positions seriously.

35b Organizing your ideas

APA encourages the use of headings to help readers follow the organization of a paper. For an original research report, the major headings often follow a standard model: Method, Results, Discussion. For a review of the literature, headings will vary, depending on the topic. For examples of headings in APA papers, see pages 200 and 203.

35c Using sources to inform and support your argument

Sources can play several different roles as you develop your points.

Providing background information or context You can use facts and statistics to support generalizations or to establish the importance of your topic.

Explaining terms or concepts Explain words, phrases, or ideas that might be unfamiliar to your readers. Quoting or paraphrasing a source can help you define terms and concepts in accessible language.

Supporting your claims Back up your assertions with facts, examples, and other evidence from your research.

Lending authority to your argument Expert opinion can give weight to your argument. But don't rely on experts to make your argument for you. Construct your argument in your own words and cite authorities in the field to support your position.

Anticipating and countering other interpretations Do not ignore sources that seem contrary to your position or that offer interpretations different from your own. Instead, use them to give voice to opposing ideas and interpretations before you counter them.

36 Avoiding plagiarism

Your research paper is a collaboration between you and your sources. To be fair and ethical, you must acknowledge your debt to the writers of those sources. When you acknowledge your sources, you avoid plagiarism, a serious academic offense.

Three different acts are considered plagiarism: (1) failing to cite quotations and borrowed ideas, (2) failing to enclose borrowed language in quotation marks, and (3) failing to put summaries and paraphrases in your own words.

36a Citing quotations and borrowed ideas

When you cite sources, you give credit to writers from whom you've borrowed words and ideas. You also let your readers know where your information comes from, so that they can evaluate the original source.

You must cite anything you borrow from a source, including direct quotations; statistics and other specific facts; visuals such as cartoons, graphs, and diagrams; and any ideas you present in a summary or a paraphrase.

The only exception is common knowledge—information that your readers may know or could easily locate in general sources. For example, most general encyclopedias

PRACTICE hackerhandbooks.com/pocket
> APA > 36–1 to 36–5

will tell readers that Sigmund Freud wrote *The Interpretation of Dreams* and that chimpanzees can learn American Sign Language. When you have seen certain information repeatedly in your reading, you don't need to cite it. However, when information has appeared in only a few sources, when it is highly specific (as with statistics), or when it is controversial, you should cite the source.

APA recommends an author-date style of citations. Here, briefly, is how the author-date system usually works. See 38 for a detailed discussion of variations.

1. The source is introduced by a signal phrase that includes the last name of the author followed by the date of publication in parentheses.
2. The material being cited is followed by a page number in parentheses.
3. At the end of the paper, an alphabetized list of references gives publication information for the source.

IN-TEXT CITATION

As researchers Yanovski and Yanovski (2002) have explained, obesity was once considered "either a moral failing or evidence of underlying psychopathology" (p. 592).

ENTRY IN THE LIST OF REFERENCES

Yanovski, S. Z., & Yanovski, J. A. (2002). Drug therapy: Obesity. *The New England Journal of Medicine, 346*, 591-602.

36b Enclosing borrowed language in quotation marks

To show that you are using a source's exact phrases or sentences, you must enclose them in quotation marks. To omit the quotation marks is to claim—falsely—that the language is your own. Such an omission is plagiarism even if you have cited the source.

ORIGINAL SOURCE

> In an effort to seek the causes of this disturbing trend, experts have pointed to a range of important potential contributors to the rise in childhood obesity that are unrelated to media.
>
> —Henry J. Kaiser Family Foundation, "The Role of Media in Childhood Obesity" (2004), p. 1

PLAGIARISM

According to the Henry J. Kaiser Family Foundation (2004), experts have pointed to a range of important potential contributors to the rise in childhood obesity that are unrelated to media (p. 1).

BORROWED LANGUAGE IN QUOTATION MARKS

According to the Henry J. Kaiser Family Foundation (2004), "experts have pointed to a range of important potential contributors to the rise in childhood obesity that are unrelated to media" (p. 1).

NOTE: When quoted sentences are set off from the text by indenting, quotation marks are not needed (see p. 170).

36c Putting summaries and paraphrases in your own words

A summary condenses information; a paraphrase conveys information in about the same number of words as in the original source. When you summarize or paraphrase, you must name the source and restate the source's meaning in your own words. You commit plagiarism if you half-copy the author's sentences—either by mixing the author's phrases with your own without using quotation marks or by plugging your own synonyms into the author's sentence structure. The following paraphrases are plagiarized—even though the source is cited—because their language and structure are too close to those of the source.

ORIGINAL SOURCE

> In an effort to seek the causes of this disturbing trend, experts have pointed to a range of important potential contributors to the rise in childhood obesity that are unrelated to media.
> —Henry J. Kaiser Family Foundation, "The Role of Media in Childhood Obesity" (2004), p. 1

PLAGIARISM: UNACCEPTABLE BORROWING OF PHRASES

According to the Henry J. Kaiser Family Foundation (2004), experts have indicated a range of significant potential contributors to the rise in childhood obesity that are not linked to media (p. 1).

PLAGIARISM: UNACCEPTABLE BORROWING OF STRUCTURE

According to the Henry J. Kaiser Family Foundation (2004), experts have identified a variety of significant factors causing a rise in childhood obesity, factors that are not linked to media (p. 1).

To avoid plagiarizing an author's language, don't look at the source while you are summarizing or paraphrasing. After you've restated the author's ideas in your own words, return to the source and check that you haven't used the author's language or sentence structure or misrepresented the author's ideas.

ACCEPTABLE PARAPHRASE

A report by the Henry J. Kaiser Family Foundation (2004) described sources other than media for the childhood obesity crisis (p. 1).

37 Integrating sources

Quotations, summaries, paraphrases, and facts will help you develop your argument, but they cannot speak for you. You can use several strategies to integrate information from research sources into your paper while maintaining your own voice.

37a Using quotations appropriately

Limiting your use of quotations In your writing, keep the emphasis on your own words. Do not quote excessively. It is not always necessary to quote full sentences from a source. Often you can integrate words or phrases from a source into your own sentence structure.

As researchers continue to face a number of unknowns about obesity, it may be helpful to envision treating the disorder, as Yanovski and Yanovski (2002) suggested, "in the same manner as any other chronic disease" (p. 592).

Using the ellipsis mark To condense a quoted passage, you can use the ellipsis mark (three periods, with spaces

PRACTICE hackerhandbooks.com/pocket
> APA > 37-1 to 37-4

between) to indicate that you have omitted words. What remains must be grammatically complete.

Roman (2003) reported that "social factors are nearly as significant as individual metabolism in the formation of . . . dietary habits of adolescents" (p. 345).

The writer has omitted the words *both healthy and unhealthy* from the source.

When you want to omit a full sentence or more, use a period before the three ellipsis dots.

According to Sothern and Gordon (2003), "Environmental factors may contribute as much as 80% to the causes of childhood obesity. . . . Research suggests that obese children demonstrate decreased levels of physical activity and increased psychosocial problems" (p. 104).

Ordinarily, do not use an ellipsis mark at the beginning or at the end of a quotation. Readers will understand that the quoted material is taken from a longer passage. The only exception occurs when you have dropped words at the end of the final quoted sentence. In such cases, put three ellipsis dots before the closing quotation mark.

Using brackets Brackets allow you to insert your own words into quoted material to clarify a confusing reference or to make the quoted words fit grammatically into the context of your writing.

The cost of treating obesity currently totals $117 billion per year—a price, according to the surgeon general, "second only to the cost of [treating] tobacco use" (Carmona, 2004).

To indicate an error such as a misspelling in a quotation, insert [*sic*], italicized and with brackets around it, right after the error.

Setting off long quotations When you quote forty or more words, set off the quotation by indenting it one-half inch from the left margin. Use the normal right margin and do not single-space.

Long quotations should be introduced by an informative sentence, usually followed by a colon. Quotation marks are unnecessary because the indented format tells readers that the passage is taken from the source.

Yanovski and Yanovski (2002) have traced the history of treatments for obesity:

> For many years, obesity was approached as if it were either a moral failing or evidence of underlying psychopathology. With the advent of behavioral treatments for obesity in the 1960s, hope arose that modification of maladaptive eating and exercise habits would lead to sustained weight loss, and that time-limited programs would produce permanent changes in weight. (p. 592)

At the end of the indented quotation, the parenthetical citation goes outside the final punctuation mark.

37b Using signal phrases

Whenever you include a direct quotation, a paraphrase, or a summary in your paper, prepare readers for it with a signal phrase. A signal phrase usually names the author of the source, gives the publication date in parentheses, and often provides some context. It is generally acceptable in the social sciences to call authors by their last name only, even on first mention. If your paper refers to two authors with the same last name, use their initials as well.

See the chart on page 172 for a list of verbs commonly used in signal phrases.

Marking boundaries Avoid dropping quotations into your text without warning. Provide clear signal phrases, including at least the author's name and the date of publication. Signal phrases mark the boundaries between source material and your own words and ideas.

DROPPED QUOTATION

Obesity was once considered in a very different light. "For many years, obesity was approached as if it were either a moral failing or evidence of underlying psychopathology" (Yanovski & Yanovski, 2002, p. 592).

QUOTATION WITH SIGNAL PHRASE

As researchers Yanovski and Yanovski (2002) have explained, obesity was once considered "either a moral failing or evidence of underlying psychopathology" (p. 592).

Using signal phrases in APA papers

To avoid monotony, try to vary both the language and the placement of your signal phrases.

Model signal phrases

In the words of Carmona (2004), ". . ."

As Yanovski and Yanovski (2002) have noted, ". . ."

Hoppin and Taveras (2004), medical researchers, pointed out that ". . ."

". . . ," claimed Critser (2003).

". . . ," wrote Duenwald (2004), ". . ."

Researchers McDuffie et al. (2003) have offered a compelling argument for this view: ". . ."

Hilts (2002) answered these objections with the following analysis: ". . ."

Verbs in signal phrases

Are you providing background, explaining a concept, supporting a claim, lending authority, or refuting a belief? Choose a verb that is appropriate for the way you are using the source.

admitted	contended	reasoned
agreed	declared	refuted
argued	denied	rejected
asserted	emphasized	reported
believed	insisted	responded
claimed	noted	suggested
compared	observed	thought
confirmed	pointed out	wrote

NOTE: In APA style, use the past tense or present perfect tense to introduce quotations and other source material: *Davis (2005) noted* or *Davis (2005) has noted*, not *Davis (2005) notes*. Use the present tense only to discuss the results of an experiment (*the results show*) or knowledge that has clearly been established (*researchers agree*).

Putting source material in context Provide context for any source material that appears in your paper. A signal phrase can help you connect your own ideas with those of another writer by clarifying how the source will contribute to your paper. It's a good idea to embed source material, especially long quotations, between sentences of your own that interpret the source and link the source to your argument.

QUOTATION WITH EFFECTIVE CONTEXT

A report by the Henry J. Kaiser Family Foundation (2004) outlined trends that may have contributed to the childhood obesity crisis, including food advertising for children as well as

> a reduction in physical education classes . . . , an increase in the availability of sodas and snacks in public schools, the growth in the number of fast-food outlets . . . , and the increasing number of highly processed high-calorie and high-fat grocery products. (p. 1)

Addressing each of these areas requires more than a doctor armed with a prescription pad; it requires a broad mobilization not just of doctors and concerned parents but of educators, food industry executives, advertisers, and media representatives.

NOTE: When you bring other sources into a conversation about your research topic, you are synthesizing sources. For more on synthesis, see 31c.

Integrating statistics and other facts When you are citing a statistic or another specific fact, a signal phrase is often not necessary. In most cases, readers will understand that the citation refers to the statistic or fact (not the whole paragraph).

In purely financial terms, the drugs cost more than $3 a day on average (Duenwald, 2004).

There is nothing wrong, however, with using a signal phrase.

Duenwald (2004) pointed out that in purely financial terms, the drugs cost more than $3 a day on average.

38 APA documentation style

In most social science classes, you will be asked to use the APA system for documenting sources, which is set forth in the *Publication Manual of the American Psychological Association*, 6th ed. (Washington, DC: APA, 2010).

PRACTICE hackerhandbooks.com/pocket
> APA > 38-1 to 38-3

Directory to APA in-text citation models

1. A quotation — 174
2. A summary or a paraphrase — 175
3. Two authors — 175
4. Three to five authors — 175
5. Six or more authors — 175
6. Unknown author — 176
7. Organization as author — 176
8. Authors with the same last name — 176
9. Two or more works by the same author in the same year — 176
10. Two or more works in the same parentheses — 177
11. Personal communication — 177
12. Electronic source — 177
13. Indirect source (source quoted in another source) — 178

38a APA in-text citations

APA's in-text citations provide at least the author's last name and the year of publication. For direct quotations and some summaries and paraphrases, a page number is given as well. In the following models, the elements of the in-text citation are highlighted.

NOTE: APA style requires the use of the past tense or the present perfect tense in signal phrases introducing cited material: *Smith (2005) reported, Smith (2005) has argued.*

■ **1. A quotation** Ordinarily, introduce the quotation with a signal phrase that includes the author's last name followed by the year of publication in parentheses. Put the page number, preceded by "p." (or "pp." for more than one page), in parentheses after the quotation.

Critser (2003) noted that many health care providers still "remain either in ignorance or outright denial about the health danger to the poor and the young" (p. 5).

If the author is not named in the signal phrase, place the author's name, the year, and the page number in parentheses after the quotation: (Critser, 2003, p. 5). (See item 12 on p. 177 for citing parts of electronic sources.)

NOTE: Do not include a month, even if the entry in the reference list includes the month.

■ **2. A summary or a paraphrase** Include the author's last name and the year in a signal phrase introducing the material or in parentheses following it. Give a page number to help readers find the passage. For online sources without page numbers, see "No page numbers" on page 178.

Yanovski and Yanovski (2002) explained that sibutramine suppresses appetite by blocking the reuptake of the neurotransmitters serotonin and norepinephrine in the brain (p. 594).

Sibutramine suppresses appetite by blocking the reuptake of the neurotransmitters serotonin and norepinephrine in the brain (Yanovski & Yanovski, 2002, p. 594).

■ **3. Two authors** Name both authors in the signal phrase or in parentheses each time you cite the work. In the parentheses, use "&" between the authors' names; in the signal phrase, use "and."

According to Sothern and Gordon (2003), "Environmental factors may contribute as much as 80% to the causes of childhood obesity" (p. 104).

Obese children often engage in limited physical activity (Sothern & Gordon, 2003, p. 104).

■ **4. Three to five authors** Identify all authors in the signal phrase or in parentheses the first time you cite the source.

In 2003, Berkowitz, Wadden, Tershakovec, and Cronquist concluded that sibutramine "must be carefully monitored . . . to control increases in [blood pressure] and pulse rate" (p. 1811).

In subsequent citations, use the first author's name followed by "et al." in either the signal phrase or the parentheses.

As Berkowitz et al. (2003) advised, "Until more extensive safety and efficacy data are available, . . . weight-loss medications should be used only on an experimental basis for adolescents" (p. 1811).

■ **5. Six or more authors** Use the first author's name followed by "et al." in the signal phrase or in parentheses.

McDuffie et al. (2002) tested 20 adolescents, aged 12-16, over a three-month period and found that orlistat, combined with behavioral therapy, produced an average weight loss of 4.4 kg, or 9.7 pounds (p. 646).

6. Unknown author

If the author is unknown, mention the work's title in the signal phrase or give the first word or two of the title in the parenthetical citation. Titles of short works such as articles and chapters are put in quotation marks; titles of long works such as books and reports are italicized.

Children struggling to control their weight must also struggle with the pressures of television advertising that, on the one hand, encourages the consumption of junk food and, on the other, celebrates thin celebrities ("Television," 2002).

NOTE: In the rare case when "Anonymous" is specified as the author, treat it as if it were a real name: (Anonymous, 2009). In the list of references, also use the name Anonymous as author.

7. Organization as author

If the author is a government agency or another organization, name the organization in the signal phrase or in the parenthetical citation the first time you cite the source.

Obesity puts children at risk for a number of medical complications, including Type 2 diabetes, hypertension, sleep apnea, and orthopedic problems (Henry J. Kaiser Family Foundation, 2004, p. 1).

If the organization has a familiar abbreviation, you may include it in brackets the first time you cite the source and use the abbreviation alone in later citations.

FIRST CITATION	(National Institute of Mental Health [NIMH], 2010)
LATER CITATIONS	(NIMH, 2010)

8. Authors with the same last name

To avoid confusion, use initials with the last names if your reference list includes two or more authors with the same last name.

Research by E. Smith (1989) revealed that. . . .

9. Two or more works by the same author in the same year

When your list of references includes more than

one work by the same author in the same year, use lowercase letters ("a," "b," and so on) with the year to order the entries in the reference list. (See item 7 on p. 182.) Use those same letters with the year in the in-text citation.

Research by Durgin (2003b) has yielded new findings about the role of counseling in treating childhood obesity.

■ **10. Two or more works in the same parentheses** When your parenthetical citation names two or more works, put them in the same order that they appear in the reference list, separated with semicolons.

Researchers have indicated that studies of pharmacological treatments for childhood obesity are inconclusive (Berkowitz et al., 2003; McDuffie et al., 2002).

■ **11. Personal communication** Cite interviews, memos, letters, e-mail, and similar unpublished person-to-person communications in the text only, not in the reference list.

One of Atkinson's colleagues, who has studied the effect of the media on children's eating habits, has contended that advertisers for snack foods will need to design ads responsibly for their younger viewers (F. Johnson, personal communication, October 20, 2004).

■ **12. Electronic source** Cite electronic sources, including online sources, as you would any other sources, giving the author and the year when they are available.

Atkinson (2001) found that children who spent at least four hours a day watching TV were less likely to engage in adequate physical activity during the week.

Electronic sources may lack page numbers, authors' names, or dates. Here are APA's guidelines for handling sources without these details.

Unknown author

If no author is named in the source, mention the title of the source in a signal phrase or give the first word or two of the title in parentheses (see also item 6). (If an organization serves as the author, see item 7.)

The body's basal metabolic rate, or BMR, is a measure of its at-rest energy requirement ("Exercise," 2003).

Unknown date

When the date is unknown, use the abbreviation "n.d." (for "no date").

Attempts to establish a definitive link between television programming and children's eating habits have been problematic (Magnus, n.d.).

No page numbers

APA ordinarily requires page numbers for quotations, summaries, and paraphrases. When an electronic source lacks stable numbered pages, include paragraph numbers or headings to help readers locate the passage being cited.

If the source has numbered paragraphs, use the paragraph number preceded by the abbreviation "para.": (Hall, 2009, para. 5). If the source contains headings, cite the appropriate heading in parentheses; you may also indicate which paragraph under that heading you are referring to.

Hoppin and Taveras (2004) pointed out that several other medications were classified by the Drug Enforcement Administration as having the "potential for abuse" (Weight-Loss Drugs section, para. 6).

NOTE: PDF documents often have stable page numbers. For such sources, give the page number in the parenthetical citation.

■ **13. Indirect source (source quoted in another source)**
If you use a source that was cited in another source (a secondary source), name the original source in your signal phrase. List the secondary source in your reference list and include it in your parenthetical citation, preceded by the words "as cited in." In the following example, Satcher is the original source; Critser is the secondary source, given in the reference list.

Former surgeon general Dr. David Satcher described "a nation of young people seriously at risk of starting out obese and dooming themselves to the difficult task of overcoming a tough illness" (as cited in Critser, 2003, p. 4).

38b APA references

In APA style, the alphabetical list of works cited, which appears at the end of the paper, is titled "References." For advice on preparing the list, see pages 197–98. For sample references lists, see pages 201, 204, and 206.

Alphabetize entries in the list of references by authors' last names; if a work has no author, alphabetize it by its title. The first element of each entry is important because citations in the text of the paper refer to it and readers will be looking for it in the alphabetized list. The date of publication appears immediately after the first element of the citation.

In APA references, titles of books are italicized; titles of articles are neither italicized nor put in quotation marks. (For rules on capitalization of titles, see p. 196.)

General guidelines for listing authors (print and online) In APA style, all authors' names are inverted (the last name comes first), and initials are used for all first and middle names.

NAME AND YEAR CITED IN TEXT
Duncan (2008) has reported that. . . .

BEGINNING OF ENTRY IN THE LIST OF REFERENCES
Duncan, B. (2008).

Directory to APA reference list models

GENERAL GUIDELINES FOR LISTING AUTHORS (PRINT AND ONLINE)

1.	Single author	181
2.	Two to seven authors	181
3.	Eight or more authors	181
4.	Organization as author	181
5.	Unknown author	182
6.	Two or more works by the same author	182
7.	Two or more works by the same author in the same year	182

ARTICLES IN PERIODICALS (PRINT)

8.	Article in a journal paginated by volume	183
9.	Article in a journal paginated by issue	183
	Citation at a glance 184	
10.	Article in a magazine	183

PRACTICE hackerhandbooks.com/pocket
> APA > 38–4 to 38–8

ARTICLES IN PERIODICALS (PRINT) (CONTINUED)
11. Article in a newspaper — 183
12. Letter to the editor — 183
13. Editorial or other unsigned article — 183
14. Review — 183

BOOKS (PRINT)
15. Basic format for a book — 185
    Citation at a glance 186
16. Book with an editor — 185
17. Book with an author and an editor — 185
18. Book with an author and a translator — 185
19. Edition other than the first — 185
20. Article or chapter in an edited book or an anthology — 185
21. Multivolume work — 187
22. Book with a title in its title — 187

ONLINE SOURCES
23. Article in an online journal — 187
24. Article in an online magazine — 187
25. Article in an online newspaper — 188
26. Article from a database — 188
    Citation at a glance 190
27. Online book — 188
28. Chapter in an online book — 188
29. Report or long document from a Web site — 188
30. Section in a Web document — 189
    Citation at a glance 192
31. Short work from a Web site — 189
32. Podcast — 189
33. Blog (Weblog) post — 191
34. Online audio or video file — 191
35. Entry in a wiki — 191
36. Data set or graphic representation — 191
37. E-mail — 193
38. Online posting — 193

OTHER SOURCES (INCLUDING ONLINE VERSIONS)
39. Dissertation from a database — 194
40. Government document — 194
41. Report from a private organization — 194
42. Conference proceedings — 194
43. Map, chart, or illustration — 194
44. Advertisement — 194
45. Lecture, speech, or address — 194
46. Brochure, pamphlet, or fact sheet — 195
47. Film or video (motion picture) — 195
48. Television program — 195
49. Computer software or video game — 195

1. Single author

author: last name + initial(s) | *year* | *title (book)*
Egeland, J. (2008). *A billion lives: An eyewitness report from the*

place of publication | *publisher*
frontlines of humanity. New York, NY: Simon & Schuster.

2. Two to seven authors
List up to seven authors by last names followed by initials. Use an ampersand (&) before the name of the last author.

all authors: last name + initial(s) | *year* | *title (book)*
Musick, M. A., & Wilson, J. (2007). *Volunteers: A social profile*.

place of publication | *publisher*
Bloomington: Indiana University Press.

all authors: last name + initial(s)
Diessner, R., Solom, R. C., Frost, N. K., Parsons, L., & Davidson, J.

year | *title (article)*
(2008). Engagement with beauty: Appreciating natural,

journal title
artistic, and moral beauty. *The Journal of Psychology*,

volume | *page(s)*
142, 303-329.

3. Eight or more authors
List the first six authors followed by three ellipsis dots and the last author's name.

Mulvaney, S. A., Mudasiru, E., Schlundt, D. G., Baughman, C. L., Fleming, M., VanderWoude, A., . . . Rothman, R. (2008). Self-management in Type 2 diabetes: The adolescent perspective. *The Diabetes Educator, 34*, 118-127.

4. Organization as author

author: organization name | *year* | *title (book)*
American Psychiatric Association. (1994). *Diagnostic and statistical*

edition number | *place of publication*
manual of mental disorders (4th ed.). Washington, DC:

organization as author and publisher
Author.

If the publisher is not the same as the author, give the publisher's name at the end as you would for any other source.

■ 5. Unknown author
Begin the entry with the work's title.

New concise world atlas. (2007). New York, NY: Oxford University Press.

- title (book): *New concise world atlas*.
- year: (2007).
- place of publication: New York, NY:
- publisher: Oxford University Press.

■ 6. Two or more works by the same author
Use the author's name for all entries. List the entries by year, the earliest first.

Barry, P. (2007, December 8). Putting tumors on pause. *Science News, 172,* 365.

Barry, P. (2008, August 2). Finding the golden genes. *Science News, 174,* 16-21.

■ 7. Two or more works by the same author in the same year
List the works alphabetically by title. In the parentheses, following the year add "a," "b," and so on. Use these same letters when giving the year in the in-text citation. (See also pp. 197–98.)

Elkind, D. (2008a, Spring). Can we play? *Greater Good, 4*(4), 14-17.

Elkind, D. (2008b, June 27). The price of hurrying children [Web log post]. Retrieved from http://blogs.psychologytoday.com/blog/digital-children

Articles in periodicals (print) Periodicals include journals, magazines, and newspapers. For a journal or a magazine, give only the volume number if the publication is paginated continuously throughout each volume; give the volume and issue numbers if each issue of the volume begins on page 1. Italicize the volume number and put the issue number, not italicized, in parentheses.

For all periodicals, when an article appears on consecutive pages, provide the range of pages. When an article does not appear on consecutive pages, list all pages on which the article appears: A1, A17.

Some print articles include a DOI (digital object identifier), often on the first page of the article. For such an article, give the DOI at the end of the reference list entry, following the print publication information. See item 8.

For an illustrated citation of an article in a print journal or magazine, see page 184.

■ 8. Article in a journal paginated by volume

Holtug, N. (2010). Immigration and the politics of social cohesion. *Ethnicities, 10*, 435-451. doi:10.1177/1468796810378320

■ 9. Article in a journal paginated by issue

Black, J. (2010). Big government: Good and bad. *The New Criterion, 28*(5), 24-27.

■ 10. Article in a magazine
Give the year and the month for monthly magazines; add the day for weekly magazines.

McKibben, B. (2007, October). Carbon's new math. *National Geographic, 212*(4), 32-37.

■ 11. Article in a newspaper
Use "p." (or "pp." for more than one page) before page numbers.

Svoboda, E. (2008, October 21). Deep in the rain forest, stalking the next pandemic. *The New York Times*, p. D5.

■ 12. Letter to the editor

Park, T. (2008, August). Defining the line [Letter to the editor]. *Scientific American, 299*(2), 10.

■ 13. Editorial or other unsigned article

The global justice movement [Editorial]. (2005). *Multinational Monitor, 26*(7/8), 6.

■ 14. Review
If the review has no author or title, use the material in brackets as the title.

Applebaum, A. (2008, February 14). A movie that matters [Review of the motion picture *Katyn*, 2007]. *The New York Review of Books, 55*(2), 13-15.

Agents of change. (2008, February 2). [Review of the book *The power of unreasonable people: How social entrepreneurs create markets that change the world*, by J. Elkington & P. Hartigan]. *The Economist, 386*(8565), 94.

Citation at a glance

Article in a journal or magazine (APA)

To cite an article in a print journal or magazine in APA style, include the following elements:

1. Author
2. Year of publication for journal; complete date for magazine
3. Title and subtitle of article
4. Name of journal or magazine
5. Volume number; issue number, if required (see p. 182)
6. Page number(s) of article
7. DOI, if there is one

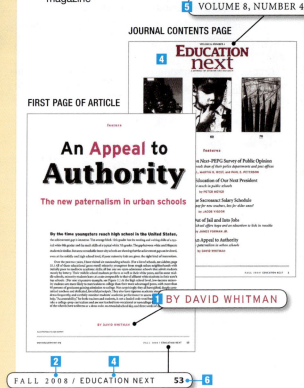

REFERENCE LIST ENTRY FOR A JOURNAL OR MAGAZINE ARTICLE

Whitman, D. (2008). An appeal to authority: The new paternalism in urban schools. *Education Next, 8*(4), 53-58.

For variations on citing articles in print journals or magazines in APA style, see pages 182 and 183.

Books (print) Give the city and the state (abbreviated) for all US cities or the city and the country (not abbreviated) for all non-US cities; also include the province (not abbreviated) for Canadian cities. Do not give a state if the publisher's name includes it (as in many university presses). For an illustrated citation of a print book, see page 186.

■ 15. Basic format for a book

McKenzie, F. R. (2008). *Theory and practice with adolescents: An applied approach.* Chicago, IL: Lyceum Books.

■ 16. Book with an editor
Use the abbreviation "Ed." for one editor; use "Eds." for more than one.

Aronson, J., & Aronson, E. (Eds.). (2008). *Readings about the social animal* (10th ed.). New York, NY: Worth.

■ 17. Book with an author and an editor
Use the abbreviation "Ed." for one editor; use "Eds." for more than one.

McLuhan, M. (2003). *Understanding me: Lectures and interviews* (S. McLuhan & D. Staine, Eds.). Toronto, Ontario, Canada: McClelland & Stewart.

■ 18. Book with an author and a translator
Use "Trans." for one or more translators.

Steinberg, M. D. (2003). *Voices of revolution, 1917* (M. Schwartz, Trans.). New Haven, CT: Yale University Press. (Original work published 2001)

■ 19. Edition other than the first

O'Brien, J. A. (Ed.). (2006). *The production of reality: Essays and readings on social interaction* (4th ed.). Thousand Oaks, CA: Pine Forge Press.

■ 20. Article or chapter in an edited book or an anthology
Use the abbreviation "Ed." for one editor; use "Eds." for more than one.

Denton, N. A. (2006). Segregation and discrimination in housing. In R. G. Bratt, M. E. Stone, & C. Hartman (Eds.), *A right to housing: Foundation of a new social agenda* (pp. 61-81). Philadelphia, PA: Temple University Press.

Citation at a glance
Book (APA)

To cite a print book in APA style, include the following elements:

1. Author
2. Year of publication
3. Title and subtitle
4. Place of publication
5. Publisher

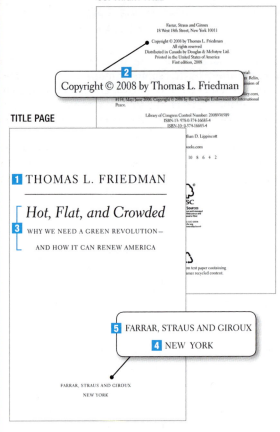

REFERENCE LIST ENTRY FOR A PRINT BOOK

Friedman, T. L. (2008). *Hot, flat, and crowded: Why we need a green revolution—And how it can renew America*. New York, NY: Farrar, Straus and Giroux.

For more on citing print books in APA style, see pages 185 and 187.

■ 21. Multivolume work

Luo, J. (Ed.). (2005). *China today: An encyclopedia of life in the People's Republic* (Vols. 1-2). Westport, CT: Greenwood Press.

■ 22. Book with a title in its title
If the book title contains another book title or an article title, neither italicize the internal title nor place it in quotation marks.

Marcus, L. (Ed.). (1999). *Sigmund Freud's* The interpretation of dreams*: New interdisciplinary essays.* Manchester, England: Manchester University Press.

Online sources   Online articles and books sometimes include a DOI (digital object identifier). APA uses the DOI, when available, in place of a URL in reference list entries.

If a source has no publication date, use "n.d." (for "no date"). Use a retrieval date for an online source only if the content is likely to change. Most of the examples in this section do not show a retrieval date because the content of the sources is stable; if you are unsure about whether to use a retrieval date, consult your instructor.

■ 23. Article in an online journal

Whitmeyer, J. M. (2000). Power through appointment. *Social Science Research, 29,* 535-555. doi:10.1006/ssre.2000.0680

If there is no DOI, include the URL for the journal's home page.

Ashe, D. D., & McCutcheon, L. E. (2001). Shyness, loneliness, and attitude toward celebrities. *Current Research in Social Psychology, 6,* 124-133. Retrieved from http://www.uiowa.edu/~grpproc/crisp/crisp.html

■ 24. Article in an online magazine
Include the URL for the magazine's home page.

Shelburne, E. C. (2008, September). The great disruption. *The Atlantic, 302*(2). Retrieved from http://www.theatlantic.com/

Rupley, S. (2010, February 26). The myth of the benign monopoly. *Salon*. Retrieved from http://www.salon.com/

25. Article in an online newspaper
Include the URL for the newspaper's home page.

Watson, P. (2008, October 19). Biofuel boom endangers orangutan habitat. *Los Angeles Times*. Retrieved from http://www.latimes.com/

26. Article from a database
If the database gives a DOI for the article, use the DOI at the end. For an illustrated citation of an article from a database, see pages 190–91.

all authors: last name + initial(s) | *year* | *article title*
Eskritt, M., & McLeod, K. (2008). Children's note taking as a mnemonic tool. *Journal of Experimental Child Psychology, 101,* 52-74. doi:10.1016/jecp.2008.05.007

journal title — *volume* — *page(s)* — *DOI*

If there is no DOI, include the URL for the home page of the journal. If the URL is not included in the database entry, you can search for it on the Web.

Howard, K. R. (2007). Childhood overweight: Parental perceptions and readiness for change. *The Journal of School Nursing, 23,* 73-79. Retrieved from http://jsn.sagepub.com/

27. Online book
Adams, B. (2004). *The theory of social revolutions*. Retrieved from http://www.gutenberg.org/catalog/world/readfile?fk_files=44092 (Original work published 1913)

28. Chapter in an online book
Clinton, S. J. (1999). What can be done to prevent childhood obesity? In *Understanding childhood obesity* (pp. 81-98). Retrieved from http://www.questia.com/

29. Report or long document from a Web site

Source with date

all authors: last name + initial(s) | *online publication date* | *document title* | *URL*
Cain, A., & Burris, M. (1999, April). *Investigation of the use of mobile phones while driving*. Retrieved from http://www.cutr.usf.edu/pdf/mobile_phone_text.PDF

Source with no date

Archer, D. (n.d.). *Exploring nonverbal communication*. Retrieved from http://nonverbal.ucsc.edu

■ 30. Section in a Web document

[author (organization)] [year] [title of section] [title of Web document] [URL]

National Institute on Media and the Family. (2009). Mobile networking. In *Guide to social networking: Risks*. Retrieved from http://www.mediafamily.org/network_pdf/MediaWise _Guide_to_Social_Networking_Risks_09.pdf

For an illustrated citation of a section in a Web document, see pages 192–93.

■ 31. Short work from a Web site

NATO statement endangers patients in Afghanistan. (2010, March 11). *Médecins sans frontières/Doctors without borders*. Retrieved from http://www.doctorswithoutborders.org/

■ 32. Podcast

[organization as producer] [date of posting] [podcast title] [descriptive label] [series title] [URL]

National Academies (Producer). (2007, June 6). Progress in preventing childhood obesity: How do we measure up? [Audio podcast]. *The sounds of science podcast*. Retrieved from http://media.nap.edu/podcasts/

[writer/presenter] [date of posting] [podcast title] [podcast number] [descriptive label] [Web site hosting podcast] [URL]

Chesney, M. (2007, September 13). Gender differences in the use of complementary and alternative medicine (No. 12827) [Audio podcast]. Retrieved from University of California Television website: http://www.uctv.tv/ondemand

Citation at a glance
Article from a database (APA)

To cite an article from a database in APA style, include the following elements:

1 Author(s)
2 Date of publication
3 Title of article
4 Name of periodical
5 Volume number; issue number, if required (see p. 182)
6 Page number(s)
7 DOI (digital object identifier)
8 URL for journal's home page (if there is no DOI)

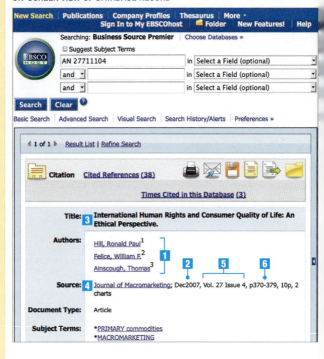

REFERENCE LIST ENTRY FOR AN ARTICLE FROM A DATABASE

Hill, R. P., Felice, W. F., & Ainscough, T. (2007). International human rights and consumer quality of life: An ethical perspective. *Journal of Macromarketing, 27*, 370-379. doi:10.1177/027614670307128

[1] Author — [2] Date — [3] Title of article — [4] Title of journal — [5] Volume — [6] Pages — [7] DOI

For more on citing articles from a database in APA style, see item 26.

■ **33. Blog (Weblog) post** Give the writer's name, the date of the post, the subject, the label "Web log post" in brackets, and the URL. For a response to a post, use the label "Web log comment."

Kellermann, M. (2007, May 23). Disclosing clinical trials [Web log post]. Retrieved from http://www.iq.harvard.edu/blog/sss/archives/2007/05

■ **34. Online audio or video file**

Chomsky, N. (n.d.). The new imperialism [Audio file]. Retrieved from http://www.rhapsody.com/noamchomsky

Zakaria, F. (Host), & McCullough, C. (Writer). (2007, March 6). In focus: American teens, Rwandan truths [Video file]. Retrieved from http://www.pulitzercenter.org/showproject.cfm?id=26

■ **35. Entry in a wiki** Include the date of retrieval; wiki content can change frequently. If an author or an editor is identified, include that name at the beginning of the entry.

Ethnomethodology. (n.d.). Retrieved June 18, 2010, from http://stswiki.org/index.php?title=Ethnomethodology

■ **36. Data set or graphic representation**

U.S. Department of Agriculture, Economic Research Service. (2009). *Eating and health module (ATUS): 2007 data* [Data set]. Retrieved from http://www.ers.usda.gov/Data/ATUS/Data/2007/2007data.htm

Gallup. (2008, October 23). *No increase in proportion of first-time voters* [Graphs]. Retrieved from http://www.gallup.com/poll/111331/No-Increase-Proportion-First-Time-Voters.aspx

Citation at a glance
Section in a Web document (APA)

To cite a section in a Web document in APA style, include the following elements:

1. Author
2. Date of publication or most recent update
3. Title of section
4. Title of document
5. URL of section or of document

BROWSER PRINTOUT OF WEB SITE

2008 Minnesota Health Statistics Annual Summary – Minnesota Dept. of Health

[1] Minnesota Department of Health
Protecting, maintaining and improving the health of all Minnesotans

MDH

[4] 2008 Minnesota Health Statistics Annual Summary

The Minnesota "Annual Summary" or "Minnesota Health Statistics" is a report published yearly. The most recent version of this report is ***2008 Minnesota Health Statistics***, published January 2010. This report provides statistical data on the following subjects for the state of Minnesota.

[2] published January 2010.

To view the PDF files, you will need Adobe Acrobat R[eader] site).

- Introduction, Technical Notes, Definitions (PDF: 42KB/7 pages)
- Overview of 2008 Annual Summary (PDF: 66KB/11 pages)
- Live Births (PDF: 196KB/21 pages)
- Fertility (PDF: 26KB/2 pages) ● [3]
- Infant Mortality and Fetal Deaths (PDF: 188KB/15 pages)
- General Mortality (PDF: 333KB/40 pages)
- Marriage/Dissolution of Marriage Divorce (PDF: 25KB/2 pages)
- Population (PDF: 73KB/12 pages)

Note: Induced abortion statistics previously reported in this publication are now published separately.
See Report to the Legislature: Induced Abortions in Minnesota

See also Minnesota Health Statistics Annual Summary Main Page

For further information about the Annual Summary, please contact:

Center for Health Statistics
Minnesota Department of Health
Golden Rule Building, 3rd Floor
85 East Seventh Place

http://www.health.state.mn.us/divs/chs/annsum/08annsum/index.html

ON-SCREEN VIEW OF DOCUMENT

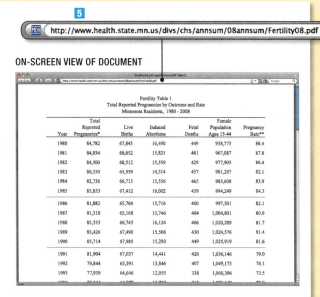

REFERENCE LIST ENTRY FOR A SECTION IN A WEB DOCUMENT

Minnesota Department of Health. (2010, January). Fertility. In *2008 Minnesota health statistics annual summary*. Retrieved from http://www.health.state.mn.us/divs/chs/annsum/08annsum/Fertility08.pdf

For more on citing documents from Web sites in APA style, see pages 188–91.

37. E-mail
E-mail messages, letters, and other personal communications are not included in the list of references. (See item 11 on p. 177 for citing these sources in the text of your paper.)

38. Online posting

McKinney, J. (2006, December 19). Adult education-healthcare partnerships [Electronic mailing list message]. Retrieved from http://www.nifl.gov/pipermail/healthliteracy/2006/000524.html

Other sources (including online versions)

■ 39. Dissertation from a database

Hymel, K. M. (2009). *Essays in urban economics* (Doctoral dissertation). Available from ProQuest Dissertations and Theses database. (AAT 3355930)

■ 40. Government document

U.S. Census Bureau. (2006). *Statistical abstract of the United States.* Washington, DC: Government Printing Office.

U.S. Census Bureau, Bureau of Economic Analysis. (2008, August). *U.S. international trade in goods and services* (Report No. CB08-121, BEA08-37, FT-900). Retrieved from http://www.census.gov/foreign-trade/Press-Release/2008pr/06/ftdpress.pdf

■ 41. Report from a private organization
If the report has a number, put it in parentheses following the title. (See also item 4 on pp. 181–82.)

Ford Foundation. (n.d.). *Helping citizens to understand and influence state budgets.* Retrieved from http://www.fordfound.org/pdfs/impact/evaluations/state_fiscal_initiative.pdf

■ 42. Conference proceedings

Stahl, G. (Ed.). (2002). *Proceedings of CSCL '02: Computer support for collaborative learning.* Hillsdale, NJ: Erlbaum.

■ 43. Map, chart, or illustration

Ukraine [Map]. (2008). Retrieved from the University of Texas at Austin Perry-Castañeda Library Map Collection website: http://www.lib.utexas.edu/maps/cia08/ukraine_sm_2008.gif

■ 44. Advertisement

Xbox 360 [Advertisement]. (2007, February). *Wired, 15*(2), 71.

■ 45. Lecture, speech, or address

Fox, V. (2008, March 5). *Economic growth, poverty, and democracy in Latin America: A president's perspective.* Address at the Freeman Spogli Institute, Stanford University, Stanford, CA.

■ 46. Brochure, pamphlet, or fact sheet

National Council of State Boards of Nursing. (n.d.).
Professional boundaries [Brochure]. Retrieved from
https://www.ncsbn.org/Professional_Boundaries
_2007_Web.pdf

World Health Organization. (2007, October). *Health of indigenous peoples* (No. 326) [Fact sheet]. Retrieved from http://www.who.int/mediacentre/factsheets/fs326/en/index.html

■ 47. Film or video (motion picture)

Guggenheim, D. (Director), & Bender, L. (Producer). (2006). *An inconvenient truth* [DVD]. United States: Paramount Home Entertainment.

Spurlock, M. (Director). (2004). *Super size me* [Motion picture]. Available from IDP Films, 1133 Broadway, Suite 926, New York, NY 10010

■ 48. Television program

Pratt, C. (Executive producer). (2008, October 5). *Face the nation* [Television broadcast]. Washington, DC: CBS News.

Smith, M. (Writer/producer). (2008). Heat [Television series episode]. In D. Fanning (Executive producer), *Frontline*. Boston, MA: WGBH.

■ 49. Computer software or video game

Sims 2 [Computer software]. (2005). New York, NY: Maxis.

39 APA manuscript format; sample pages

The American Psychological Association makes a number of recommendations for formatting a paper and preparing a list of references. The following guidelines are consistent with advice given in the *Publication Manual of the American Psychological Association*, 6th ed. (Washington, DC: APA, 2010).

39a APA manuscript format

Formatting the paper The explanations and examples in 39a and 39b for formatting student papers in the social sciences are consistent with APA's guidelines for papers prepared for publication and with typical requirements for undergraduate papers.

Title page Most instructors will want you to include a title page. See pages 199 and 202.

Page numbers and running head Number all pages with arabic numerals (1, 2, 3, and so on) in the upper right corner about one-half inch from the top of the page. Flush with the left margin and on the same line as the page number, type a running head consisting of the title of the paper (shortened to no more than fifty characters) in all capital letters. (See pp. 200–01 and 203–04.) On the title page only, include the words "Running head" followed by a colon before the title. (See pp. 199 and 202.)

Margins and line spacing Use margins of one inch on all sides of the page. Left-align the text. Double-space throughout the paper.

Capitalization, italics, and quotation marks Capitalize all words of four letters or more in titles of works and in headings that appear in the text of the paper. Capitalize the first word after a colon if the word begins a complete sentence.

Italicize the titles of books, periodicals, and other long works, such as Web sites. Use quotation marks around the titles of periodical articles, short stories, poems, and other short works.

NOTE: APA has different requirements for titles in the reference list. See page 198.

Long quotations and footnotes See page 170 for APA's guidelines for formatting long quotations. Place footnotes at the bottom of the page on which the text reference occurs. Begin each note with the superscript arabic numeral that corresponds to the number in the text. Indent the first line one-half inch. See page 200.

Abstract If your instructor requires one, include an abstract on its own page after the title page. Center the word "Abstract" one inch from the top of the page.

An abstract is a 100-to-150-word overview of your essay. It should express your main idea and key points; it might also suggest any implications or applications of the research you discuss in the paper.

Headings Although headings are not always necessary, their use is encouraged in the social sciences. For college papers, one level of heading is usually sufficient.

In APA style, major headings are centered and boldface. Second-level headings, if any, are flush left and boldface. Capitalize the first word of the heading, along with all other words except articles, short prepositions, and coordinating conjunctions.

Visuals APA classifies visuals as tables and figures (figures include graphs, charts, drawings, and photographs).

Label each table with an arabic numeral (Table 1, Table 2) and provide a clear title. The label and title should appear on separate lines above the table, flush left and double-spaced. Below the table, give its source in a note.

Note. From "Innovation Roles: From Souls of Fire to Devil's Advocates," by M. Meyer, 2000, *The Journal of Business Communication, 37*, p. 338.

For each figure, place a label and a caption below the figure, flush left and double-spaced. They need not appear on separate lines.

Preparing the list of references Begin your list of references on a new page at the end of the paper. Center the title "References" one inch from the top of the page. Double-space throughout. For sample reference lists, see pages 201, 204, and 206.

Indenting entries Type the first line of each entry flush left and indent any additional lines one-half inch, as shown on pages 201, 204, and 206.

Alphabetizing the list Alphabetize the reference list by the last names of the authors (or editors); when a work has no author or editor, alphabetize by the first word of the title other than *A*, *An*, or *The*.

If you list two or more works by the same author, arrange the entries by year, the earliest first. If you include two or more works by the same author in the same year, arrange them alphabetically by title. Add the letters "a," "b," and so on in the parentheses after the year. For journal articles, use only the year and the letter: (2009a). For articles in magazines and newspapers, use the full date and the letter in the reference list: (2009a, July 17); use only the year and the letter in in-text citations.

Authors' names Invert all authors' names and use initials instead of first names. Separate the names with commas. With two to seven authors, use an ampersand (&) before the last author's name. If there are eight or more authors, give the first six authors, three ellipsis dots, and the last author (see item 3, p. 181).

Titles of books and articles Italicize the titles and subtitles of books. Do not italicize or use quotation marks around the titles of articles. Capitalize only the first word of the title and subtitle (and all proper nouns). Capitalize names of periodicals as you would capitalize them normally (see 22c).

Abbreviations for page numbers Abbreviations for "page" and "pages" ("p." and "pp.") are used before page numbers of newspaper articles and articles in edited books (see item 11 on p. 183 and item 20 on p. 185) but not before page numbers of articles in magazines and scholarly journals (see items 8–10 on p. 183).

Breaking a URL or DOI When a URL or a DOI (digital object identifier) must be divided, break it after a double slash or before any other mark of punctuation. Do not insert a hyphen, and do not add a period at the end.

39b Sample APA pages

On the following pages are excerpts from a review of the literature paper written for a psychology class, a nursing practice paper, and a paper written for a business class.

MODELS hackerhandbooks.com/pocket
> Model papers > APA papers: Mirano
> APA annotated bibliography: Haddad
> APA nursing practice paper: Riss
> APA business proposal: Ratajczak

Sample APA title page

Running head: CAN MEDICATION CURE OBESITY IN CHILDREN?   1

Can Medication Cure Obesity in Children?
A Review of the Literature
Luisa Mirano
Northwest-Shoals Community College

Author Note

This paper was prepared for Psychology 108, Section B, taught by Professor Kang.

---

[1] Short title in all capital letters on all pages; words "Running head" on title page only. [2] Arabic page number on all pages. [3] Full title and writer's name and affiliation, centered. [4] Author's note (optional) for extra information.

(Annotations indicate APA-style formatting and effective writing.)

Can Medication Cure Obesity in Children?
A Review of the Literature

In March 2004, U.S. Surgeon General Richard Carmona called attention to a health problem in the United States that, until recently, has been overlooked: childhood obesity. Carmona said that the "astounding" 15% child obesity rate constitutes an "epidemic." Since the early 1980s, that rate has "doubled in children and tripled in adolescents." Now more than 9 million children are classified as obese.[1] This literature review considers whether the use of medication is a promising approach for solving the childhood obesity problem by responding to the following questions:

1. What are the implications of childhood obesity?
2. Is medication effective at treating childhood obesity?
3. Is medication safe for children?
4. Is medication the best solution?

Understanding the limitations of medical treatments for children highlights the complexity of the childhood obesity problem in the United States and underscores the need for physicians, advocacy groups, and policymakers to search for other solutions.

What Are the Implications of Childhood Obesity?

Obesity can be a devastating problem from both an individual and a societal perspective. Obesity puts children at risk for a number of medical complications, including Type 2 diabetes, hypertension,

---

[1] Obesity is measured in terms of body-mass index (BMI): weight in kilograms divided by square of height in meters. An adolescent with a BMI in the 95th percentile for his or her age and gender is considered obese.

Sample APA list of references

CAN MEDICATION CURE OBESITY IN CHILDREN? 9

References

Berkowitz, R. I., Wadden, T. A., Tershakovec, A. M., & Cronquist, J. L. (2003). Behavior therapy and sibutramine for the treatment of adolescent obesity. *Journal of the American Medical Association, 289*, 1805-1812.

Carmona, R. H. (2004, March 2). *The growing epidemic of childhood obesity*. Testimony before the Subcommittee on Competition, Foreign Commerce, and Infrastructure of the U.S. Senate Committee on Commerce, Science, and Transportation. Retrieved from http://www.hhs.gov/asl/testify/t040302.html

Critser, G. (2003). *Fat land*. Boston, MA: Houghton Mifflin.

Duenwald, M. (2004, January 6). Slim pickings: Looking beyond ephedra. *The New York Times*, p. F1. Retrieved from http://nytimes.com/

Henry J. Kaiser Family Foundation. (2004, February). *The role of media in childhood obesity*. Retrieved from http://www.kff.org/entmedia/7030.cfm

Hilts, P. J. (2002, March 20). Petition asks for removal of diet drug from market. *The New York Times*, p. A26. Retrieved from http://nytimes.com/

Hoppin, A. G., & Taveras, E. M. (2004, June 25). Assessment and management of childhood and adolescent obesity. *Clinical Update*. Retrieved from http://www.medscape.com/viewarticle/481633

McDuffie, J. R., Calis, K. A., Uwaifo, G. I., Sebring, N. G., Fallon, E. M., Hubbard, V. S., & Yanovski, J. A. (2002). Three-month tolerability of orlistat in adolescents with obesity-related comorbid conditions. *Obesity Research, 10*, 642-650.

---

1 Reference list on new page, heading centered.
2 Authors' names inverted and alphabetized. **3** First line of entry flush left, subsequent lines indented ½". **4** Double-spaced throughout.

Sample APA title page

Running head: ALL AND HTN IN ONE CLIENT   1

Acute Lymphoblastic Leukemia and Hypertension in One Client:
A Nursing Practice Paper
Julie Riss
George Mason University

Author Note

This paper was prepared for Nursing 451, taught by Professor Durham. The author wishes to thank the nursing staff of Milltown General Hospital for help in understanding client care and diagnosis.

---

[1] Short title in all capital letters on all pages; words "Running head" on title page only. [2] Arabic page number on all pages. [3] Full title and writer's name and affiliation, centered. [4] Author's note (optional) for extra information.

(Annotations indicate APA-style formatting and effective writing.)

ALL AND HTN IN ONE CLIENT

Acute Lymphoblastic Leukemia and Hypertension in One Client:
A Nursing Practice Paper

Historical and Physical Assessment

Physical History

E.B. is a 16-year-old white male 5'10" tall weighing 190 lb. He was admitted to the hospital on April 14, 2006, due to decreased platelets and a need for a PRBC transfusion. He was diagnosed in October 2005 with T-cell acute lymphoblastic leukemia (ALL), after a 2-week period of decreased energy, decreased oral intake, easy bruising, and petechia. The client had experienced a 20-lb weight loss in the previous 6 months. At the time of diagnosis, his CBC showed a WBC count of 32, an H & H of 13/38, and a platelet count of 34,000. He began induction chemotherapy on October 12, 2005, receiving vincristine, 6-mercaptopurine, doxorubicin, intrathecal methotrexate, and then high-dose methotrexate per protocol. During his hospital stay he required packed red cells and platelets on two different occasions. He was diagnosed with hypertension (HTN) due to systolic blood pressure readings consistently ranging between 130s and 150s and was started on nifedipine. E.B. has a history of mild ADHD, migraines, and deep vein thrombosis (DVT). He has tolerated the induction and consolidation phases of chemotherapy well and is now in the maintenance phase.

Psychosocial History

There is a possibility of a depressive episode a year previously when he would not attend school. He got into serious trouble and was sent to a shelter for 1 month. He currently lives with his mother, father, and 14-year-old sister.

Family History

Paternal: prostate cancer and hypertension in grandfather

ALL AND HTN IN ONE CLIENT   10

                              References

Hockenberry, M. (2003). *Wong's nursing care of infants and children*.
    St. Louis, MO: Mosby.

Lemone, P., & Burke, K. (2004). *Medical surgical nursing: Critical
    thinking in client care*. Upper Saddle River, NJ: Pearson
    Education.

Sample proposal, APA style

[1] MEMORANDUM

To: Jay Crosson, Senior Vice President, Human Resources
From: Kelly Ratajczak, Intern, Purchasing Department
Subject: Proposal to Add a Wellness Program
Date: April 24, 2006

Health care costs are rising. In the long run, implementing a wellness [2] program in our corporate culture will decrease the company's health care costs.

Research indicates that nearly 70% of health care costs are from common illnesses related to high blood pressure, overweight, lack of exercise, high cholesterol, stress, poor nutrition, and other preventable health [3] issues (Hall, 2006). Health care costs are a major expense for most businesses, and they do not reflect costs due to the loss of productivity or absenteeism. A wellness program would address most, if not all, of these health care issues and related costs.

Benefits of Healthier Employees [4]

Not only would a wellness program substantially reduce costs associated with employee health care, but our company would prosper through many other benefits. Businesses that have wellness programs show a lower cost in production, fewer sick days, and healthier employees ("Workplace Health," 2006). Our healthier employees will help to cut not only our production and absenteeism costs but also potential costs such as higher turnover because of low employee morale.

Implementing the Program

Implementing a good wellness program means making small changes to the work environment, starting with a series of information sessions.

---

[1] First page in memo format. [2] Clear point in first paragraph.
[3] Introduction provides background information. [4] Headings define sections.

(Annotations indicate typical business-style formatting and effective writing.)

Wellness Program Proposal 3

References

Hall, B. (2006). Good health pays off! Fundamentals of health promotion incentives. *Journal of Deferred Compensation 11*(2), 16-26. Retrieved from http://www.aspenpublishers.com/

Springer, D. (2005, October 28). Key to business success? *La Crosse Tribune*. Retrieved from http://lacrossetribune.com/

Workplace health and productivity programs lower absenteeism, costs. (2006). *Managing benefit plans 6*(2), 1-4. Retrieved from http://www.ioma.com/

Chicago Papers

40 Supporting a thesis 208
41 Avoiding plagiarism 210
42 Integrating sources 213
43 *Chicago* documentation style 217

Directory to *Chicago*-style notes and bibliography entries 219

44 *Chicago* manuscript format 235
SAMPLE PAGES 239

Many history instructors and some humanities instructors require the *Chicago*-style footnotes or endnotes explained in section 43. When you write a paper using sources, you face three main challenges in addition to documenting those sources: (1) supporting a thesis, (2) avoiding plagiarism, and (3) integrating quotations and other source material.

40 Supporting a thesis

Most assignments ask you to form a thesis, or main idea, and to support that thesis with well-organized evidence.

40a Forming a thesis

A thesis is a one-sentence (or occasionally a two-sentence) statement of your central idea. Usually your thesis will appear at the end of the first paragraph (see the example on p. 240).

The thesis of your paper will be your reasoned and informed answer to the central research question you pose, as in the following examples.

RESEARCH QUESTION

To what extent was Confederate Major General Nathan Bedford Forrest responsible for the massacre of Union troops at Fort Pillow?

POSSIBLE THESIS

Although we will never know whether Nathan Bedford Forrest directly ordered the massacre of Union troops at Fort Pillow, evidence suggests that he was responsible for it.

RESEARCH QUESTION

How did the 365-day combat tour affect soldiers' experiences of the Vietnam War?

POSSIBLE THESIS

Letters and diaries written by combat soldiers in Vietnam reveal that when soldiers' tours of duty were shortened, their investment in the war shifted from fighting for victory to fighting for survival.

PRACTICE hackerhandbooks.com/pocket
> *Chicago* > 40–1 and 40–2

Each of these thesis statements expresses a view on a debatable issue—an issue about which intelligent, well-meaning people might disagree. The writer's job is to convince such readers that this view is worth taking seriously.

40b Organizing your ideas

The body of your paper will consist of evidence in support of your thesis. To get started, sketch an informal plan that organizes your evidence. The student who wrote about Fort Pillow used a simple list of questions as the blueprint for his paper. These questions became headings that help readers follow the writer's line of argument.

What happened at Fort Pillow?

Did Forrest order the massacre?

Can Forrest be held responsible for the massacre?

40c Using sources to inform and support your argument

Sources can play several different roles as you develop your points.

Providing background information or context You can use facts and statistics to support generalizations or to establish the importance of your topic.

Explaining terms or concepts Explain words, phrases, or ideas important to your topic that may be unfamiliar to readers. Quoting or paraphrasing a source can help you define terms and concepts in accessible language.

Supporting your claims Back up your assertions with facts, examples, and other evidence from your research.

Lending authority to your argument Expert opinion can give weight to your argument. But don't rely on experts to make your argument for you. Construct your argument in your own words and cite authorities in the field to support your position.

Anticipating and countering objections Do not ignore sources that seem contrary to your position or that offer arguments different from your own. Instead, use them to raise opposing ideas and interpretations before you counter them.

41 Avoiding plagiarism

Your research paper is a collaboration between you and your sources. To be fair and ethical, you must acknowledge your debt to the writers of those sources. When you acknowledge your sources, you avoid plagiarism, a serious academic offense.

Three different acts are considered plagiarism: (1) failing to cite quotations and borrowed ideas, (2) failing to enclose borrowed language in quotation marks, and (3) failing to put summaries and paraphrases in your own words.

41a Citing quotations and borrowed ideas

When you cite sources, you give credit to writers from whom you've borrowed words and ideas. You also let your readers know where your information comes from so that they can evaluate the original source.

You must cite anything you borrow from a source, including direct quotations; statistics and other specific facts; visuals such as cartoons, graphs, and diagrams; and any ideas you present in a summary or a paraphrase.

The only exception is common knowledge—information your readers could easily locate. For example, most encyclopedias will tell readers that the Korean War ended in 1953 and that President Theodore Roosevelt was the first American to receive a Nobel Prize. When you have seen certain general information repeatedly in your reading, you don't need to cite it. However, when information has appeared in only a few sources, when it is highly specific (as with statistics), or when it is controversial, you should cite it.

Chicago citations consist of superscript numbers in the text of the paper that refer readers to notes with corresponding numbers either at the foot of the page (footnotes) or at the end of the paper (endnotes).

PRACTICE hackerhandbooks.com/pocket
> *Chicago* > 41–1 to 41–5

TEXT

Governor John Andrew was not allowed to recruit black soldiers from out of state. "Ostensibly," writes Peter Burchard, "no recruiting was done outside Massachusetts, but it was an open secret that Andrew's agents were working far and wide."[1]

NOTE

1. Peter Burchard, *One Gallant Rush: Robert Gould Shaw and His Brave Black Regiment* (New York: St. Martin's, 1965), 85.

For detailed advice on using *Chicago* notes, see 43a. When you use footnotes or endnotes, you will usually need to provide a bibliography as well (see 43b).

41b Enclosing borrowed language in quotation marks

To show that you are using a source's exact phrases or sentences, you must enclose them in quotation marks. To omit the quotation marks is to claim—falsely—that the language is your own. Such an omission is plagiarism even if you have cited the source.

ORIGINAL SOURCE

> For many Southerners it was psychologically impossible to see a black man bearing arms as anything but an incipient slave uprising complete with arson, murder, pillage, and rapine.
>
> —Dudley Taylor Cornish, *The Sable Arm: Negro Troops in the Union Army, 1861–1865*, p. 158

PLAGIARISM

According to Civil War historian Dudley Taylor Cornish, for many Southerners it was psychologically impossible to see a black man bearing arms as anything but an incipient slave uprising complete with arson, murder, pillage, and rapine.[2]

BORROWED LANGUAGE IN QUOTATION MARKS

According to Civil War historian Dudley Taylor Cornish, "For many Southerners it was psychologically impossible to see a black man bearing arms as anything but an incipient slave uprising complete with arson, murder, pillage, and rapine."[2]

NOTE: When quoted sentences are set off from the text by indenting, quotation marks are not needed (see p. 214).

41c Putting summaries and paraphrases in your own words

A summary condenses information; a paraphrase conveys information in about the same number of words as in the original source. When you summarize or paraphrase, you must name the source and restate the source's meaning in your own words.

In the following example, the paraphrase is plagiarized—even though the source is cited—because too much of its language is borrowed from the source without quotation marks. The underlined phrases have been copied exactly (without quotation marks). In addition, the writer has closely followed the sentence structure of the original source, merely making a few substitutions (such as *Fifty percent* for *Half* and *angered and perhaps frightened* for *enraged and perhaps terrified*).

ORIGINAL SOURCE

> Half of the force holding Fort Pillow were Negroes, former slaves now enrolled in the Union Army. Toward them Forrest's troops had the fierce, bitter animosity of men who had been educated to regard the colored race as inferior and who for the first time had encountered that race armed and fighting against white men. The sight enraged and perhaps terrified many of the Confederates and aroused in them the ugly spirit of a lynching mob.
>
> —Albert Castel, "The Fort Pillow Massacre," pp. 46–47

PLAGIARISM: UNACCEPTABLE BORROWING

Albert Castel suggests that much of the brutality at Fort Pillow can be traced to racial attitudes. Fifty percent of the troops <u>holding Fort Pillow were Negroes, former slaves</u> who had joined <u>the Union Army. Toward them Forrest's</u> soldiers displayed the savage hatred <u>of men who had been</u> taught the inferiority of blacks <u>and who for the first time had</u> confronted them <u>armed and fighting against white men.</u> The vision angered and perhaps frightened <u>the Confederates and aroused in them the ugly spirit of a lynching mob.</u>[3]

To avoid plagiarizing an author's language, don't look at the source while you are summarizing or paraphrasing. After you've restated the author's idea in your own words, return to the source and check that you haven't used the author's language or sentence structure or misrepresented the author's ideas.

ACCEPTABLE PARAPHRASE

Albert Castel suggests that much of the brutality at Fort Pillow can be traced to racial attitudes. Nearly half of the Union troops were blacks, men whom the Confederates had been raised to consider their inferiors. The shock and perhaps fear of facing armed ex-slaves in battle for the first time may well have unleashed the fury that led to the massacre.[3]

42 Integrating sources

Quotations, summaries, paraphrases, and facts will support your argument, but they cannot speak for you. You can use several strategies to integrate information from research sources into your paper while maintaining your own voice.

42a Using quotations appropriately

Limiting your use of quotations In your writing, keep the emphasis on your own words. Do not quote excessively. It is not always necessary to quote full sentences from a source. Often you can integrate words or phrases from a source into your own sentence structure.

As Hurst has pointed out, until "an outcry erupted in the Northern press," even the Confederates did not deny that there had been a massacre at Fort Pillow.[4]

Union surgeon Dr. Charles Fitch testified that after he was in custody he "saw" Confederate soldiers "kill every negro that made his appearance dressed in Federal uniform."[5]

Using the ellipsis mark You can use the ellipsis mark (three periods, with spaces between) to condense a quoted passage and indicate that you have omitted words. What remains must be grammatically complete.

Union surgeon Fitch's testimony that all women and children had been evacuated from Fort Pillow before the attack conflicts with Forrest's report: "We captured . . . about 40 negro women and children."[6]

PRACTICE hackerhandbooks.com/pocket
> *Chicago* > 42–1 to 42–4

The writer has omitted several words not relevant to the issue at hand: *164 Federals, 75 negro troops, and.*

When you want to omit a full sentence or more, use a period before the three ellipsis dots. For an example, see the long quotation at the bottom of this page.

You do not need an ellipsis mark at the beginning or at the end of a quotation. Readers will understand that the quoted material is taken from a longer passage.

Using brackets   Brackets allow you to insert your own words into quoted material to clarify a confusing reference or to make the quoted words fit grammatically into the context of your writing.

According to Albert Castel, "It can be reasonably argued that he [Forrest] was justified in believing that the approaching steamships intended to aid the garrison [at Fort Pillow]."[7]

NOTE: Use [*sic*], italicized and with brackets around it, to indicate that an error in a quoted sentence appears in the original source. (See the example below.)

Setting off long quotations   *Chicago* style allows you to set off a long quotation or run it into your text. For emphasis, you may want to set off a quotation of more than five lines; you should always set off quotations of ten lines or more. To set off a quotation, indent it one-half inch from the left margin and keep the standard right margin. Double-space the quotation.

Introduce long quotations with an informative sentence, usually ending in a colon. Because the indented format tells readers that the words are taken directly from the source, you don't need quotation marks.

In a letter home, Confederate officer Achilles V. Clark recounted what happened at Fort Pillow:

> Words cannot describe the scene. The poor deluded negroes would run up to our men fall upon their knees and with uplifted hands scream for mercy but they were ordered to their feet and then shot down. The whitte [*sic*] men fared but little better. . . . I with several others tried to stop the butchery and at one time had partially succeeded, but Gen. Forrest ordered them shot down like dogs, and the carnage continued.[8]

42b Using signal phrases

Whenever you include a direct quotation, a paraphrase, or a summary in your paper, prepare readers for it with a *signal phrase*. A signal phrase usually names the author of the source and often provides some context for the source material. The first time you mention an author, use the full name: *Shelby Foote argues*. . . . When you refer to the author again, you may use the last name only: *Foote raises an important question*.

See the chart on page 216 for a list of verbs commonly used in signal phrases. Note that *Chicago* style calls for verbs in the present tense or present perfect tense (*points out* or *has pointed out*) to introduce source material unless you include a date that specifies the time of the original author's writing.

Marking boundaries Avoid dropping quotations into your text without warning. Provide clear signal phrases, including at least the author's name. A signal phrase indicates the boundary between your words and the source's words.

DROPPED QUOTATION
Unionists claimed that their troops had abandoned their arms and were in full retreat. "The Confederates, however, all agreed that the Union troops retreated to the river with arms in their hands."[9]

QUOTATION WITH SIGNAL PHRASE
Unionists claimed that their troops had abandoned their arms and were in full retreat. "The Confederates, however," writes historian Albert Castel, "all agreed that the Union troops retreated to the river with arms in their hands."[9]

Introducing summaries and paraphrases Introduce most summaries and paraphrases with a signal phrase that mentions the author and places the material in context. Readers will then understand where the summary or paraphrase begins.

The signal phrase (highlighted) in the following example shows that the whole paragraph, not just the last sentence, is based on the source.

According to Jack Hurst, official Confederate policy was that black soldiers were to be treated as runaway slaves; in addition,

Using signal phrases in *Chicago* papers

To avoid monotony, try to vary both the language and the placement of your signal phrases.

Model signal phrases

In the words of historian James M. McPherson, ". . ."[1]

As Dudley Taylor Cornish has argued, ". . ."[2]

In a letter to his wife, a Confederate soldier who witnessed the massacre wrote that ". . ."[3]

". . . ," claims Benjamin Quarles.[4]

". . . ," writes Albert Castel, ". . ."[5]

Shelby Foote offers an intriguing interpretation: ". . ."[6]

Verbs in signal phrases

Are you providing background, explaining a concept, supporting a claim, lending authority, or refuting a belief? Choose a verb that is appropriate for the way you are using the source.

admits	contends	reasons
agrees	declares	refutes
argues	denies	rejects
asserts	emphasizes	reports
believes	insists	responds
claims	notes	suggests
compares	observes	thinks
confirms	points out	writes

NOTE: In *Chicago* style, use the present tense or present perfect tense to introduce quotations or other material from nonfiction sources: *Foote points out* or *Foote has pointed out.* Use the past tense only to emphasize that the author's language or opinion was articulated in the past.

---

the Confederate Congress decreed that white Union officers commanding black troops be killed. Confederate Lieutenant General Kirby Smith went one step further, declaring that he would kill all captured black troops. Smith's policy never met with strong opposition from the Richmond government.[10]

Putting source material in context Provide context for any source material that appears in your paper. A signal phrase can help you connect your own ideas with those of another writer by clarifying how the source will contribute to your paper. It's a good idea to embed source material, especially long quotations, between sentences of your own that interpret the source and link the source to your argument.

QUOTATION WITH EFFECTIVE CONTEXT

In a respected biography of Nathan Bedford Forrest, Hurst suggests that the temperamental Forrest "may have ragingly ordered a massacre and even intended to carry it out — until he rode inside the fort and viewed the horrifying result" and ordered it stopped.[11] While this is an intriguing interpretation of events, even Hurst would probably admit that it is merely speculation.

NOTE: When you bring other sources into a conversation about your research topic, you are synthesizing sources. For more on synthesis, see 31c.

Integrating statistics and other facts   When you cite a statistic or another specific fact, a signal phrase is often not necessary. In most cases, readers will understand that the citation refers to the statistic or fact (not the whole paragraph).

Of 295 white troops garrisoned at Fort Pillow, 168 were taken prisoner. Black troops fared worse, with only 58 of 262 captured and most of the rest presumably killed or wounded.[12]

There is nothing wrong, however, with using a signal phrase.

43   Chicago documentation style (notes and bibliography)

In history and some humanities courses, you may be asked to use the documentation system set forth in *The Chicago Manual of Style*, 16th ed. (Chicago: University of Chicago Press, 2010). In *Chicago* style, superscript numbers in the text of the paper refer readers to notes with corresponding numbers either at the bottom of the page (footnotes) or at the end of the paper (endnotes). A bibliography is often required as well.

PRACTICE   hackerhandbooks.com/pocket
> *Chicago* > 43–1 to 43–8

43a First and subsequent notes for a source

The first time you cite a source, the note should include publication information for that work as well as the page number on which the passage you cite may be found.

   1. Peter Burchard, *One Gallant Rush: Robert Gould Shaw and His Brave Black Regiment* (New York: St. Martin's, 1965), 85.

For subsequent references to a source you have already cited, you may simply give the author's last name, a short form of the title, and the page or pages cited. A short form of the title of a book is italicized; a short form of the title of an article is put in quotation marks.

   4. Burchard, *One Gallant Rush*, 31.

When you have two consecutive notes from the same source, you may use "Ibid." (meaning "in the same place") and the page number for the second note. Use "Ibid." alone if the page number is the same.

   5. Jack Hurst, *Nathan Bedford Forrest: A Biography* (New York: Knopf, 1993), 8.

   6. Ibid., 174.

43b *Chicago*-style bibliography

A bibliography, which appears at the end of your paper, lists every work you have cited in your notes; in addition, it may include works that you consulted but did not cite. For advice on constructing the list, see pages 237–38. A sample bibliography appears on page 242.

NOTE: If you include a bibliography, *The Chicago Manual of Style* suggests that you shorten all notes, including the first reference to a source, as described in 43a. Check with your instructor, however, to see whether using a shortened note for a first reference to a source is acceptable.

43c Model notes and bibliography entries

The following models are consistent with guidelines in *The Chicago Manual of Style*, 16th ed. For each type of source, a note appears first, followed by a bibliography entry. The note shows the format you should use when citing a source for the first time. For subsequent citations of a source, use shortened notes (see 43a).

Some online sources, especially periodical articles, contain a permanent locator called a digital object identifier (DOI). Use the DOI, when available, in place of a URL in citations of online sources.

Directory to *Chicago*-style notes and bibliography entries

BOOKS (PRINT AND ONLINE)

1.	Basic format for a print book	220
	Citation at a glance 221	
2.	Basic format for an online book	220
3.	Basic format for an e-book (electronic book)	220
4.	Two or three authors	222
5.	Four or more authors	222
6.	Unknown author	222
7.	Multiple works by the same author	222
8.	Edited work without an author	222
9.	Edited work with an author	222
10.	Translated work	223
11.	Edition other than the first	223
12.	Volume in a multivolume work	223
13.	Selection in an anthology	223
14.	Letter in a published collection	223
	Citation at a glance 224	
15.	Work in a series	226
16.	Encyclopedia or dictionary entry	226
17.	Sacred text	226
18.	Source quoted in another source	226

ARTICLES IN PERIODICALS (PRINT AND ONLINE)

19.	Article in a print journal	226
	Citation at a glance 227	
20.	Article in an online journal	229
21.	Journal article from a database	229
	Citation at a glance 228	
22.	Article in a print magazine	230
23.	Article in an online magazine	230
24.	Magazine article from a database	230
25.	Article in a print newspaper	230
26.	Article in an online newspaper	230
27.	Newspaper article from a database	231
28.	Unsigned newspaper article	231
29.	Book review	231

ONLINE SOURCES

30.	Web site	231
31.	Short work from a Web site	233
	Citation at a glance 232	
32.	Online posting or e-mail	233
33.	Blog (Weblog) post	233
34.	Podcast	234
35.	Online audio or video	234

OTHER SOURCES (INCLUDING ONLINE VERSIONS)

36.	Government document	234
37.	Unpublished dissertation	235
38.	Personal communication	235
39.	Published or broadcast interview	235
40.	Video (DVD, Blu-ray Disc)	235
41.	Sound recording	235

Books (print and online)

■ 1. Basic format for a print book

1. Mary N. Woods, *Beyond the Architect's Eye: Photographs and the American Built Environment* (Philadelphia: University of Pennsylvania Press, 2009).

Woods, Mary N. *Beyond the Architect's Eye: Photographs and the American Built Environment.* Philadelphia: University of Pennsylvania Press, 2009.

For an illustrated citation of a print book, see page 221.

■ 2. Basic format for an online book

2. John Dewey, *Democracy and Education* (1916; ILT Digital Classics, 1994), chap. 4, http://www.ilt.columbia.edu/publications/dewey.html.

Dewey, John. *Democracy and Education.* 1916. ILT Digital Classics, 1994. http://www.ilt.columbia.edu/publications/dewey.html.

■ 3. Basic format for an e-book (electronic book)

3. Leo Tolstoy, *War and Peace*, trans. Richard Pevear and Larissa Volokhonsky (New York: Knopf, 2007), Kindle edition, vol. 1, pt. 1, chap. 3.

Tolstoy, Leo. *War and Peace.* Translated by Richard Pevear and Larissa Volokhonsky. New York: Knopf, 2007. Kindle edition.

Citation at a glance
Book (*Chicago*)

To cite a print book in *Chicago* style, include the following elements:

1 Author
2 Title and subtitle
3 City of publication
4 Publisher
5 Year of publication
6 Page number(s) cited (for notes)

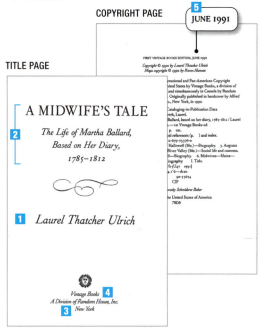

NOTE

1. Laurel Thatcher Ulrich, *A Midwife's Tale: The Life of Martha Ballard, Based on Her Diary, 1785-1812* (New York: Vintage, 1991), 174.

BIBLIOGRAPHY

Ulrich, Laurel Thatcher. *A Midwife's Tale: The Life of Martha Ballard, Based on Her Diary, 1785-1812*. New York: Vintage, 1991.

For more on citing print books in *Chicago* style, see pages 220–26.

4. Two or three authors

4. Chris Stringer and Peter Andrews, *The Complete World of Human Evolution* (London: Thames and Hudson, 2005), 45.

Stringer, Chris, and Peter Andrews. *The Complete World of Human Evolution*. London: Thames and Hudson, 2005.

5. Four or more authors
In the note, give the first author's name followed by "et al." (for "and others"); in the bibliography entry, list all authors' names.

5. Lynn Hunt et al., *The Making of the West: Peoples and Cultures,* 3rd ed. (Boston: Bedford/St. Martin's, 2009), 541.

Hunt, Lynn, Thomas R. Martin, Barbara H. Rosenwein, R. Po-chia Hsia, and Bonnie G. Smith. *The Making of the West: Peoples and Cultures*. 3rd ed. Boston: Bedford/St. Martin's, 2009.

6. Unknown author

6. *The Men's League Handbook on Women's Suffrage* (London, 1912), 23.

The Men's League Handbook on Women's Suffrage. London, 1912.

7. Multiple works by the same author
In the bibliography, use six hyphens in place of the author's name in the second and subsequent entries. Arrange the entries alphabetically by title.

Harper, Raymond L. *A History of Chesapeake, Virginia*. Charleston, SC: History Press, 2008.

------. *South Norfolk, Virginia, 1661-2005*. Charleston, SC: History Press, 2005.

8. Edited work without an author

8. Jack Beatty, ed., *Colossus: How the Corporation Changed America* (New York: Broadway Books, 2001), 127.

Beatty, Jack, ed. *Colossus: How the Corporation Changed America*. New York: Broadway Books, 2001.

9. Edited work with an author

9. Ted Poston, *A First Draft of History*, ed. Kathleen A. Hauke (Athens: University of Georgia Press, 2000), 46.

Poston, Ted. *A First Draft of History*. Edited by Kathleen A. Hauke. Athens: University of Georgia Press, 2000.

10. Translated work

10. Tonino Guerra, *Abandoned Places*, trans. Adria Bernardi (Barcelona: Guernica, 1999), 71.

Guerra, Tonino. *Abandoned Places*. Translated by Adria Bernardi. Barcelona: Guernica, 1999.

11. Edition other than the first

11. Walter Muir Whitehill and Lawrence W. Kennedy, *Boston: A Topographical History,* 3rd ed. (Cambridge, MA: Belknap Press of Harvard University Press, 2000), 58.

Whitehill, Walter Muir, and Lawrence W. Kennedy. *Boston: A Topographical History*. 3rd ed. Cambridge, MA: Belknap Press of Harvard University Press, 2000.

12. Volume in a multivolume work

12. Charles Reagan Wilson, ed., *Myth, Manner, and Memory*, vol. 4 of *The New Encyclopedia of Southern Culture* (Chapel Hill: University of North Carolina Press, 2006), 198.

Wilson, Charles Reagan, ed. *Myth, Manner, and Memory*. Vol. 4 of *The New Encyclopedia of Southern Culture*. Chapel Hill: University of North Carolina Press, 2006.

13. Selection in an anthology

Begin with the author and title of the selection and then give the title and editor (if any) of the anthology.

13. Zora Neale Hurston, "From *Dust Tracks on a Road*," in *The Norton Book of American Autobiography*, ed. Jay Parini (New York: Norton, 1999), 336.

Hurston, Zora Neale. "From *Dust Tracks on a Road*." In *The Norton Book of American Autobiography*, edited by Jay Parini, 333-43. New York: Norton, 1999.

14. Letter in a published collection

If the letter writer's name is part of the book title, begin the note with the writer's last name but begin the bibliography entry with the full name. (For an illustrated citation of a letter in a published collection, see pp. 224–25.)

14. Mitford to Esmond Romilly, 29 July 1940, in *Decca: The Letters of Jessica Mitford*, ed. Peter Y. Sussman (New York: Knopf, 2006), 55-56.

Mitford, Jessica. *Decca: The Letters of Jessica Mitford*. Edited by Peter Y. Sussman. New York: Knopf, 2006.

Citation at a glance
Letter in a published collection (*Chicago*)

To cite a letter in a published collection in *Chicago* style, include the following elements:

1. Author of letter
2. Recipient of letter
3. Date of letter
4. Title of collection
5. Editor of collection
6. City of publication
7. Publisher
8. Year of publication
9. Page number(s) cited (for notes); page range of letter (for bibliography)

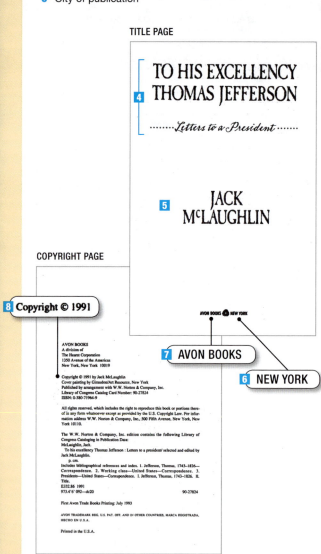

FIRST AND LAST PAGES OF LETTER

> Washington 30th. Oct 1805
>
> His Excellency Ths. Jefferson
> Sir,
> I have not the honor to be personally known to your Excellency therefore you will no doubt think it strange to receive this letter from a person of whom you have not the smallest knowledge. But in order to state to your Excellency in as few words as possible the purport of this address, I am a young man, a Roman Catholic who had been born and partly educated in Ireland but finding like many others who had been compelled to Migrate from that Kingdom in consequence of the late troubles which had almost overwhelmed that unhappy Nation That it was impossible for me to do anything in my Native Country. I came into this Country a few years since as an adventurer but having had the [m]isfortune not to be bred to any particular profession which

> Patronage   61
>
> your Excellency this very prolix letter which should it please your Excellency to give me some little Office or appointment in that extensive Country of Louisiana It should be my constant endeavour to merit the same by fidelity and an indefatigable attention to whatever business I should be assigned. May I have the satisfaction in whatsoever Country or situation [I] may be in to hear of your Excellencies long continuence of your Natural powers unempaired to conduct the Helm of this Extensive Country which are the sincere wishes of your Excellencies Mo. Obt. Hum. Servt.
>
>   John O'Neill

NOTE

1. John O'Neill to Thomas Jefferson, 30 October 1805, in *To His Excellency Thomas Jefferson: Letters to a President*, ed. Jack McLaughlin (New York: Avon Books, 1991), 61.

BIBLIOGRAPHY

O'Neill, John. John O'Neill to Thomas Jefferson, 30 October 1805. In *To His Excellency Thomas Jefferson: Letters to a President*, edited by Jack McLaughlin, 59-61. New York: Avon Books, 1991.

For another citation of a letter in *Chicago* style, see item 14.

■ 15. Work in a series

15. R. Keith Schoppa, *The Columbia Guide to Modern Chinese History*, Columbia Guides to Asian History (New York: Columbia University Press, 2000), 256-58.

Schoppa, R. Keith. *The Columbia Guide to Modern Chinese History*. Columbia Guides to Asian History. New York: Columbia University Press, 2000.

■ 16. Encyclopedia or dictionary entry

16. *Encyclopaedia Britannica*, 15th ed., s.v. "Monroe Doctrine."

The abbreviation "s.v." is for the Latin *sub verbo* ("under the word"). Reference works are usually not included in the bibliography.

■ 17. Sacred text

17. Matt. 20:4-9 (Revised Standard Version).

17. Qur'an 18:1-3.

Sacred texts are usually not included in the bibliography.

■ 18. Source quoted in another source

18. Ron Grossman and Charles Leroux, "A Local Outpost of Democracy," *Chicago Tribune,* March 5, 1996, quoted in William Julius Wilson and Richard P. Taub, *There Goes the Neighborhood: Racial, Ethnic, and Class Tensions in Four Chicago Neighborhoods and Their Meaning for America* (New York: Knopf, 2006), 18.

Grossman, Ron, and Charles Leroux. "A Local Outpost of Democracy." *Chicago Tribune,* March 5, 1996. Quoted in William Julius Wilson and Richard P. Taub, *There Goes the Neighborhood: Racial, Ethnic, and Class Tensions in Four Chicago Neighborhoods and Their Meaning for America* (New York: Knopf, 2006), 18.

Articles in periodicals (print and online)

■ 19. Article in a print journal

Include the volume and issue numbers and the date; end the bibliography entry with the page range of the article. (For an illustrated citation of an article in a print journal, see p. 227.)

19. T. H. Breen, "Will American Consumers Buy a Second American Revolution?," *Journal of American History* 93, no. 2 (2006): 405.

Breen, T. H. "Will American Consumers Buy a Second American Revolution?" *Journal of American History* 93, no. 2 (2006): 404-8.

Citation at a glance
Article in a journal (*Chicago*)

To cite an article in a print journal in *Chicago* style, include the following elements:

1. Author
2. Title of article
3. Title of journal
4. Volume and issue numbers
5. Date of publication
6. Page number(s) cited (for notes); page range of article (for bibliography)

TITLE PAGE OF JOURNAL

[4] VOLUME 113 · NUMBER 2 · APRIL 2008 **[5]**

[3] The American Historical Review
AMERICAN HISTORICAL ASSOCIATION

FIRST PAGE OF ARTICLE

[2] An Age of Imperial Revolutions

[1] JEREMY ADELMAN

WHEN THE VENEZUELAN CREOLE FRANCISCO DE MIRANDA led an expeditionary force to the shores of his native land to liberate it from Spanish rule in the summer of 1806, he brought with him a new weapon for making revolutions: a printing press. He hoped that his band of white, black, and mulatto patriots would start a revolt to free a continent with an alliance of swords and ideas. After dawdling for ten days, Miranda learned that royal troops (also white, black, and mulatto) were marching from Caracas. He withdrew before the two multiracial forces could clash. Consider Miranda's reasons for retreat: The nation he sought to free from its chains was not, in his opinion, a nation at all. While Venezuelans yearned for "Civil Liberty," they did not know how to grasp and protect it. They needed a liberation that would tutor them in the ways of liberty and fraternity, to create a nation of virtuous citizens out of a colony of subjects. This was why Miranda treated the printing press, a portable factory of words about liberty and sovereignty, as part of the arsenal of change: he wanted to create public opinion where there was none. But faced with the prospect of a violent clash and a scourge of "opposition and internal divisions," of a war waged mainly with swords, he preferred to pull out and bide his time.[1]

Miranda's dilemma—whether or not to move forward knowing how revolutions worked in imperial settings when their protagonists did not presume that their cause was self-evidently bound to triumph—evokes questions about the embedded politics of what we might now call, with a wince, "regime change." As empires gave way to successor systems in their colonies, those regimes began to call themselves nations not in order to cause imperial crises, but as the result of such crises. The study of imperial crises and the study of the origins of nationalism in colonial societies should inform each other more than they do. Bringing these two separate fields of scholarship together, and questioning the tacit and not-so-tacit beliefs upon which they rest, can help us reframe the complex passages from empires to successor states, free

[6] 319

NOTE

1. Jeremy Adelman, "An Age of Imperial Revolutions," *American Historical Review* 113, no. 2 (2008): 321.

BIBLIOGRAPHY

Adelman, Jeremy. "An Age of Imperial Revolutions." *American Historical Review* 113, no. 2 (2008): 319-40.

For more on citing articles from journals in *Chicago* style, see pages 226–29.

Citation at a glance
Journal article from a database (*Chicago*)

To cite a journal article from a database in *Chicago* style, include the following elements:

1. Author
2. Title of article
3. Title of journal
4. Volume and issue numbers
5. Year of publication
6. Page number(s) cited (for notes); page range of article (for bibliography)
7. DOI; *or* database name and article number; *or* "stable" or "persistent" URL for article

ON-SCREEN VIEW OF DATABASE RECORD

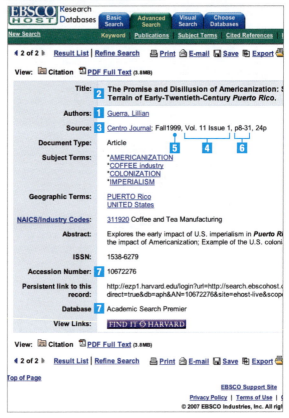

NOTE

1. Lillian Guerra, "The Promise and Disillusion of Americanization: Surveying the Socioeconomic Terrain of Early-Twentieth-Century Puerto Rico," *Centro Journal* 11, no. 1 (1999): 10. Academic Search Premier (10672276).

BIBLIOGRAPHY

Guerra, Lillian. "The Promise and Disillusion of Americanization: Surveying the Socioeconomic Terrain of Early-Twentieth-Century Puerto Rico." *Centro Journal* 11, no. 1 (1999): 8-31. Academic Search Premier (10672276).

For more on citing journal, magazine, and newspaper articles from databases in *Chicago* style, see items 21, 24, and 27.

■ **20. Article in an online journal**   Give the DOI if the article has one; if there is no DOI, give the URL for the article.

20. Brian Lennon, "New Media Critical Homologies," *Postmodern Culture* 19, no. 2 (2009), http://pmc.iath.virginia.edu/text-only/issue.109/19.2lennon.txt.

Lennon, Brian. "New Media Critical Homologies." *Postmodern Culture* 19, no. 2 (2009). http://pmc.iath.virginia.edu /text-only/issue.109/19.2lennon.txt.

■ **21. Journal article from a database**   Give whatever identifying information is available in the database listing: a DOI for the article; or the name of the database and the number assigned by the database; or a "stable" or "persistent" URL for the article. (For an illustrated citation of a journal article from a database, see pp. 228–29.)

21. Constant Leung, "Language and Content in Bilingual Education," *Linguistics and Education* 16, no. 2 (2005): 239, doi:10.1016/j.linged.2006.01.004.

Leung, Constant. "Language and Content in Bilingual Education." *Linguistics and Education* 16, no. 2 (2005): 238-52. doi:10.1016/j.linged.2006.01.004.

■ 22. Article in a print magazine

22. Tom Bissell, "Improvised, Explosive, and Divisive," *Harper's*, January 2006, 42.

Bissell, Tom. "Improvised, Explosive, and Divisive." *Harper's*, January 2006, 41-54.

■ 23. Article in an online magazine
Include the URL for the article.

23. Katharine Mieszkowski, "A Deluge Waiting to Happen," *Salon*, July 3, 2008, http://www.salon.com/news/feature/2008/07/03/floods/index.html.

Mieszkowski, Katharine. "A Deluge Waiting to Happen." *Salon*, July 3, 2008. http://www.salon.com/news/feature/2008/07/03/floods/index.html.

■ 24. Magazine article from a database
Give whatever identifying information is available in the database listing: a DOI for the article; or the name of the database and the number assigned by the database; or a "stable" or "persistent" URL for the article.

24. "Facing Facts in Afghanistan," *National Review*, November 2, 2009, 14, Expanded Academic ASAP (A209905060).

"Facing Facts in Afghanistan." *National Review*, November 2, 2009, 14. Expanded Academic ASAP (A209905060).

■ 25. Article in a print newspaper
Page numbers are not necessary; a section letter or number, if available, is sufficient.

25. Randal C. Archibold, "These Neighbors Are Good Ones without a New Fence," *New York Times*, October 22, 2008, sec. A.

Archibold, Randal C. "These Neighbors Are Good Ones without a New Fence." *New York Times*, October 22, 2008, sec. A.

■ 26. Article in an online newspaper
Include the URL for the article; if the URL is very long, use the URL for the newspaper's home page. Omit page numbers, even if the source provides them.

26. Doyle McManus, "The Candor War," *Chicago Tribune*, July 29, 2010, http://www.chicagotribune.com/.

McManus, Doyle. "The Candor War." *Chicago Tribune*, July 29, 2010. http://www.chicagotribune.com/.

■ 27. Newspaper article from a database
Give whatever identifying information is available in the database listing: a DOI for the article; or the name of the database and the number assigned by the database; or a "stable" or "persistent" URL for the article.

27. Clifford J. Levy, "In Kyrgyzstan, Failure to Act Adds to Crisis," *New York Times*, June 18, 2010, General OneFile (A229196045).

Levy, Clifford J. "In Kyrgyzstan, Failure to Act Adds to Crisis." *New York Times*, June 18, 2010. General OneFile (A229196045).

■ 28. Unsigned newspaper article
Begin the note with the title of the article; begin the bibliography entry with the name of the newspaper.

28. "Renewable Energy Rules," *Boston Globe*, August 11, 2003, sec. A.

Boston Globe. "Renewable Energy Rules." August 11, 2003, sec. A.

■ 29. Book review

29. Benjamin Wittes, "Remember the Titan," review of *Louis D. Brandeis: A Life*, by Melvin T. Urofsky, *Wilson Quarterly* 33, no. 4 (2009): 100.

Wittes, Benjamin. "Remember the Titan." Review of *Louis D. Brandeis: A Life*, by Melvin T. Urofsky. *Wilson Quarterly* 33, no. 4 (2009): 100-101.

Online sources For most Web sites, include an author if a site has one, the title of the site, the sponsor, the date the site was last modified or updated, and the site's URL. Do not italicize a Web site title unless the site is an online book or periodical. Use quotation marks for the titles of sections or pages in a Web site. If a site does not have a date, give the date you accessed the site ("accessed January 3, 2011").

■ 30. Web site

30. Chesapeake and Ohio Canal National Historical Park, National Park Service, last modified April 9, 2010, http://www.nps.gov/choh/index.htm.

Chesapeake and Ohio Canal National Historical Park. National Park Service. Last modified April 9, 2010. http://www.nps.gov/choh/index.htm.

Citation at a glance
Primary source from a Web site (*Chicago*)

To cite a primary source (or another document) from a Web site in *Chicago* style, include as many of the following elements as are available:

1 Author
2 Title of document
3 Title of site
4 Sponsor of site
5 Update or modified date (date of access if none)
6 URL of document

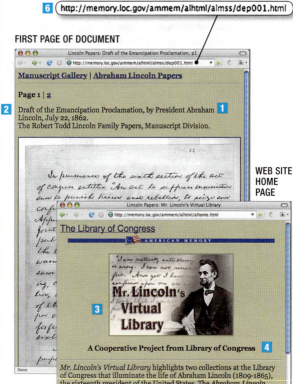

NOTE

1. Abraham Lincoln, "Draft of the Emancipation Proclamation," Mr. Lincoln's Virtual Library, Library of Congress, accessed July 24, 2010, http://memory.loc.gov/ammem/alhtml/almss/dep001.html.

BIBLIOGRAPHY

Lincoln, Abraham. "Draft of the Emancipation Proclamation." Mr. Lincoln's Virtual Library. Library of Congress. Accessed July 24, 2010. http://memory.loc.gov/ammem/alhtml/almss/dep001.html.

For more on citing documents from Web sites in *Chicago* style, see pages 231–34.

■ 31. Short work from a Web site

31. George P. Landow, "Victorian and Victorianism," Victorian Web, last modified August 2, 2009, http://victorianweb.org/vn/victor4.html.

Landow, George P. "Victorian and Victorianism." Victorian Web. Last modified August 2, 2009. http://victorianweb.org/vn/victor4.html.

(For an illustrated citation of a primary source from a Web site, see pp. 232–33.)

■ 32. Online posting or e-mail

E-mails that are not part of an online discussion are treated as personal communications (see item 38). Online postings and e-mails are not included in the bibliography.

32. Susanna J. Sturgis to Copyediting-L discussion list, July 17, 2010, http://listserv.indiana.edu/archives/copyediting-l.html.

■ 33. Blog (Weblog) post

Treat as a short work from a Web site (item 31). Put the title of the posting in quotation marks; italicize the name of the blog. Insert the word "blog" in parentheses after the name if it is not part of the name.

33. Miland Brown, "The Flawed Montevideo Convention of 1933," *World History Blog*, May 31, 2008, http://www.worldhistoryblog.com/2008/05/flawed-montevideo-convention-of-1933.html.

Brown, Miland. "The Flawed Montevideo Convention of 1933." *World History Blog*. May 31, 2008. http://www.worldhistoryblog.com/2008/05/flawed-montevideo-convention-of-1933.html.

■ **34. Podcast** Treat as a short work from a Web site (item 31), including the following, if available: the author's (or speaker's) name; the title of the podcast, in quotation marks; an identifying number, if any; the title of the site on which the podcast appears; the sponsor of the site; and the URL. Before the URL, identify the type of podcast or file format and the date of posting or your date of access.

34. Paul Tiyambe Zeleza, "Africa's Global Past," Episode 40, Africa Past and Present, African Online Digital Library, podcast audio, April 29, 2010, http://afripod.aodl.org/.

Zeleza, Paul Tiyambe. "Africa's Global Past." Episode 40. Africa Past and Present. African Online Digital Library. Podcast audio. April 29, 2010. http://afripod.aodl.org/.

■ **35. Online audio or video** Cite as a short work from a Web site (see item 31). If the source is a downloadable file, identify the file format or medium before the URL.

35. Richard B. Freeman, "Global Capitalism, Labor Markets, and Inequality," Institute of International Studies, University of California at Berkeley, October 31, 2007, http://www.youtube.com/watch?v=cgNCFsXGUa0.

Freeman, Richard B. "Global Capitalism, Labor Markets, and Inequality." Institute of International Studies, University of California at Berkeley. October 31, 2007. http://www.youtube.com/watch?v=cgNCFsXGUa0.

Other sources (including online versions)

■ **36. Government document**

36. U.S. Department of State, *Foreign Relations of the United States: Diplomatic Papers, 1943* (Washington, DC: GPO, 1965), 562.

U.S. Department of State. *Foreign Relations of the United States: Diplomatic Papers, 1943*. Washington, DC: GPO, 1965.

■ 37. Unpublished dissertation

37. Stephanie Lynn Budin, "The Origins of Aphrodite" (PhD diss., University of Pennsylvania, 2000), 301-2, ProQuest (AAT 9976404).

Budin, Stephanie Lynn. "The Origins of Aphrodite." PhD diss., University of Pennsylvania, 2000. ProQuest (AAT 9976404).

■ 38. Personal communication

38. Sara Lehman, e-mail message to author, August 13, 2003.

Personal communications are not included in the bibliography.

■ 39. Published or broadcast interview

39. Robert Downey Jr., interview by Graham Norton, *The Graham Norton Show*, BBC America, December 14, 2009.

Downey, Robert, Jr. Interview by Graham Norton. *The Graham Norton Show*. BBC America, December 14, 2009.

■ 40. Video (DVD, Blu-ray Disc)

40. *The Secret of Roan Inish*, directed by John Sayles (1993; Culver City, CA: Columbia TriStar Home Video, 2000), DVD.

The Secret of Roan Inish. Directed by John Sayles. 1993; Culver City, CA: Columbia TriStar Home Video, 2000. DVD.

■ 41. Sound recording

41. Gustav Holst, *The Planets*, Royal Philharmonic Orchestra, conducted by André Previn, Telarc 80133, compact disc.

Holst, Gustav. *The Planets*. Royal Philharmonic Orchestra. Conducted by André Previn. Telarc 80133. Compact disc.

44 *Chicago* manuscript format; sample pages

44a *Chicago* manuscript format

The guidelines in this section for formatting a *Chicago* paper and preparing endnotes and a bibliography are based on *The Chicago Manual of Style*, 16th ed. (Chicago:

University of Chicago Press, 2010). For pages from a sample paper, see 44b.

Formatting the paper

Title page Include the full title of your paper, your name, the course title, the instructor's name, and the date. Do not number the title page but count it in the manuscript numbering; that is, the first page of the text will be numbered 2. See page 239 for a sample title page.

Pagination Using arabic numerals, number all pages except the title page in the upper right corner. You may also place your last name to the left of the page number.

Margins and line spacing Leave margins of at least one inch at the top, bottom, and sides of the page. Double-space the entire manuscript, including long, indented quotations. (For line spacing in notes and the bibliography, see pp. 237 and 238.) Left-align the text.

Long quotations See page 214 for *Chicago* guidelines for setting off long quotations from the text.

Capitalization and italics In titles of works, capitalize all words except articles (*a, an, the*), prepositions (*at, from, between*, and so on), coordinating conjunctions (*and, but, or, nor, for, so, yet*), and *to* and *as*—unless one of these words is first or last in the title or subtitle.

Lowercase the first word following a colon even if the word begins a complete sentence. When the colon introduces a series of sentences or questions, capitalize all sentences in the series, including the first.

Italicize the titles of books, periodicals, and other long works. Use quotation marks around the titles of periodical articles, short stories, poems, and other short works.

Visuals Visuals are tables and figures, which include drawings, photographs, maps, and charts.

Label each table with an arabic numeral (Table 1, Table 2, and so on) and provide a clear title that identifies the subject. The label and title should appear on separate lines above the table, flush left. Below the table, give its source in a note like this one:

Source: Edna Bonacich and Richard P. Appelbaum, *Behind the Label* (Berkeley: University of California Press, 2000), 145.

For each figure, place a label and a caption below the figure, flush left. The label and caption need not appear on separate lines. The word "Figure" may be abbreviated as "Fig."

Place visuals as close as possible to the sentences that relate to them unless your instructor prefers that visuals appear in an appendix.

URLs (Web addresses) When a URL must be divided at the end of a line, do not insert a hyphen or break at a hyphen if the URL contains one. Instead, break the URL after a colon or a double slash or before any other mark of punctuation. If your word processing program automatically turns URLs into links (by underlining them and changing the color), turn off this feature.

Headings *Chicago* does not provide guidelines for the use of headings in student papers. If you would like to insert headings in a long essay or research paper, check first with your instructor. See page 240 for typical placement and formatting of headings.

Preparing the endnotes Begin the endnotes on a new page at the end of the paper. Center the title "Notes" about one inch from the top of the page, and number the pages consecutively with the rest of the manuscript. See page 241 for an example.

Indenting and numbering Indent the first line of each note one-half inch from the left margin; do not indent additional lines. Begin the note with the arabic numeral that corresponds to the number in the text. Put a period after the number.

Line spacing Single-space each note and double-space between notes (unless your instructor prefers double-spacing throughout).

Preparing the bibliography Typically, the notes in *Chicago* papers are followed by a bibliography, an alphabetically arranged list of all the works cited or consulted. Center the title "Bibliography" about one inch from the top of the page. Number bibliography pages consecutively with the rest of the paper. See page 242 for an example.

Alphabetizing the list Alphabetize the bibliography by the last names of the authors (or editors); when a work has no author or editor, alphabetize by the first word of the title other than *A*, *An*, or *The*.

If your list includes two or more works by the same author, use six hyphens instead of the author's name in all entries after the first. Arrange the entries alphabetically by title. See item 7 on page 222.

Indenting and line spacing Begin each entry at the left margin, and indent any additional lines one-half inch. Single-space each entry and double-space between entries (unless your instructor prefers double-spacing throughout).

44b Sample pages from a *Chicago* paper

On the following pages is an excerpt from a research paper written for a history class.

MODELS hackerhandbooks.com/pocket
> Model papers > *Chicago* papers: Bishop; Benjamin

Sample *Chicago* title page

The Massacre at Fort Pillow:
Holding Nathan Bedford Forrest Accountable

Ned Bishop

History 214
Professor Citro
March 22, 2008

Bishop 2

Although Northern newspapers of the time no doubt exaggerated some of the Confederate atrocities at Fort Pillow, most modern sources agree that a massacre of Union troops took place there on April 12, 1864. It seems clear that Union soldiers, particularly black soldiers, were killed after they had stopped fighting or had surrendered or were being held prisoner. Less clear is the role played by Major General Nathan Bedford Forrest in leading his troops. Although we will never know whether Forrest directly ordered the massacre, evidence suggests that he was responsible for it.

What happened at Fort Pillow?

Fort Pillow, Tennessee, which sat on a bluff overlooking the Mississippi River, had been held by the Union for two years. It was garrisoned by 580 men, 292 of them from United States Colored Heavy and Light Artillery regiments, 285 from the white Thirteenth Tennessee Cavalry. Nathan Bedford Forrest commanded about 1,500 troops.[1]

The Confederates attacked Fort Pillow on April 12, 1864, and had virtually surrounded the fort by the time Forrest arrived on the battlefield. At 3:30 p.m., Forrest demanded the surrender of the Union forces: "The conduct of the officers and men garrisoning Fort Pillow has been such as to entitle them to being treated as prisoners of war. . . . Should my demand be refused, I cannot be responsible for the fate of your command."[2] Union Major William Bradford, who had replaced Major Booth, killed earlier by sharpshooters, asked for an hour to consider the demand. Forrest, worried that vessels in the river were bringing in more Union troops, "shortened the time to twenty minutes."[3] Bradford refused to surrender, and Forrest quickly ordered the attack.

The Confederates charged to the fort, scaled the parapet, and fired on

---

1 Writer's thesis. **2** Headings (centered) guide readers.
3 Quotation cited with endnote.

Bishop 8

Notes

[1] 1. John Cimprich and Robert C. Mainfort Jr., eds., "Fort Pillow Revisited: New Evidence about an Old Controversy," *Civil War History* 28, no. 4 (1982): 293-94.

[2] 2. Quoted in Brian Steel Wills, *A Battle from the Start: The Life of Nathan Bedford Forrest* (New York: HarperCollins, 1992), 182.

3. Ibid., 183.

4. Shelby Foote, *The Civil War, a Narrative: Red River to Appomattox* (New York: Vintage, 1986), 110.

5. Nathan Bedford Forrest, "Report of Maj. Gen. Nathan B. Forrest, C. S. Army, Commanding Cavalry, of the Capture of Fort Pillow," Shotgun's Home of the American Civil War, accessed March 6, 2008, http://www.civilwarhome.com/forrest.htm.

[3] 6. Jack Hurst, *Nathan Bedford Forrest: A Biography* (New York: Knopf, 1993), 174.

7. Foote, *Civil War*, 111.

[4] 8. Cimprich and Mainfort, "Fort Pillow," 295.

9. Ibid., 305.

10. Ibid., 299.

11. Foote, *Civil War*, 110.

12. Quoted in Wills, *Battle from the Start*, 187.

[5] 13. Albert Castel, "The Fort Pillow Massacre: A Fresh Examination of the Evidence," *Civil War History* 4, no. 1 (1958): 44-45.

14. Cimprich and Mainfort, "Fort Pillow," 300.

---

[1] First line of note indented ½". **[2]** Note number not raised, followed by period. **[3]** Authors' names not inverted. **[4]** Last names and shortened title refer to earlier note by same authors. **[5]** Single-space notes; double-space between them.

Sample Chicago bibliography

Bishop 10

Bibliography

[1] Castel, Albert. "The Fort Pillow Massacre: A Fresh Examination of the Evidence." *Civil War History* 4, no. 1 (1958): 37-50.

Cimprich, John, and Robert C. Mainfort Jr., eds. "Fort Pillow Revisited: New Evidence about an Old Controversy." *Civil War History* 28, no. 4 (1982): 293-306.

[2] Cornish, Dudley Taylor. *The Sable Arm: Black Troops in the Union Army, 1861-1865*. Lawrence: University Press of Kansas, 1987.

Foote, Shelby. *The Civil War, a Narrative: Red River to Appomattox*. New York: Vintage, 1986.

Forrest, Nathan Bedford. "Report of Maj. Gen. Nathan B. Forrest, C. S. Army, Commanding Cavalry, of the Capture of Fort Pillow." Shotgun's Home of the American Civil War. Accessed March 6, 2008. http://www.civilwarhome.com/forrest.htm.

[3] Hurst, Jack. *Nathan Bedford Forrest: A Biography*. New York: Knopf, 1993.

McPherson, James M. *Battle Cry of Freedom: The Civil War Era*. New York: Oxford University Press, 1988.

Wills, Brian Steel. *A Battle from the Start: The Life of Nathan Bedford Forrest*. New York: HarperCollins, 1992.

---

[1] Alphabetize by authors' last names. [2] First line of each entry at left margin; additional lines indented ½". [3] Single-space entries; double-space between them.

CSE Papers

45 **CSE documentation style** 244

Directory to CSE in-text citation models 244

Directory to CSE reference list models 247

46 **CSE manuscript format** 256

45 CSE documentation style

In many science classes, you may be asked to use one of three systems of documentation recommended by the Council of Science Editors (CSE) in *Scientific Style and Format: The CSE Manual for Authors, Editors, and Publishers*, 7th ed. (Reston: CSE, 2006).

45a CSE documentation systems

The three CSE documentation systems specify the ways that sources are cited in the text of the paper and in the reference list at the end of the paper.

In the citation-sequence system, each source is given a superscript number the first time it appears in the paper. Any subsequent references to that source are marked with the same number. At the end of the paper, a list of references provides full publication information for each numbered source. Entries in the reference list are numbered in the order in which they are mentioned in the paper.

In the citation-name system, the list of references is created first, with entries alphabetized by authors' last names. The entries are numbered according to their alphabetical order, and the numbers are used in the text to cite the sources from the list.

In the name-year system, the author of the source is named in the text or in parentheses, and the date is given in parentheses. The reference list at the end of the paper is arranged alphabetically by authors' last names.

Sections 45b and 45c describe formatting of in-text citations and the reference list, respectively, in all three systems.

Directory to CSE in-text citation models

1. Basic format — 245
2. Author named in the text — 245
3. Specific part of source — 245
4. Work by two authors — 245
5. Work by three or more authors — 246
6. Multiple works by one author — 246
7. Organization as author — 246

45b CSE in-text citations

In-text citations in all three CSE systems refer readers to the reference list at the end of the paper. The reference list is organized differently in the three systems (see 45c).

■ 1. Basic format

Citation-sequence or citation-name system

Scientists are beginning to question the validity of linking genes to a number of human traits and disorders [1].

Name-year

Scientists are beginning to question the validity of linking genes to a number of human traits and disorders (Allen 2009).

■ 2. Author named in the text

Citation-sequence or citation-name

Smith [2], studying three species of tree frogs, identified variations in coloring over a small geographic area.

Name-year

Smith (2010), studying three species of tree frogs, identified variations in coloring over a small geographic area.

■ 3. Specific part of source

Citation-sequence or citation-name

Our data differed markedly from Markam's study [3(Figs. 2,7)] on the same species in North Dakota.

Researchers observed an immune response in "19 of 20 people who ate a potato vaccine aimed at the Norwalk virus," according to Langridge [4(p. 68)].

Name-year

Our data differed markedly from Markam's study (2010, Figs. 2, 7) on the same species in North Dakota.

Researchers observed an immune response in "19 of 20 people who ate a potato vaccine aimed at the Norwalk virus," according to Langridge (2009, p. 68).

■ 4. Work by two authors

Citation-sequence or citation-name

Follow item 1, 2, or 3, depending on the way you are using the source in your paper.

Name-year

Self-organization plays a complex role in the evolution of biological systems (Johnson and Lam 2010).

Johnson and Lam (2010) explored the complex role of self-organization in evolution.

■ 5. Work by three or more authors

Citation-sequence or citation-name

Follow item 1, 2, or 3 on page 245, depending on the way you are using the source in your paper.

Name-year

Orchid seed banking is a promising method of conservation to preserve species in situ (Seaton et al. 2010).

Seaton et al. (2010) provided a range of in situ techniques for orchid seed banking as a method of conservation of species.

■ 6. Multiple works by one author

Citation-sequence or citation-name

Gawande's work [4,5,6] deals not just with the practice of modern medicine but more broadly with the way we rely on human expertise in every aspect of society.

Name-year: works in different years

Gawande's work (2003, 2007, 2009) deals not just with the practice of modern medicine but more broadly with the way we rely on human expertise in every aspect of society.

Name-year: works in the same year

The works are arranged in the reference list in chronological order, the earliest first. The letters "a," "b," and so on are added after the year, in both the reference list and the in-text citation. (See also the name-year model at the top of p. 250.)

Scientists have investigated the role of follicle stimulating hormone (FSH) in the growth of cancer cells beyond the ovaries and testes (Seppa 2010a).

■ 7. Organization as author

Citation-sequence or citation-name

Follow item 1, 2, or 3 on page 245, depending on the way you are using the source in your paper.

Name-year

Developing standards for handling and processing biospecimens is essential to ensure the validity of cancer research and, ultimately, treatment (OBBR 2010).

The reference list entry gives the abbreviation for the organization's name, followed by the full name of the organization (Office of Biorepositories and Biospecimen Research); only the abbreviation is used in the in-text citation. (See item 3 on pp. 248–49.)

Directory to CSE reference list models

BASIC GUIDELINES
1. Single author — 248
2. Two or more authors — 248
3. Organization as author — 248
4. Two or more works by the same author — 249
5. Two or more works by the same author in the same year — 249

BOOKS
6. Print book — 250
7. Online book — 250
8. Book with an editor — 250
9. Edition other than the first — 251
10. Article or chapter in an edited volume — 251

ARTICLES
11. Article in a print journal — 251
12. Article in an online journal — 251
13. Article in a print magazine — 252
14. Article in an online magazine — 252
15. Article in a print newspaper — 252
16. Article in an online newspaper — 252
17. Article from a database — 253

OTHER SOURCES
18. Home page of a Web site — 253
19. Short work from a Web site — 253
20. Report from a government agency (print and online) — 254
21. Conference presentation (print and online) — 254
22. DVD or Blu-ray Disc (BD) — 255
23. Online video — 255
24. Podcast — 256
25. E-mail — 256

45c CSE references

In the citation-sequence system, entries in the reference list are numbered in the order in which they appear in the text of the paper. In the citation-name system, entries in the reference list are put into alphabetical order and then numbered in that order. In the name-year system, entries are listed alphabetically in the reference list; they are not numbered. See 45b for examples of in-text citations using all three systems. See 46b for details about formatting the reference list.

Basic guidelines

■ 1. Single author

Citation-sequence or citation-name

1. Bliss M. The making of modern medicine: turning points in the treatment of disease. Chicago: University of Chicago Press; 2011.

Name-year

Bliss M. 2011. The making of modern medicine: turning points in the treatment of disease. Chicago: University of Chicago Press.

■ 2. Two or more authors

For a source with two to ten authors, list all authors' names; for a source with more than ten authors, list the first ten authors followed by a comma and "et al." (for "and others").

Citation-sequence or citation-name

2. Seaton PT, Hong H, Perner H, Pritchard HW. Ex situ conservation of orchids in a warming world. Bot Rev. 2010;76(2):193-203.

Name-year

Seaton PT, Hong H, Perner H, Pritchard HW. 2010. Ex situ conservation of orchids in a warming world. Bot Rev. 76(2):193-203.

■ 3. Organization as author

Citation-sequence or citation-name

3. American Cancer Society. Cancer facts and figures for African Americans 2005-2006. Report. Atlanta (GA): The Society; 2005.

Name-year

Give the abbreviation of the organization name in brackets at the beginning of the entry; alphabetize the entry by the first word of the full name. (For an in-text citation, see the name-year model at the top of p. 247.)

[ACS] American Cancer Society. 2005. Cancer facts and figures for
African Americans 2005-2006. Report. Atlanta (GA): The Society.

■ 4. Two or more works by the same author

Citation-sequence or citation-name

In the citation-sequence system, list the works in the order in which they appear in the paper. In the citation-name system, order the works alphabetically by title. (The following examples are presented in the citation-name system.)

4. Gawande A. Better: a surgeon's notes on performance. New York: Metropolitan; 2007.

5. Gawande A. The checklist manifesto: how to get things right. New York: Metropolitan; 2009.

6. Gawande A. Complications: a surgeon's notes on an imperfect science. New York: Picador; 2003.

Name-year

List the works chronologically, the earliest first.

Gawande A. 2003. Complications: a surgeon's notes on an imperfect
science. New York: Picador.

Gawande A. 2007. Better: a surgeon's notes on performance. New
York: Metropolitan.

Gawande A. 2009. The checklist manifesto: how to get things right.
New York: Metropolitan.

■ 5. Two or more works by the same author in the same year

Citation-sequence or citation-name

In the citation-sequence system, list the works in the order in which they appear in the paper. In the citation-name system, order the works alphabetically by title. (The following examples are presented in the citation-sequence system.)

5. Seppa N. Protein implicated in many cancers. Sci News [Internet]. 2010 Oct 20 [cited 2011 Jan 22]; [11 paragraphs]. Available from: http://www.sciencenews.org/view/generic/id/64426

8. Seppa N. Anticancer protein might combat HIV. Sci News. 2010 Nov 20;178(11):9.

Name-year

List the works in chronological order, the earliest first, and add the letters "a," "b," and so on after the year. If the works have only a year but not exact dates, arrange the entries alphabetically by title.

Seppa N. 2010a. Fish oil may fend off breast cancer: other supplements studied show no signs of protection. Sci News. Jul 31;178(3):13.

Seppa N. 2010b. Ovary removal boosts survival: procedure shown to benefit women with BRCA mutations. Sci News. Sep 25;178(7):12.

Books

■ 6. Print book

Citation-sequence or citation-name
6. Tobin M. Endangered: biodiversity on the brink. Golden (CO): Fulcrum; 2010.

Name-year
Tobin M. 2010. Endangered: biodiversity on the brink. Golden (CO): Fulcrum.

■ 7. Online book

Citation-sequence or citation-name
7. Wilson DE, Reeder DM, editors. Mammal species of the world [Internet]. Washington (DC): Smithsonian Institution; 3rd ed. Baltimore (MD): Johns Hopkins University Press; c2005 [cited 2010 Oct 14]; [about 200 screens]. Available from: http://vertebrates.si.edu/mammals/msw/.

Name-year
Wilson DE, Reeder DM, editors. c2005. Mammal species of the world [Internet]. Washington (DC): Smithsonian Institution; 3rd ed. Baltimore (MD): Johns Hopkins University Press; [cited 2010 Oct 14]; [about 200 screens]. Available from: http://vertebrates.si.edu/mammals/msw/.

■ 8. Book with an editor

Citation-sequence or citation-name
8. Kurimoto N, Fielding D, Musani A, editors. Endobronchial ultrasonography. New York: Wiley-Blackwell; 2011.

Name-year

Kurimoto N, Fielding D, Musani A, editors. 2011. Endobronchial ultrasonography. New York: Wiley-Blackwell.

■ 9. Edition other than the first

Citation-sequence or citation-name

9. Mai J, Paxinos G, Assheuer J. Atlas of the human brain. 2nd ed. Burlington (MA): Elsevier; 2004.

Name-year

Mai J, Paxinos G, Assheuer J. 2004. Atlas of the human brain. 2nd ed. Burlington (MA): Elsevier.

■ 10. Article or chapter in an edited volume

Citation-sequence or citation-name

10. Underwood AJ, Chapman MG. Intertidal ecosystems. In: Levin SA, editor. Encyclopedia of biodiversity. Vol. 3. San Diego: Academic Press; 2000. p. 485-499.

Name-year

Underwood AJ, Chapman MG. 2000. Intertidal ecosystems. In: Levin SA, editor. Encyclopedia of biodiversity. Vol. 3. San Diego: Academic Press; p. 485-499.

Articles

■ 11. Article in a print journal

Citation-sequence or citation-name

11. Wasserman EA, Blumberg MS. Designing minds: how should we explain the origins of novel behaviors. Am Sci. 2010;98(3):183-185.

Name-year

Wasserman EA, Blumberg MS. 2010. Designing minds: how should we explain the origins of novel behaviors. Am Sci. 98(3):183-185.

■ 12. Article in an online journal

Citation-sequence or citation-name

12. Leslie M. The power of one. Science [Internet]. 2011 Jan 7 [cited 2011 Feb 3];331(6013):24-26. Available from: http://www.sciencemag.org/content/331/6013/24.1.summary doi:10.1126/science.331.6013.24-a

Name-year

Leslie M. The power of one. Science [Internet]. 2011 Jan 7 [cited 2011 Feb 3];331(6013):24-26. Available from: http://www.sciencemag.org/content/331/6013/24.1.summary doi:10.1126/science.331.6013.24-a

■ 13. Article in a print magazine

Citation-sequence or citation-name

13. Quammen D. Great migrations. Natl Geogr. 2010 Nov:31-51.

Name-year

Quammen D. 2010 Nov. Great migrations. Natl Geogr. 31-51.

■ 14. Article in an online magazine

Citation-sequence or citation-name

14. Matson J. Twisted light could enable black hole detection. Sci Am [Internet]. 2011 Feb 14 [cited 2011 Feb 28]; [8 paragraphs]. Available from: http://www.scientificamerican.com/article.cfm?id=twisting-light-oam

Name-year

Matson J. 2011 Feb 14. Twisted light could enable black hole detection. Sci Am [Internet]. [cited 2011 Feb 28]; [8 paragraphs]. Available from: http://www.scientificamerican.com/article.cfm?id=twisting-light-oam

■ 15. Article in a print newspaper

Citation-sequence or citation-name

15. Wald M. Scientists call for new sources of critical elements. New York Times (New York Ed.). 2011 Feb 19;B5 (col. 1).

Name-year

Wald M. 2011 Feb 19. Scientists call for new sources of critical elements. New York Times (New York Ed.). B5 (col. 1).

■ 16. Article in an online newspaper

Citation-sequence or citation-name

16. Wade N. Human DNA contamination seen in genome databases. New York Times [Internet]. 2011 Feb 16; [17 paragraphs]. Available from: http://www.nytimes.com/2011/02/17/science/17genome.html?ref=science

Name-year

Wade N. 2011 Feb 16. Human DNA contamination seen in genome databases. New York Times [Internet]. [17 paragraphs]. Available from: http://www.nytimes.com/2011/02/17/science/17genome.html?ref=science

17. Article from a database

Citation-sequence or citation-name

17. Logan CA. A review of ocean acidification and America's response. BioScience [Internet]. 2010 [cited 2011 Jun 17];60(10):819-828. General OneFile. Available from: http://find.galegroup.com.ezproxy.bpl.org/. Document No.: A241952492.

Name-year

Logan CA. 2010. A review of ocean acidification and America's response. BioScience [Internet]. [cited 2011 Jun 17];60(10):819-828. General OneFile. Available from: http://find.galegroup.com.ezproxy.bpl.org/. Document No.: A241952492.

Other sources

18. Home page of a Web site

Citation-sequence or citation-name

18. American Society of Gene and Cell Therapy [Internet]. Milwaukee (WI): The Society; c2000-2011 [cited 2011 Jan 16]. Available from: http://www.asgt.org/.

Name-year

[ASGCT] American Society of Gene and Cell Therapy [Internet]. c2000-2011. Milwaukee (WI): The Society; [cited 2010 Jan 16]. Available from: http://www.asgt.org/.

19. Short work from a Web site

Citation-sequence or citation-name

19. Cleveland Clinic [Internet]. Cleveland (OH): The Clinic; c1995-2011. Diabetes and smoking; [cited 2010 Feb 8]; [8 paragraphs]. Available from: http://my.clevelandclinic.org/tobacco/diabetes_and_smoking.aspx

Name-year

Cleveland Clinic [Internet]. c1995-2011. Cleveland (OH): The Clinic. Diabetes and smoking; [cited 2010 Feb 8]; [8 paragraphs]. Available from: http://my.clevelandclinic.org/tobacco/diabetes_and_smoking.aspx

■ 20. Report from a government agency (print and online)

Citation-sequence or citation-name

20. National Institute on Drug Abuse (US). Inhalant abuse. Bethesda (MD): National Institutes of Health (US); 2010 Jul. NIH Pub. No.: 10-3818. Available from: National Clearinghouse on Alcohol and Drug Information, Rockville, MD 20852.

20. National Institute on Drug Abuse (US). Inhalant abuse [Internet]. Bethesda (MD): National Institutes of Health (US); [revised 2010 Jul; cited 2011 Jan 23]; [about 13 pages]. NIH Pub. No.: 10-3818. Available from: http://www.drugabuse.gov/ResearchReports/Inhalants/inhalants.html

Name-year

[NIDA] National Institute on Drug Abuse (US). 2010 Jul. Inhalant abuse. Bethesda (MD): National Institutes of Health (US). NIH Pub. No.: 10-3818. Available from: National Clearinghouse on Alcohol and Drug Information, Rockville, MD 20852.

[NIDA] National Institute on Drug Abuse (US). 2010 Jul. Inhalant abuse [Internet]. Bethesda (MD): National Institutes of Health (US); [cited 2010 Jan 23]; [about 13 pages]. NIH Pub. No.: 10-3818. Available from: http://www.drugabuse.gov/ResearchReports/Inhalants/inhalants.html

■ 21. Conference presentation (print and online)

Citation-sequence or citation-name

21. Pendleton L. The cost of beach water monitoring errors in southern California. In: Proceedings of the 2004 National Beaches Conference; 2004 Oct 13-15; San Diego, CA. Washington (DC): Environmental Protection Agency (US); 2005 Mar. p. 104-110.

21. Pendleton L. The cost of beach water monitoring errors in southern California [conference presentation on the Internet]. In: Proceedings of the 2004 National Beaches Conference [Internet]; 2004 Oct 13-15; San Diego, CA. Washington (DC): Environmental

Protection Agency (US); 2005 Mar [cited 2011 Jan 30]. p. 104-110. Available from: http://water.epa.gov/type/oceb/beaches/ upload/2008_10_28_beaches_meetings_2004_part1.pdf

Name-year

Pendleton L. 2005 Mar. The cost of beach water monitoring errors in southern California. In: Proceedings of the 2004 National Beaches Conference; 2004 Oct 13-15; San Diego, CA. Washington (DC): Environmental Protection Agency (US). p. 104-110.

Pendleton L. 2005 Mar. The cost of beach water monitoring errors in southern California [conference presentation on the Internet]. In: Proceedings of the 2004 National Beaches Conference [Internet]; 2004 Oct 13-15; San Diego, CA. Washington (DC): Environmental Protection Agency (US); [cited 2011 Jan 30]. p. 104-110. Available from: http:// water.epa.gov/type/oceb/beaches/upload/ 2008_10_28_beaches_meetings_2004_part1.pdf

■ 22. DVD or Blu-ray Disc (BD)

Citation-sequence or citation-name

22. NOVA: secrets beneath the ice [DVD]. Seifferlein B, editor; Hochman G, producer. Boston: WGBH Educational Foundation; 2010. 1 DVD: 52 min., sound, color.

Name-year

NOVA: secrets beneath the ice [DVD]. 2010. Seifferlein B, editor; Hochman G, producer. Boston: WGBH Educational Foundation. 1 DVD: 52 min., sound, color.

■ 23. Online video

Citation-sequence or citation-name

23. Life: creatures of the deep: nemertean worms and sea stars [video on the Internet]. Gunton M, executive producer; Holmes M, series producer. [place unknown]: Discovery Channel/BBC; 2010 Mar 21 [cited 2011 Feb 4]. 2:55 min. Available from: http:// dsc.discovery.com/videos/life-the-series-videos/?bcid=73073289001

Name-year

Life: creatures of the deep: nemertean worms and sea stars [video on the Internet]. 2010 Mar 21. Gunton M, executive producer; Holmes M, series producer. [place unknown]:

Discovery Channel/BBC; [cited 2011 Feb 4]. 2:55 min.
Available from: http://dsc.discovery.com/videos/
life-the-series-videos/?bcid=73073289001

■ 24. Podcast

Citation-sequence or citation-name

24. The spirit of innovation: from high school to the moon [podcast on the Internet]. Mirsky S, host; Conrad N, interviewee. New York: Scientific American; 2011 Feb 17 [cited 2011 Feb 27]. 19:26 min. Available from: http://www.scientificamerican.com/podcast/episode.cfm?id=from-high-school-innovation-to-the-11-02-17

Name-year

The spirit of innovation: from high school to the moon [podcast
   on the Internet]. 2011 Feb 17. Mirsky S, host; Conrad N,
   interviewee. New York: Scientific American; [cited 2011
   Feb 27]. 19:26 min. Available from: http://
   www.scientificamerican.com/podcast/
   episode.cfm?id=from-high-school-innovation-to-the-11-02-17

■ **25. E-mail**   CSE recommends not including personal communications such as e-mail in the reference list. A parenthetical note in the text usually suffices: (2010 e-mail to me; unreferenced).

46 CSE manuscript format

The guidelines in this section are adapted from advice given in *Scientific Style and Format: The CSE Manual for Authors, Editors, and Publishers*, 7th ed. (Reston: CSE, 2006). When in doubt about the formatting required in your course, check with your instructor.

46a Formatting the paper

Materials and typeface   Use good-quality 8½" × 11" white paper. If your instructor does not require a specific font, choose one that is standard and easy to read (such as Times New Roman).

MODELS hackerhandbooks.com/pocket
 > Model papers > CSE papers: Martin; Johnson/Arnold

Title page Center all information on the title page: the title of your paper, your name, the course name, and the date.

Pagination The title page is counted as page 1, although a number does not appear. Number the first page of the text of the paper as page 2. Type a shortened form of the title followed by the page number in the top right corner of each page.

Margins, spacing, and indentation Leave margins of at least one inch on all sides of the page. Double-space throughout the paper. Indent the first line of each paragraph one-half inch. When a quotation is set off from the text, indent the entire quotation one-half inch from the left margin.

Abstract An abstract is a single paragraph at the beginning of the paper that summarizes the paper and might include your research methods, findings, and conclusions. Do not include bibliographic references in the abstract.

Headings CSE encourages the use of headings to help readers follow the organization of a paper. Common headings for papers reporting research are Introduction, Methods, Results, and Discussion.

Visuals A visual, such as a table, figure, or chart, should be placed as close as possible to the text that discusses it. In general, try to place visuals at the top of a page.

Appendixes Appendixes may be used for relevant information that is too long to include in the body of the paper. Label each appendix and give it a title (for example, Appendix 1: Methodologies of Previous Researchers).

Acknowledgments An acknowledgments section is common in scientific writing because research is often conducted with help from others. Place the acknowledgments at the end of the paper before the reference list.

46b Formatting the reference list

Basic format Center the title "References" and then list the works you have cited in the paper. Double-space throughout.

Organization of the list In the citation-sequence system, number the entries in the order in which they appear in the text. In the citation-name system, first alphabetize all the entries by authors' last names (or by organization name or by title for works with no author, ignoring any initial *A*, *An*, or *The*); for two or more works by the same author, arrange the entries alphabetically by title. Then number the entries in the order in which they appear in the list. Make the entire entry flush with the left margin. In both systems, use the number from the reference list whenever you refer to the source in the text of the paper.

In the name-year system, alphabetize the entries by authors' last names (or by organization name or by title for works with no author, ignoring any initial *A*, *An*, or *The*). Place the year after the last author's name, followed by a period. For two or more works by the same author, arrange the entries by year, the earliest first. For two or more works by the same author in the same year, see item 5 at the top of page 250. Unless your instructor prefers otherwise, type the first line of each entry flush left, and indent any additional lines one-half inch.

Authors' names Give the last name first; use initials for first and middle names, with no periods after the initials and no space between them. Do not use a comma between the last name and the initials. For a work with up to ten authors, use all authors' names; for a work with eleven or more authors, list the first ten names followed by a comma and "et al." (for "and others").

Titles of books and articles Capitalize only the first word and all proper nouns in the title of a book or an article. Do not underline or italicize titles of books; do not place titles of articles in quotation marks.

Titles of journals Abbreviate titles of journals that consist of more than one word. Omit the words *the* and *of* and apostrophes. Capitalize all the words or abbreviated words in the title; do not underline or italicize the title: Science, Sci Am, N Engl J Med, Womens Health.

Page ranges Do not abbreviate page ranges for articles in journals or periodicals or for chapters in edited volumes. When an article appears on discontinuous pages, list all pages or page ranges, separated by commas: 145-149, 162-174. For chapters in edited volumes, use the abbreviation "p." before the numbers (p. 63-90).

Breaking a URL or DOI When a URL or a DOI (digital object identifier) must be divided, break it only after a double slash or a slash. Do not insert a hyphen, and do not add a period at the end unless a URL ends in a slash.

Glossaries

47 Glossary of usage 260
48 Glossary of grammatical terms 270

47 Glossary of usage

This glossary includes words commonly confused, words commonly misused, and words that are nonstandard. It also lists colloquialisms that may be appropriate in informal speech but are inappropriate in formal writing.

a, an Use *an* before a vowel sound, *a* before a consonant sound: *an apple, a peach*. Problems sometimes arise with words beginning with *h* or *u*. If the *h* is silent, the word begins with a vowel sound, so use *an*: *an hour, an heir, an honest senator*. If the *h* is pronounced, the word begins with a consonant sound, so use *a*: *a hospital, a historian, a hotel*. Words such as *university* and *union* begin with a consonant sound, so use *a*: *a union*. Words such as *uncle* and *umbrella* begin with a vowel sound, so use *an*: *an underground well*. When an abbreviation or acronym begins with a vowel sound, use *an*: *an EKG, an MRI*.

accept, except *Accept* is a verb meaning "to receive." *Except* is usually a preposition meaning "excluding." *I will accept all the packages except that one. Except* is also a verb meaning "to exclude." *Please except that item from the list.*

adapt, adopt *Adapt* means "to adjust or become accustomed"; it is usually followed by *to*. *Adopt* means "to take as one's own." *Our family adopted a Vietnamese child, who quickly adapted to his new life.*

adverse, averse *Adverse* means "unfavorable." *Averse* means "opposed" or "reluctant"; it is usually followed by *to*. *I am averse to your proposal because it could have an adverse impact on the economy.*

advice, advise *Advice* is a noun, *advise* a verb. *We advise you to follow John's advice.*

affect, effect *Affect* is usually a verb meaning "to influence." *Effect* is usually a noun meaning "result." *The drug did not affect the disease, and it had adverse side effects. Effect* can also be a verb meaning "to bring about." *Only the president can effect such a change.*

all ready, already *All ready* means "completely prepared." *Already* means "previously." *Susan was all ready for the concert, but her friends had already left.*

all right *All right*, written as two words, is correct. *Alright* is nonstandard.

all together, altogether *All together* means "everyone gathered." *Altogether* means "entirely." *We were not altogether sure that we could bring the family all together for the reunion.*

allusion, illusion An *allusion* is an indirect reference; an *illusion* is a misconception or false impression. *Did you catch my allusion to Shakespeare? Mirrors give the room an illusion of depth.*

a lot *A lot* is two words. Do not write *alot*.

among, between Ordinarily, use *among* with three or more entities, *between* with two. *The prize was divided among several contestants. You have a choice between carrots and beans.*

amoral, immoral *Amoral* means "neither moral nor immoral"; it also means "not caring about moral judgments." *Immoral* means "morally wrong." *Many business courses are taught from an amoral perspective. Murder is immoral.*

amount, number Use *amount* with quantities that cannot be counted; use *number* with those that can. *This recipe calls for a large amount of sugar. We have a large number of toads in our garden.*

an See *a, an*.

and/or Avoid *and/or* except in technical or legal documents.

anxious *Anxious* means "worried" or "apprehensive." In formal writing, avoid using *anxious* to mean "eager." *We are eager* (not *anxious*) *to see your new house.*

anybody, anyone See pages 21 and 31.

anyone, any one *Anyone*, an indefinite pronoun, means "any person at all." *Any one* refers to a particular person or thing in a group. *Anyone in the class may choose any one of the books to read.*

anyways, anywheres *Anyways* and *anywheres* are nonstandard for *anyway* and *anywhere*.

as *As* is sometimes used to mean "because." But do not use it if there is any chance of ambiguity. *We canceled the picnic because* (not *as*) *it began raining. As* here could mean "because" or "when."

as, like See *like, as*.

averse See *adverse, averse*.

awful The adjective *awful* and the adverb *awfully* are too colloquial for formal writing.

awhile, a while *Awhile* is an adverb; it can modify a verb, but it cannot be the object of a preposition such as *for*. The two-word form *a while* is a noun preceded by an article and therefore can be the object of a preposition. *Stay awhile. Stay for a while.*

USAGE hackerhandbooks.com/pocket
  > Language Debates > Pronoun-antecedent agreement

back up, backup *Back up* is a verb phrase. *Back up the car carefully. Be sure to back up your hard drive. Backup* is a noun often meaning "duplicate of electronically stored data." *Keep your backup in a safe place. Backup* can also be used as an adjective. *I regularly create backup disks.*

bad, badly *Bad* is an adjective, *badly* an adverb. *They felt bad about being early and ruining the surprise. Her arm hurt badly after she slid into second.* See section 13.

being as, being that *Being as* and *being that* are nonstandard expressions. Write *because* instead.

beside, besides *Beside* is a preposition meaning "at the side of" or "next to." *Annie sleeps with a flashlight beside her bed. Besides* is a preposition meaning "except" or "in addition to." *No one besides Terrie can have that ice cream. Besides* is also an adverb meaning "in addition." *I'm not hungry; besides, I don't like ice cream.*

between See *among, between*.

bring, take Use *bring* when an object is being transported toward you, *take* when it is being moved away. *Please bring me a glass of water. Please take these magazines to Mr. Scott.*

can, may *Can* is traditionally reserved for ability, *may* for permission. *Can you speak French? May I help you?*

capital, capitol *Capital* refers to a city, *capitol* to a building where lawmakers meet. *The residents of the state capital protested the development plans. The capitol has undergone extensive renovations. Capital* also refers to wealth or resources.

censor, censure *Censor* means "to remove or suppress material considered objectionable." *Censure* means "to criticize severely." *The school's policy of censoring books has been censured by the media.*

cite, site *Cite* means "to quote as an authority or example." *Site* is usually a noun meaning "a particular place." *He cited the zoning law in his argument against the proposed site of the gas station.* Locations on the Internet are usually referred to as *sites*.

coarse, course *Coarse* means "crude" or "rough in texture." *The hand-knit sweater had a coarse weave. Course* usually refers to a path, a playing field, or a unit of study. *I plan to take a course in car repair this summer.* The expression *of course* means "certainly."

complement, compliment *Complement* is a verb meaning "to go with or complete" or a noun meaning "something

USAGE hackerhandbooks.com/pocket
> Language Debates > *bad* versus *badly*

that completes." As a verb, *compliment* means "to flatter"; as a noun, it means "flattering remark." *Her skill at rushing the net complements his skill at volleying. Sheiying's music arrangements receive many compliments.*

conscience, conscious *Conscience* is a noun meaning "moral principles"; *conscious* is an adjective meaning "aware or alert." *Let your conscience be your guide. Were you conscious of his love for you?*

continual, continuous *Continual* means "repeated regularly and frequently." *She grew weary of the continual telephone calls. Continuous* means "extended or prolonged without interruption." *The broken siren made a continuous wail.*

could care less *Could care less* is a nonstandard expression. Write *couldn't care less* instead.

could of *Could of* is nonstandard for *could have*.

council, counsel A *council* is a deliberative body, and a *councilor* is a member of such a body. *Counsel* usually means "advice" and can also mean "lawyer"; a *counselor* is one who gives advice or guidance. *The councilors met to draft the council's position paper. The pastor offered wise counsel to the troubled teenager.*

criteria *Criteria* is the plural of *criterion*, which means "a standard, rule, or test on which a judgment or decision can be based." *The only criterion for the scholarship is ability.*

data *Data* is a plural noun meaning "facts or results." But *data* is increasingly being accepted as a singular noun. *The new data suggest* (or *suggests*) *that our theory is correct.* (The singular *datum* is rarely used.)

different from, different than Ordinarily, write *different from. Your sense of style is different from Jim's.* However, *different than* is acceptable to avoid an awkward construction. *Please let me know if your plans are different than* (to avoid *from what*) *they were six weeks ago.*

don't *Don't* is the contraction for *do not. I don't want milk. Don't* should not be used as the contraction for *does not*, which is *doesn't. He doesn't* (not *don't*) *want milk.*

due to *Due to* is an adjective phrase and should not be used as a preposition meaning "because of." *The trip was canceled because of* (not *due to*) *lack of interest. Due to* is acceptable as a subject complement and usually follows a form of the verb *be. His success was due to hard work.*

each See pages 21 and 31.

effect See *affect, effect*.

either See pages 21 and 31.

elicit, illicit *Elicit* is a verb meaning "to bring out" or "to evoke." *Illicit* is an adjective meaning "unlawful." *The reporter was unable to elicit any information from the police about illicit drug traffic.*

emigrate from, immigrate to *Emigrate* means "to leave one place to settle in another." *My great-grandfather emigrated from Russia to escape the religious pogroms.* *Immigrate* means "to enter another place and reside there." *Thousands of Bosnians immigrated to the United States in the 1990s.*

enthused As an adjective, *enthusiastic* is preferred. *The children were enthusiastic* (not *enthused*) *about going to the circus.*

etc. Avoid ending a list with *etc.* It is more emphatic to end with an example, and usually readers will understand that the list is not exhaustive. When you don't wish to end with an example, *and so on* is more graceful than *etc.*

everybody, everyone See pages 21 and 31.

everyone, every one *Everyone* is an indefinite pronoun. *Everyone wanted to go.* *Every one*, the pronoun *one* preceded by the adjective *every*, means "each individual or thing in a particular group." *Every one* is usually followed by *of*. *Every one of the missing books was found.*

except See *accept, except*.

farther, further *Farther* describes distances. *Further* suggests quantity or degree. *Detroit is farther from Miami than I thought. You extended the curfew further than necessary.*

fewer, less *Fewer* refers to items that can be counted; *less* refers to items that cannot be counted. *Fewer people are living in the city. Please put less sugar in my tea.*

firstly *Firstly* sounds pretentious, and it leads to the ungainly series *firstly, secondly, thirdly, fourthly*, and so on. Write *first, second, third* instead.

further See *farther, further*.

good, well See page 39.

graduate Both of the following uses of *graduate* are standard: *My sister was graduated from UCLA last year. My sister graduated from UCLA last year.* It is nonstandard to drop the word *from*: *My sister graduated UCLA last year.*

grow Phrases such as *to grow a business* are jargon. Usually the verb *grow* is intransitive (it does not take a direct object). *Our business has grown very quickly.* When *grow* is used in a transitive sense, with a direct object, it means "to cultivate" or "to allow to grow." *We plan to grow tomatoes. John is growing a beard.* (See also pp. 272 and 276.)

hanged, hung *Hanged* is the past-tense and past-participle form of the verb *hang,* meaning "to execute." *The prisoner was hanged at dawn. Hung* is the past-tense and past-participle form of the verb *hang,* meaning "to fasten or suspend." *The stockings were hung by the chimney with care.*

hardly Avoid expressions such as *can't hardly* and *not hardly,* which are considered double negatives. *I can* (not *can't*) *hardly describe my elation at getting the job.*

he At one time *he* was used to mean "he or she." Today such usage is inappropriate. See pages 17 and 31 for alternative constructions.

hisself *Hisself* is nonstandard. Use *himself.*

hopefully *Hopefully* means "in a hopeful manner." *We looked hopefully to the future.* Some usage experts object to the use of *hopefully* as a sentence adverb, apparently on grounds of clarity. To be safe, avoid using *hopefully* in sentences such as the following: *Hopefully, your son will recover soon.* Instead, indicate who is doing the hoping: *I hope that your son will recover soon.*

however Some writers object to *however* at the beginning of a sentence, but experts advise placing the word according to the meaning and emphasis intended. Any of the following sentences is correct, depending on the intended contrast. *Pam decided, however, to attend the lecture. However, Pam decided to attend the lecture.* (She had been considering other activities.) *Pam, however, decided to attend the lecture.* (Unlike someone else, Pam opted for the lecture.)

hung See *hanged, hung.*

illusion See *allusion, illusion.*

immigrate See *emigrate from, immigrate to.*

immoral See *amoral, immoral.*

imply, infer *Imply* means "to suggest or state indirectly"; *infer* means "to draw a conclusion." *John implied that he knew all about computers, but the interviewer inferred that John was inexperienced.*

in, into *In* indicates location or condition; *into* indicates movement or a change in condition. *They found the lost letters in a box after moving into the house.*

in regards to Use either *in regard to* or *as regards. In regard to* (or *As regards*) *the contract, ignore the first clause.*

USAGE hackerhandbooks.com/pocket
> Language Debates > Sexist language
> > *however* at the beginning of a sentence

irregardless *Irregardless* is nonstandard. Use *regardless*.

is when, is where See section 6c.

its, it's *Its* is a possessive pronoun; *it's* is a contraction for *it is*. *It's always fun to watch a dog chase its tail.*

kind of, sort of Avoid using *kind of* or *sort of* to mean "somewhat." *The movie was a little* (not *kind of*) *boring.* Do not put *a* after either phrase. *That kind of* (not *kind of a*) *salesclerk annoys me.*

lay, lie See page 25.

lead, led *Lead* is a metallic element; it is a noun. *Led* is the past tense of the verb *lead*. *He led me to the treasure.*

learn, teach *Learn* means "to gain knowledge"; *teach* means "to impart knowledge." *I must teach* (not *learn*) *my sister to read.*

leave, let *Leave* means "to exit." Avoid using it with the nonstandard meaning "to permit." *Let* (not *Leave*) *me help you with the dishes.*

less See *fewer, less*.

let, leave See *leave, let*.

liable *Liable* means "obligated" or "responsible." Do not use it to mean "likely." *You're likely* (not *liable*) *to trip if you don't tie your shoelaces.*

lie, lay See page 25.

like, as *Like* is a preposition, not a subordinating conjunction. It should be followed only by a noun or a noun phrase. *As* is a subordinating conjunction that introduces a subordinate clause. In casual speech, you may say *She looks like she has not slept.* But in formal writing, use *as*. *She looks as if she has not slept.*

loose, lose *Loose* is an adjective meaning "not securely fastened." *Lose* is a verb meaning "to misplace" or "to not win." *Did you lose your only loose pair of work pants?*

may See *can, may*.

maybe, may be *Maybe* is an adverb meaning "possibly"; *may be* is a verb phrase. *Maybe the sun will shine tomorrow. Tomorrow may be a brighter day.*

may of, might of *May of* and *might of* are nonstandard for *may have* and *might have*.

media, medium *Media* is the plural of *medium*. *Of all the media that cover the Olympics, television is the medium that best captures the spectacle of the events.*

USAGE hackerhandbooks.com/pocket
> Language Debates > *lie* versus *lay*

must of *Must of* is nonstandard for *must have*.

myself *Myself* is a reflexive or intensive pronoun. Reflexive: *I cut myself.* Intensive: *I will drive you myself.* Do not use *myself* in place of *I* or *me*: *He gave the plants to Melinda and me* (not *myself*).

neither See pages 21 and 31.

none See page 21.

nowheres *Nowheres* is nonstandard for *nowhere*.

number See *amount, number*.

off of *Off* is sufficient. Omit *of*.

passed, past *Passed* is the past tense of the verb *pass*. *Emily passed me a slice of cake.* *Past* usually means "belonging to a former time" or "beyond a time or place." *Our past president spoke until past 10:00. The hotel is just past the station.*

plus *Plus* should not be used to join independent clauses. *This raincoat is dirty; moreover* (not *plus*), *it has a hole in it.*

precede, proceed *Precede* means "to come before." *Proceed* means "to go forward." *As we proceeded up the mountain, we saw evidence that some hikers had preceded us.*

principal, principle *Principal* is a noun meaning "the head of a school or an organization" or "a sum of money." It is also an adjective meaning "most important." *Principle* is a noun meaning "a basic truth or law." *The principal expelled her for three principal reasons. We believe in the principle of equal justice for all.*

proceed, precede See *precede, proceed*.

quote, quotation *Quote* is a verb; *quotation* is a noun. Avoid using *quote* as a shortened form of *quotation*. *Her quotations* (not *quotes*) *from Shakespeare intrigued us.*

real, really *Real* is an adjective; *really* is an adverb. *Real* is sometimes used informally as an adverb, but avoid this use in formal writing. *She was really* (not *real*) *angry.* See also section 13.

reason . . . is because See section 6c.

reason why The expression *reason why* is redundant. *The reason* (not *The reason why*) *Jones lost the election is clear.*

respectfully, respectively *Respectfully* means "showing or marked by respect." *He respectfully submitted his opinion.* *Respectively* means "each in the order given." *John, Tom, and Larry were a butcher, a baker, and a lawyer, respectively.*

USAGE hackerhandbooks.com/pocket
> Language Debates > *myself*
> *none*

sensual, sensuous *Sensual* means "gratifying the physical senses," especially those associated with sexual pleasure. *Sensuous* means "pleasing to the senses," especially involving art, music, and nature. *The sensuous music and balmy air led the dancers to more sensual movements.*

set, sit *Set* means "to put" or "to place"; *sit* means "to be seated." *She set the dough in a warm corner of the kitchen. The cat sits in the warmest part of the room.*

should of *Should of* is nonstandard for *should have*.

since Do not use *since* to mean "because" if there is any chance of ambiguity. *Because* (not *Since*) *we won the game, we have been celebrating with a pitcher of root beer. Since* here could mean "because" or "from the time that."

sit See *set, sit*.

site, cite See *cite, site*.

somebody, someone, something See pages 21 and 31.

suppose to Write *supposed to*.

sure and *Sure and* is nonstandard for *sure to*. *Be sure to* (not *sure and*) *bring a gift for the host.*

take See *bring, take*.

than, then *Than* is a conjunction used in comparisons; *then* is an adverb denoting time. *That pizza is more than I can eat. Tom laughed, and then we recognized him.*

that See *who, which, that*.

that, which Many writers reserve *that* for restrictive clauses, *which* for nonrestrictive clauses. (See pp. 57–58.)

theirselves *Theirselves* is nonstandard for *themselves*.

them The use of *them* in place of *those* is nonstandard. *Please send those* (not *them*) *letters to the sponsors.*

then See *than, then*.

there, their, they're *There* is an adverb specifying place; it is also an expletive (placeholder). Adverb: *Sylvia is sitting there patiently.* Expletive: *There are two plums left.* (See also p. 272.) *Their* is a possessive pronoun. *Fred and Jane finally washed their car. They're* is a contraction of *they are. They're late today.*

to, too, two *To* is a preposition; *too* is an adverb; *two* is a number. *Too many of your shots slice to the left, but the last two were right on the mark.*

USAGE hackerhandbooks.com/pocket
> Language Debates > *that* versus *which*

toward, towards *Toward* and *towards* are generally interchangeable, although *toward* is preferred in American English.

try and *Try and* is nonstandard for *try to*. *I will try to* (not *try and*) *be better about writing to you.*

unique See page 40.

use to Write *used to*. *We used to live in an apartment.*

utilize *Utilize* is often a pretentious substitute for *use*; in most cases, *use* is sufficient. *I used* (not *utilized*) *the best workers to get the job done fast.*

wait for, wait on *Wait for* means "to be in readiness for" or "await." *Wait on* means "to serve." *We're waiting for* (not *waiting on*) *Ruth before we can leave.*

ways *Ways* is colloquial when used in place of *way* to mean "distance." *The city is a long way* (not *ways*) *from here.*

weather, whether The noun *weather* refers to the state of the atmosphere. *Whether* is a conjunction indicating a choice between alternatives. *We wondered whether the weather would clear up in time for our picnic.*

well, good See page 39.

where Do not use *where* in place of *that*. *I heard that* (not *where*) *the crime rate is increasing.*

which See *that, which* and *who, which, that*.

while Avoid using *while* to mean "although" or "whereas" if there is any chance of ambiguity. *Although* (not *While*) *Gloria lost money in the slot machine, Tom won it at roulette.* Here *While* could mean either "although" or "at the same time that."

who, which, that Use *who*, not *which*, to refer to persons. Generally, use *that* to refer to things or, occasionally, to a group or class of people. *The player who* (not *that* or *which*) *made the basket at the buzzer was named MVP. The team that scores the most points in this game will win the tournament.*

who, whom See section 12d.

who's, whose *Who's* is a contraction of *who is*; *whose* is a possessive pronoun. *Who's ready for more popcorn? Whose coat is this?*

would of *Would of* is nonstandard for *would have*.

USAGE hackerhandbooks.com/pocket
> Language Debates
> Absolute concepts such as *unique*
> *who* versus *which* or *that*
> *who* versus *whom*

you See pages 33–34.

your, you're *Your* is a possessive pronoun; *you're* is a contraction of *you are*. Is that *your* bike? *You're* in the finals.

48 Glossary of grammatical terms

This glossary gives definitions for parts of speech, such as nouns; parts of sentences, such as subjects; and types of sentences, clauses, and phrases.

If you are looking up the name of an error (sentence fragment, for example), consult the index or the table of contents instead.

absolute phrase A word group that modifies a whole clause or sentence, usually consisting of a noun followed by a participle or participial phrase: *Her words echoing in the large arena*, the senator mesmerized the crowd.

active vs. passive voice When a verb is in the active voice, the subject of the sentence does the action: *Hernando caught* the ball. In the passive voice, the subject receives the action: The *ball was caught* by Hernando. Often the actor does not appear in a passive-voice sentence: The *ball was caught*. See also section 2.

adjective A word used to modify (describe) a noun or pronoun: the *frisky* horse, *rare old* stamps, *sixteen* candles. Adjectives usually answer one of these questions: Which one? What kind of? How many or how much? See also section 13.

adjective clause A subordinate clause that modifies a noun or pronoun. An adjective clause begins with a relative pronoun (*who, whom, whose, which, that*) or a relative adverb (*when, where*) and usually appears right after the word it modifies: The book *that goes unread* is a writer's worst nightmare.

adverb A word used to modify a verb, an adjective, or another adverb: rides *smoothly*, *unusually* attractive, *very* slowly. An adverb usually answers one of these questions: When? Where? How? Why? Under what conditions? To what degree? See also section 13.

adverb clause A subordinate clause that modifies a verb (or occasionally an adjective or adverb). An adverb clause begins with a subordinating conjunction such as *although, because, if, unless,* or *when* and usually appears at the beginning or the end of a sentence: *When the sun went down*, the hikers

USAGE hackerhandbooks.com/pocket
> Language Debates > *you*

prepared their camp. See also *subordinate clause; subordinating conjunction.*

agreement   See sections 10 and 12.

antecedent   A noun or pronoun to which a pronoun refers: When the *battery* wears down, we recharge *it*. The noun *battery* is the antecedent of the pronoun *it*.

appositive   A noun or noun phrase that renames a nearby noun or pronoun: Bloggers, *conversationalists at heart*, are the online equivalent of talk show hosts.

article   The word *a, an,* or *the,* used to mark a noun. Also see 16b.

case   See sections 12c and 12d.

clause   A word group containing a subject, a verb, and any objects, complements, or modifiers. See *independent clause; subordinate clause.*

collective noun   See sections 10e and 12a.

common noun   See section 22a.

complement   See *object complement; subject complement.*

complex sentence   A sentence consisting of one independent clause and one or more subordinate clauses. In the following example, the subordinate clause is italicized: We walked along the river *until we came to the bridge.*

compound-complex sentence   A sentence consisting of at least two independent clauses and at least one subordinate clause: *Jan dictated a story, and the children wrote whatever he said.* In the preceding sentence, the subordinate clause is *whatever he said.* The two independent clauses are *Jan dictated a story* and *the children wrote whatever he said.*

compound sentence   A sentence consisting of two independent clauses. The clauses are usually joined with a comma and a coordinating conjunction (*and, but, or, nor, for, so, yet*) or with a semicolon: *The car broke down,* but *a rescue van arrived within minutes. A shark was spotted near shore; people left the water immediately.*

conjunction   A joining word. See *conjunctive adverb; coordinating conjunction; correlative conjunction; subordinating conjunction.*

conjunctive adverb   An adverb used with a semicolon to connect independent clauses: The bus was stuck in traffic; *therefore*, the team was late for the game. The most commonly used conjunctive adverbs are *consequently, furthermore, however, moreover, nevertheless, then, therefore,* and *thus.* See page 62 for a longer list.

coordinating conjunction One of the following words, used to join elements of equal grammatical rank: *and, but, or, nor, for, so, yet.*

correlative conjunction A pair of conjunctions connecting grammatically equal elements: *either . . . or, neither . . . nor, whether . . . or, not only . . . but also,* and *both . . . and.* See also 3b.

count noun See pages 48–49.

demonstrative pronoun A pronoun used to identify or point to a noun: *this, that, these, those. This* is my favorite chair.

direct object A word or word group that receives the action of the verb: The hungry cat clawed *the bag of dry food.* The complete direct object is *the bag of dry food.* The simple direct object is always a noun or a pronoun, in this case *bag.*

expletive The word *there* or *it* when used at the beginning of a sentence to delay the subject: *There* are eight planes waiting to take off. *It* is healthy to eat breakfast every day. The delayed subjects are the noun *planes* and the infinitive phrase *to eat breakfast every day.*

gerund A verb form ending in *-ing* used as a noun: *Reading* aloud helps children appreciate language. The gerund *reading* is used as the subject of the verb *helps.*

gerund phrase A gerund and its objects, complements, or modifiers. A gerund phrase always functions as a noun, usually as a subject, a subject complement, or a direct object. In the following example, the phrase functions as a direct object: We tried *planting tulips.*

helping verb One of the following words, when used with a main verb: *be, am, is, are, was, were, being, been; has, have, had; do, does, did; can, will, shall, should, could, would, may, might, must.* Helping verbs always precede main verbs: *will work, is working, had worked.* See also *modal verb.*

indefinite pronoun A pronoun that refers to a nonspecific person or thing: *Something* is burning. The most common indefinite pronouns are *all, another, any, anybody, anyone, anything, both, each, either, everybody, everyone, everything, few, many, neither, nobody, none, no one, nothing, one, some, somebody, someone, something.* See also pages 21 and 31.

independent clause A word group containing a subject and a verb that can or does stand alone as a sentence. In addition to at least one independent clause, many sentences contain subordinate clauses that function as adjectives, adverbs, or nouns. See also *clause; subordinate clause.*

indirect object A noun or pronoun that names to whom or for whom the action of a sentence is done: We gave *her* some leftover yarn. An indirect object always precedes a direct object, in this case *some leftover yarn.*

infinitive The word *to* followed by the base form of a verb: *to think, to dream.*

infinitive phrase An infinitive and its objects, complements, or modifiers. An infinitive phrase can function as a noun, an adjective, or an adverb. Noun: *To live without health insurance* is risky. Adjective: The Nineteenth Amendment gave women the right *to vote.* Adverb: Volunteers knocked on doors *to rescue people from the flood.*

intensive or reflexive pronoun A pronoun ending in *-self* (or *-selves*): *myself, yourself, himself, herself, itself, ourselves, yourselves, themselves.* An intensive pronoun emphasizes a noun or another pronoun: I *myself* don't have a job. A reflexive pronoun names a receiver of an action identical with the doer of the action: Did Paula cut *herself*?

interjection A word expressing surprise or emotion: *Oh! Wow! Hey! Hooray!*

interrogative pronoun A pronoun used to introduce a question: *who, whom, whose, which, what. What* does history teach us?

intransitive verb See *transitive and intransitive verbs.*

irregular verb See *regular and irregular verbs.* See also section 11a.

linking verb A verb that links a subject to a subject complement, a word or word group that renames or describes the subject: The winner *was* a teacher. The cherries *taste* sour. The most common linking verbs are forms of *be*: *be, am, is, are, was, were, being, been.* The following sometimes function as linking verbs: *appear, become, feel, grow, look, make, seem, smell, sound, taste.* See also *subject complement.*

modal verb A helping verb that cannot be used as a main verb. There are nine modals: *can, could, may, might, must, shall, should, will,* and *would*: We *must* shut the windows before the storm. The verb phrase *ought to* is often classified as a modal as well. See also *helping verb.*

modifier A word, phrase, or clause that describes or qualifies the meaning of a word. Modifiers include adjectives, adverbs, prepositional phrases, participial phrases, some infinitive phrases, and adjective and adverb clauses.

mood See section 11c.

noncount noun See pages 49–50.

noun The name of a person, place, thing, or concept (*freedom*): The *lion* in the *cage* growled at the *zookeeper.*

noun clause A subordinate clause that functions as a noun, usually as a subject, a subject complement, or a direct object. In the following sentence, the italicized noun clause functions as the subject: *Whoever leaves the house last* must lock the door. Noun clauses usually begin with *how, who, whom, whoever, that, what, whatever, whether,* or *why*.

noun equivalent A word or word group that functions like a noun: a pronoun, a noun and its modifiers, a gerund phrase, some infinitive phrases, or a noun clause.

object See *direct object; indirect object*.

object complement A word or word group that renames or describes a direct object. It always appears after the direct object: The kiln makes clay *firm and strong*.

object of a preposition See *prepositional phrase*.

participial phrase A present or past participle and its objects, complements, or modifiers. A participial phrase always functions as an adjective describing a noun or pronoun. Usually it appears before or after the word it modifies: *Being a weight-bearing joint*, the knee is often injured. Plants *kept in moist soil* will thrive.

participle, past A verb form usually ending in *-d, -ed, -n, -en,* or *-t*: *asked, stolen, fought*. Past participles are used with helping verbs to form perfect tenses (had *spoken*) and the passive voice (were *required*). They are also used as adjectives (the *stolen* car).

participle, present A verb form ending in *-ing*. Present participles are used with helping verbs in progressive forms (is *rising*, has been *walking*). They are also used as adjectives (the *rising* tide).

parts of speech A system for classifying words. Many words can function as more than one part of speech. See *adjective, adverb, conjunction, interjection, noun, preposition, pronoun, verb*.

passive voice See *active vs. passive voice*.

personal pronoun One of the following pronouns, used to refer to a specific person or thing: *I, me, you, she, her, he, him, it, we, us, they, them*. After Julia won the award, *she* gave half of the prize money to a literacy program. See also *antecedent*.

phrase A word group that lacks a subject, a verb, or both. Most phrases function within sentences as adjectives, as adverbs, or as nouns. See *absolute phrase; appositive; gerund phrase; infinitive phrase; participial phrase; prepositional phrase*.

possessive case See section 19a.

possessive pronoun   A pronoun used to indicate ownership: *my, mine, your, yours, her, hers, his, its, our, ours, your, yours, their, theirs*. The guest made *his* own breakfast.

predicate   A verb and any objects, complements, and modifiers that go with it: The horses *exercise in the corral every day*.

preposition   A word placed before a noun or noun equivalent to form a phrase modifying another word in the sentence. The preposition indicates the relation between the noun (or noun equivalent) and the word the phrase modifies. The most common prepositions are *about, above, across, after, against, along, among, around, at, before, behind, below, beside, besides, between, beyond, by, down, during, except, for, from, in, inside, into, like, near, of, off, on, onto, out, outside, over, past, since, than, through, to, toward, under, unlike, until, up, with, within*, and *without*.

prepositional phrase   A phrase beginning with a preposition and ending with a noun or noun equivalent (called the *object of the preposition*). Most prepositional phrases function as adjectives or adverbs. Adjective phrases usually come right after the noun or pronoun they modify: The road *to the summit* was treacherous. Adverb phrases usually appear at the beginning or the end of the sentence: *To the hikers*, the brief shower was a welcome relief. The brief shower was a welcome relief *to the hikers*.

progressive verb forms   See pages 28–29 and 46–47.

pronoun   A word used in place of a noun. Usually the pronoun substitutes for a specific noun, known as the pronoun's *antecedent*. In the following example, *alarm* is the antecedent of the pronoun *it*: When the *alarm* rang, I reached over and turned *it* off. See also *demonstrative pronoun; indefinite pronoun; intensive or reflexive pronoun; interrogative pronoun; personal pronoun; possessive pronoun; relative pronoun*.

proper noun   See section 22a.

regular and irregular verbs   When a verb is regular, both the past tense and the past participle are formed by adding *-ed* or *-d* to the base form of the verb: *walk, walked, walked*. The past tense and past participle of irregular verbs are formed in a variety of other ways: *ride, rode, ridden; begin, began, begun; go, went, gone*; and so on. Also see 11a.

relative adverb   The word *when* or *where*, when used to introduce an adjective clause. See also *adjective clause*.

relative pronoun   One of the following words, when used to introduce an adjective clause: *who, whom, whose, which, that*. The writer *who* won the award refused to accept it.

sentence A word group consisting of at least one independent clause. See also *complex sentence; compound sentence; compound-complex sentence; simple sentence.*

simple sentence A sentence consisting of one independent clause and no subordinate clauses: *Without a passport, Eva could not visit her parents in Poland.*

subject A word or word group that names who or what the sentence is about. In the following example, the complete subject (the simple subject and all of its modifiers) is italicized: *The devastating effects of famine* can last for many years. The simple subject is *effects*. Also see *subject after verb; understood subject.*

subject after verb Although the subject normally precedes the verb, sentences are sometimes inverted. In the following example, the subject *the sleepy child* comes after the verb *sat*: Under the table *sat the sleepy child*. When a sentence begins with the expletive *there* or *it*, the subject always follows the verb. See also *expletive.*

subject complement A word or word group that follows a linking verb and either renames or describes the subject of the sentence. If the subject complement renames the subject, it is a noun or a noun equivalent: That signature may be *a forgery*. If it describes the subject, it is an adjective: Love is *blind*.

subjunctive mood See section 11c.

subordinate clause A word group containing a subject and a verb that cannot stand alone as a sentence. Subordinate clauses function within sentences as adjectives, adverbs, or nouns. They begin with subordinating conjunctions such as *although, because, if,* and *until* or with relative pronouns such as *who, which,* and *that*. See *adjective clause; adverb clause; independent clause; noun clause.*

subordinating conjunction A word that introduces a subordinate clause and indicates the relation of the clause to the rest of the sentence. The most common subordinating conjunctions are *after, although, as, as if, because, before, even though, if, since, so that, than, that, though, unless, until, when, where, whether,* and *while*. Note: The relative pronouns *who, whom, whose, which,* and *that* also introduce subordinate clauses.

tenses See section 11b.

transitive and intransitive verbs Transitive verbs take direct objects, nouns or noun equivalents that receive the action. In the following example, the transitive verb *wrote* takes the direct object *a story*: Each student *wrote* a story. Intransitive verbs do not take direct objects: The audience *laughed*. If any words follow an intransitive verb, they are adverbs or word groups functioning as adverbs: The audience *laughed* at the talking parrot.

understood subject The subject *you* when it is understood but not actually present in the sentence. Understood subjects occur in sentences that issue commands or advice: [*You*] Put your clothes in the hamper.

verb A word that expresses action (*jump, think*) or being (*is, was*). A sentence's verb is composed of a main verb possibly preceded by one or more helping verbs: The band *practiced* every day. The report *was* not *completed* on schedule. Verbs have five forms: the base form, or dictionary form (*walk, ride*); the past-tense form (*walked, rode*); the past participle (*walked, ridden*); the present participle (*walking, riding*); and the *-s* form (*walks, rides*).

verbal phrase See *gerund phrase; infinitive phrase; participial phrase*.

Acknowledgments

Academic OneFile, screen shot of David L. Kranz, "Tracking the Sounds of Franco Zeffirelli's *The Taming of the Shrew*." October 28, 2009. Reprinted with permission of Gale/Cengage Learning.

Louise Bogan, excerpt from "Women" from *The Blue Estuaries: Poems 1923–1968*. Copyright © 1968 by Louise Bogan. Reprinted with permission of Farrar, Straus & Giroux, LLC.

EBSCO Information Services, screen shots from *Centro Journal* 11.1 (1999): 10 and *Journal of Macromarketing* 27.4 (December 2007). Reprinted with permission of EBSCO Information Services.

Thomas Friedman, title page and copyright page from *Hot, Flat, and Crowded*. Copyright © 2008 by Thomas Friedman. Used with permission of Farrar, Straus & Giroux, a division of Macmillan Publishing.

Robert Frost, excerpt from "Fire and Ice," from *The Poetry of Robert Frost*, edited by Edward Connery Lathem. Copyright © 1916, 1936, 1942, 1944, 1951, 1956, 1958 by Robert Frost. Copyright © 1964, 1967, 1970, 1975 by Lesley Frost Ballantine. Copyright © 1916, 1923, 1928, 1930, 1939, 1947, 1969 by Henry Holt and Co., Ltd. Reprinted with permission of Henry Holt, LLC, and Random House, Ltd.

Shirley Geok-lin Lim, title page from *Asian-American Literature: An Anthology*. Copyright © 2000 by NTC/Contemporary Publishing Group, Inc. Reprinted with permission of the McGraw-Hill Companies.

Phil McKenna, "The Cyber-Bullies Are Always with You . . ." from *New Scientist* (July 2007): 26–27. Reprinted with permission of Reed Business Information.

Jack McLaughlin, ed., title page, copyright page, and pages 60–61 from *To His Excellency Thomas Jefferson: Letters to a President*. Copyght © 1991. Reprinted with permission of Avon Books, a division of HarperCollins Publishers, and W. W. Norton, Inc., original publisher of the hardcover edition.

Lydia Yuri Minatoya, first page of selection from "Transformation" from *Talking to High Monks in the Snow*. Copyright © 1992 by Lydia Yuri Minatoya. Reproduced with permission of HarperCollins Publishers, Inc.

The New Bedford Whaling Museum & Old Dartmouth Historical Society, screen shot of "Overview of American Whaling." October 27, 2009. Reprinted with permission of The New Bedford Whaling Museum & Old Dartmouth Historical Society.

Constance M. Ruzich, cover and first page of "For the Love of Joe: The Language of Starbucks" from *The Journal of Popular Culture* 41.3 (2008). Copyright © The Authors. Journal Compilation © 2008 Blackwell Publishing, Inc. Reprinted with permission of Blackwell Publishing, Inc.

Laurel Thatcher Ulrich, title page and copyright page from *A Midwife's Tale: The Life of Martha Ballard, Based on Her Diary, 1785–1812*. Copyright © 1991. Used with permission of Vintage Books, a division of Random House, Inc.

Brenda Wineapple, copyright page and title page from *White Heat: The Friendship of Emily Dickinson and Thomas Wentworth Higginson*. Copyright © 2008. Reprinted with permission of Alfred A. Knopf, a division of Random House, Inc.

Vivian H. Wright et al., "Cyberbullying: Using Virtual Scenarios to Educate and Raise Awareness" from the *Journal of Computing in Teacher Education* 26.1 (2009): 35–42. Reprinted with permission of the publisher.

Index

A

a, an, 48–50, 260. *See also the*
Abbreviations, 78–80
   capitalizing, 78
   Latin, 71, 79–80
   in MLA works cited list, 130
   periods with, 71
   plurals of, 66–67
   for titles with proper names, 78–79
Absolute concepts (such as *unique*), 40
Absolute phrases, 270
   commas with, 59
Abstracts
   in APA papers, 196–97
   in CSE papers, 257
   in databases, 90
accept, except, 260
Acknowledgments, in CSE papers, 257
Active verbs, 3–5
Active voice, 4–5, 48, 270
adapt, adopt, 260
AD, BC (*CE, BCE*), 79
Addresses. *See also* URLs (Web addresses)
   commas with, 60
   e-mail, 86
   numbers in, 80
Adjective clauses
   avoiding repetition in, 52
   defined, 270
   punctuation of, 57–58
Adjective phrases, punctuation of, 58
Adjectives
   and adverbs, 38–39
   commas with coordinate, 56
   comparative forms (with *-er* or *more*), 39–40
   defined, 270
   hyphens with, 85
   after linking verbs (subject complements), 38
   no commas with cumulative, 56–57
   with prepositions (idioms), 53
   punctuation of, 56–57
   as subject complements, 38
   superlative forms (with *-est* or *most*), 39–40
adopt. See adapt, adopt, 260
Adverb clauses, 270–71
Adverbs
   and adjectives, 38–39
   comparative forms (with *-er* or *more*), 39–40
   conjunctive, 62, 271
   defined, 270
   relative, 52, 275
   superlative forms (with *-est* or *most*), 39–40
adverse, averse, 260
advice, advise, 260
affect, effect, 260
Agreement of pronoun and antecedent, 30–32
   with collective nouns (*audience, family,* etc.), 32
   with generic nouns, 31–32
   with indefinite pronouns, 31
   and sexist language, avoiding, 17, 31
Agreement of subject and verb, 20–24
   with collective nouns (*audience, family,* etc.), 22
   with indefinite pronouns, 21
   with subject after verb, 22
   with subjects joined with *and,* 21
   with subjects joined with *or* or *nor,* 21
   with *who, which, that,* 22–23
   with words between subject and verb, 20–21
Aircraft, italics for names of, 82
all (singular or plural), 21
all ready, already, 260
all right (not *alright*), 260
all together, altogether, 260
allusion, illusion, 261
almost, placement of, 10–11
a lot (not *alot*), 261
already. See all ready, already, 260
alright (nonstandard). *See all right,* 260

279

altogether. See all together, altogether, 260
American Psychological Association. *See* APA papers
among, between, 261
amoral, immoral, 261
amount, number, 261
a.m., p.m., AM, PM, 79
am vs. *is* or *are*, 20
an, a. See a, an
and
  comma with, 55
  as coordinating conjunction, 55, 272
  no comma with, 60, 61
  no semicolon with, 63
  parallelism and, 5–6
  and subject-verb agreement, 21
and/or, 74, 261
Annotated bibliography, sample, 100–01
Anonymous. *See* Unknown author
Antecedent
  agreement of pronoun and, 30–32
  defined, 271
  pronoun reference, 32–34
  of *who, which, that*, 22–23
Anthology (edited volume), selection in
  APA citation of, 185
  Chicago citation of, 223
  citation at a glance (MLA), 142–43
  CSE citation of, 251
  MLA citation of, 127, 139–40
anxious, 261
any (singular or plural), 21
anybody (singular), 21, 31
anyone (singular), 21, 31
anyone, any one, 261
anyways, anywheres, 261
APA papers, 163–206
  abstracts in, 196–97
  citation at a glance
    article from a database, 190–91
    article in a journal or magazine, 184
    book, 186
    section in a Web document, 192–93

  citations, in-text, 174–78
    directory to models for, 174
    models for, 174–78
  evidence for, 165–66
  footnotes, 196
  manuscript format, 196–98
  numbers in, 81
  plagiarism in, avoiding, 166–69
  reference list, 179–95
    directory to models for, 179–80
    models for, 181–95
    sample, 201, 204, 206
  sample pages, 199–206
  signal phrases in, 171–73
  sources
    citing, 166–69, 174–95
    integrating, 169–73
    uses of, 165–66
  tenses in, 172, 174
  thesis in, 164–65
  title page, 196, 199, 202
  URLs (Web addresses) in, 187, 198
  visuals in, 197
Apostrophes, 65–67
Appendixes, in CSE papers, 257
Appositives (nouns that rename other nouns)
  case of pronouns with, 35
  colon with, 63–64
  defined, 271
  punctuation with, 58, 72–73
  as sentence fragments, 41
Appropriate language (avoiding jargon, slang, etc.), 15–18
Archives, digital, 92–93
  MLA citation of, 148
are vs. *is*. *See* Agreement of subject and verb
Arguments, evaluating, 98–99
Article from a database, citing in paper. *See also* Articles in periodicals
  APA style, 188
  Chicago style, 228–31
  citation at a glance, 147 (MLA), 190–91 (APA), 228–29 (*Chicago*)
  CSE style, 253
  MLA style, 146
Articles (*a, an, the*), 48–51, 271. *See also a, an; the*

Articles in periodicals. *See also* Article from a database
capitalizing titles of, 77
APA style, 196, 198
Chicago style, 236
CSE style, 258
MLA style, 156
citation at a glance
APA style, 184
Chicago style, 227
MLA style, 136
citing, 135–37
APA style, 182–84
Chicago style, 226–31
CSE style, 251–53
MLA style, 146
finding, 90–91
previewing, 95–97
quotation marks for titles of, 68
APA style, 198
Chicago style, 236
CSE style, 258
MLA style, 126, 156
Artwork, italics for title of, 81
as
ambiguous use of, 261
parallelism and, 5–6
pronoun after, 36
as, like. See like, as, 266
at, in idioms (common expressions), 53
audience. See Collective nouns
Audience (readers)
appropriate voice for, 15
purpose and, evaluating, 99
thesis and, 105–06 (MLA), 164–65 (APA), 208–09 (*Chicago*)
Auxiliary verbs. *See* Helping verbs
averse. See *adverse, averse*, 260
awful, 261
awhile, a while, 261

B

back up, backup, 262
bad, badly, 38, 261
Base form of verb, 24, 45–46
to form tenses, 45–47
modal verbs (*can, might*, etc.) with, 47–48
BC, AD (*CE, BCE*), 79

be, forms of
vs. active verbs, 3–4
and agreement with subject, 20
in conditional sentences, 30
as helping verbs, 45–47
as irregular verbs, 25, 28
as linking verbs, 38, 273
in passive voice, 48
in progressive forms, 46, 47
and subjunctive mood, 30
in tenses, 28–29
as weak verbs, 3–4
because
avoiding after *reason is*, 10
not omitting, 6
Beginning of sentences
capitalizing words at, 77–78
numbers at, 80
varying, 14
being as, being that (nonstandard), 261
beside, besides, 262
between, among. See among, between, 261
Bias, signs of, 98–99
Biased language, avoiding, 17–18
Bible (sacred text)
citing in paper, 129–30, 140–41 (MLA); 226 (*Chicago*)
no italics for, 82
punctuation between chapter and verse, 64, 129–30
Bibliography
annotated, sample, 100–01
APA style (reference list), 179–95, 201, 204, 206
Chicago style, 217–35, 237, 242
CSE style (reference list), 247–56
MLA style (works cited list), 130–54, 160, 162
working, 100–01
Block quotation. *See* Quotations, long (indented)
Blog (Weblog)
citing in paper, 149 (MLA), 191 (APA), 233–34 (*Chicago*)
as source, 93–94
Blu-ray Disc (BD), citing in paper, 151 (MLA), 235 (*Chicago*), 255 (CSE)

Book catalog, 91–92
Books
    capitalizing titles of, 77
        APA style, 196, 198
        Chicago style, 236
        CSE style, 258
        MLA style, 156
    citation at a glance
        APA style, 186
        Chicago style, 221
        MLA style, 138, 142–43
    citing
        APA style, 185–87
        Chicago style, 220–26
        CSE style, 250–51
        MLA style, 137–41, 142–43, 148
    italics for titles of, 81–82
        APA style, 196, 198
        Chicago style, 218, 236
        CSE style, 258
        MLA style, 126, 156
Borrowed language and ideas. *See* Citing sources; Plagiarism, avoiding
Boundaries. *See* Dropped quotations, avoiding
Brackets, 73; 112 (MLA); 170 (APA); 214 (*Chicago*)
Bridges. *See* Transitional expressions
bring, take, 262
but
    comma with, 55
    as coordinating conjunction, 55, 272
    no comma with, 61
    no semicolon with, 63
    parallelism and, 5–6
by, not omitting, 6

C

Call numbers, in library, 92
can, as modal verb, 47–48
can, may, 261
capital, capitol, 262
Capitalization, 76–78
    of abbreviations, 78
    after colon, 64, 78; 156 (MLA); 196 (APA); 236 (*Chicago*)
    of first word of sentence, 77–78
    in quotations, 77–78
    of titles of persons, 77
    of titles of works, 77; 156 (MLA); 196, 198 (APA); 236 (*Chicago*); 258 (CSE)
capitol. See *capital, capitol*, 262
Captions. *See* Labels, for visuals
Case. *See* Pronoun case
Catalog, library, 91–92
censor, censure, 262
Central idea. *See* Thesis
cf. (meaning "compare"), 79–80
Charts. *See* Visuals
Chicago Manual of Style, The, 217, 235–36
Chicago papers, 207–42
    bibliography
        directory to models for, 219–20
        formatting, 237
        models for, 220–35
        sample, 242
    citation at a glance
        article in a journal, 227
        book, 221
        journal article from a database, 228–29
        letter in a published collection, 224–25
        primary source from a Web site, 232–33
    evidence for, 209–10
    footnotes or endnotes, 217–18
        directory to models for, 219–20
        ibid. in, 218
        models for, 220–35
        sample, 241
    manuscript format, 235–38
    numbers in, 81
    plagiarism in, avoiding, 210–13
    sample pages, 239–42
    signal phrases in, 215–17
    sources in
        citing, 210–13, 217–35
        integrating, 213–17
        uses of, 209–10
    supporting arguments in, 209–10
    tenses in, 216
    thesis in, 208–09
    URLs (Web addresses) in, 231, 237
Choppy sentences, 13–14

Citation at a glance
  APA style
    article from a database, 190–91
    article in a journal or magazine, 184
    book, 186
    section in a Web document, 192–93
  Chicago style
    article in a journal, 227
    book, 221
    journal article from a database, 228–29
    letter in a published collection, 224–25
    primary source from a Web site, 232–33
  MLA style
    article from a database, 147
    article in a periodical, 136
    book, 138
    selection from an anthology, 142–43
    short work from a Web site, 145

Citation-name system (CSE), 244, 257–58
Citations. *See* Citation at a glance; Documenting sources
Citation-sequence system (CSE), 244, 257–58
cited in, for source quoted in another source, 178. *See also quoted in*
cite, site, 262
Citing sources. *See also* Documenting sources; Plagiarism, avoiding; Quotations
  APA style, 166–69, 174–95
  Chicago style, 210–13, 217–35
  common knowledge, 108 (MLA), 166–67 (APA), 210 (*Chicago*)
  CSE style, 245–56
  general guidelines for, 102–03
  MLA style, 107–10, 122–54
City of publication, in MLA works cited list, 130
class. *See* Collective nouns

Clauses, 271. *See also* Independent clauses; Subordinate clauses
Clichés, avoiding, 16
coarse, course, 262
Collective nouns (*audience, family,* etc.)
  agreement of pronouns with, 32
  agreement of verbs with, 22
Colons, 63–65
  capitalization after, 64, 78; 156 (MLA); 196 (APA); 236 (*Chicago*)
  to fix run-on sentences, 44
  introducing quotations, 69
Combining sentences (coordination and subordination), 13–14
Commands. *See* Imperative mood
Commas, 55–61
  with absolute phrases, 59
  in addresses, 60
  with *and, but,* etc., 55
  with contrasted elements, 59
  between coordinate adjectives, 56
  before coordinating conjunctions, 55
  in dates, 60
  with interrogative tags, 59–60
  with interruptions (*he said* etc.), 58–60
  after introductory elements, 55–56
  with items in a series, 56
  with mild interjections, 59–60
  with nonrestrictive (nonessential) elements, 57–58
  with nouns of direct address, 59
  with parenthetical expressions, 59
  to prevent confusion, 55
  with quotation marks, 60, 69–70
  with semicolons, 62–63
  to set off words or phrases, 57–60
  with titles following names, 60
  with transitional expressions, 58–59

Commas (*cont.*)
unnecessary, 60–61
with *yes* and *no*, 59
Comma splices. *See* Run-on sentences
committee. *See* Collective nouns
Common knowledge, 108 (MLA), 166–67 (APA), 210 (*Chicago*)
Common nouns, 76–77
Company names
abbreviations in, 79
agreement of verb with, 23–24
Comparative form of adjectives and adverbs (with *-er* or *more*), 39–40
Comparisons
with adjectives and adverbs, 39–40
needed words in, 7–8
parallel elements in, 5–6
with pronoun following *than* or *as*, 36
complement, compliment, 262–63
Complements, object, 274
Complements, subject. *See* Subject complements
Complex sentences, 271
compliment. *See complement, compliment*, 262–63
Compound-complex sentences, 271
Compound elements
case of pronoun in, 34–35
comma with, 55
needed words in, 6–7
no comma with, 60
parallelism and, 5–6
Compound nouns. *See* Compound words
Compound numbers, hyphens with, 85
Compound sentences
comma in, 55
defined, 271
semicolon in, 62–63
Compound subjects, agreement of verb with, 21
Compound words (*father-in-law, cross section*, etc.)
hyphens with, 85
plural of, 84
Conciseness, 2–3

Conditional sentences. *See* Subjunctive mood
Conjunctions, 271. *See also* Conjunctive adverbs; Coordinating conjunctions; Correlative conjunctions
Conjunctive adverbs (*however, therefore*, etc.)
comma with, 58–59
defined, 271
semicolon with, 62
Connections. *See* Transitional expressions
conscience, conscious, 263
Consistency. *See* Shifts, avoiding
Context, establishing, 116 (MLA), 172–73 (APA), 216–17 (*Chicago*)
continual, continuous, 263
Contractions (*can't, won't*, etc.), 66
Contrary-to-fact clauses, 30
Conversation among sources. *See* Synthesizing sources
Coordinate adjectives, comma with, 56
Coordinating conjunctions
comma with, 55
coordination and, 14
defined, 272
to fix run-on sentences, 43–44
no comma with, 60, 61
no semicolon with, 63
parallelism and, 5–6
Coordination, 14
Correlative conjunctions
defined, 272
parallelism with, 5–6
could, as modal verb, 47–48
could care less (nonstandard), 263
could of (nonstandard), 263
council, counsel, 263
Council of Science Editors. *See* CSE papers
Countering arguments, 107 (MLA), 166 (APA), 209–10 (*Chicago*)
Count nouns, articles (*a, an, the*) with, 48–49
couple. *See* Collective nouns
course. *See coarse, course*, 262
criteria, 263

Critical reading, 98–99
crowd. *See* Collective nouns
CSE papers, 243–58
   abstracts in, 257
   acknowledgments in, 257
   appendixes in, 257
   citations, in-text, 245–47
      directory to models for, 244
      models for, 245–47
   documentation systems in, 244
   manuscript format, 256–58
   numbers in, 81
   reference list, 247–56
      directory to models for, 247
      formatting, 257–58
      models for, 248–56
   sources in, citing, 245–56
   title page, 257
   URLs (Web addresses) in, 258
Cumulative adjectives, no comma with, 56–57, 61
Cuts, in quotations. *See* Brackets; Ellipsis mark

D

-d, *-ed*, verb ending, 24
Dangling modifiers, 11–12
Dashes, 72–73
data, 263
Database, article from. *See* Article from a database, citing in paper
Databases, for finding sources, 90–91. *See also* Indexes to periodicals, print
Dates
   abbreviations in, 79
   capitalization of, 76
   commas with, 60
   numbers in, 80
Definite article. *See the*
Degree. *See* Comparative form of adjectives and adverbs
Demonstrative pronouns, 272
Dependent clauses. *See* Subordinate clauses
Descriptive word groups. *See* Adjective clauses; Adjective phrases, punctuation of; Adverb clauses
Diction. *See* Words

different from, *different than*, 263
Digital archives, 92–93
   MLA citation of, 148
Digital file, MLA citation of, 150
Digital object identifier. *See* DOI (digital object identifier), in citations
Direct objects
   case of pronouns as, 34–37
   defined, 272
Directories, to documentation models
   APA style, 174, 179–80
   Chicago style, 219–20
   CSE style, 247
   MLA style, 122, 131–32
Directories, Web, 92
Division of words, 86
do
   as helping verb, 272
   irregular forms of, 26
   and subject-verb agreement, 20–24
Documenting sources
   APA style, 174–95
   Chicago style, 217–35
   CSE style, 245–56
   MLA style, 130–54
does vs. *do*. *See* Agreement of subject and verb
DOI (digital object identifier), in citations, 187, 188, 198 (APA); 219 (*Chicago*); 258 (CSE)
don't vs. *doesn't*, 20–24, 263
Dots, ellipsis. *See* Ellipsis mark
Double negatives, avoiding. *See hardly*, 265
Double subjects, avoiding, 52
Drawings. *See* Visuals
Dropped quotations, avoiding, 113 (MLA), 171 (APA), 215 (*Chicago*)
due to, 263

E

each (singular), 21, 31
-ed, verb ending, 24
effect. *See affect*, *effect*, 260
e.g. (meaning "for example"), 79–80
either (singular), 21, 31
either . . . or, 5–6, 272
-elect, hyphen with, 85

Electronic sources. *See* Online sources
elicit, illicit, 264
Ellipsis mark, 74; 111–12 (MLA); 169–70 (APA); 213–14 (*Chicago*)
emigrate from, immigrate to, 264
Empty phrases, avoiding, 2–3
Endnotes. *See Chicago* papers, footnotes or endnotes; Information notes (MLA); Reference list (CSE)
End punctuation, 71–72
enthused, 264
-*er* ending (*faster, stronger*), 39–40
ESL (English as a second language). *See* Multilingual grammar concerns
-*es*, -*s*
   spelling rules, for plurals, 84
   as verb ending, 20
-*est* ending (*fastest, strongest*), 39–40
et al. (meaning "and others"), 79–80; 125, 133 (MLA); 175 (APA); 222 (*Chicago*); 246, 248 (CSE)
etc. (meaning "and so forth"), 79–80, 264
Evaluating sources, 94–99
even, placement of, 10–11
everybody, everyone, everything (singular), 21, 31–32
everyone, every one, 264
Evidence, 106–07 (MLA), 165–66 (APA), 209–10 (*Chicago*)
ex-, hyphen with, 85
except. See *accept, except*, 260
Exclamation points, 72
   and MLA citation, 123
   no comma with, 61
   with quotation marks, 69
Exclamations. *See* Interjections
Expletives *there, it*, 272
   and subject following verb, 52
   and subject-verb agreement, 22
   and wordy sentences, 3

F

Facts
   integrating, 114–15 (MLA), 173 (APA), 217 (*Chicago*)
   scientific, and verb tense, 29

family. *See* Collective nouns
farther, further, 264
fewer, less, 264
Figures. *See* Numbers
Files, managing, 101
firstly, 264
First-person point of view, 8
Footnotes or endnotes, 155 (MLA); 196 (APA); 217–18, 237 (*Chicago*)
for. *See* Coordinating conjunctions; Prepositions
Foreign words, italics for, 82
for example, no colon after, 65
Format, manuscript, 155–58 (MLA), 196–98 (APA), 235–38 (*Chicago*), 256–58 (CSE)
Fractions
   hyphens with, 85
   numerals for, 80
Fragments, sentence, 40–42
Full stop. *See* Periods
further. See *farther, further*, 264
Fused sentences. *See* Run-on sentences
Future perfect tense, 28, 47
Future progressive forms, 29, 46–47
Future tense, 28, 46

G

Gender, and pronoun agreement, 17, 31–32
Gender-neutral language, 17
Generic *he*, 17, 265
Generic nouns, 31–32
Geographic names, *the* with, 51
Gerund phrases, 272
Gerunds, 36–37, 272
Glossary of grammatical terms, 270–77
Glossary of usage, 260–70
good, well, 39
graduate, 264
Grammar, mixed. *See* Mixed constructions
Grammar, multilingual concerns with. *See* Multilingual grammar concerns
Graphic narrative, MLA citation of, 139
Graphs. *See* Visuals
grow, 264

H

hanged, hung, 265
hardly, 10–11, 265
has vs. *have*. *See* Agreement of subject and verb
have
  forming tenses with, 47
  irregular forms of, 26
  and perfect tenses, 28–29, 47
  and subject-verb agreement, 20–24
Headings, in papers, 157 (MLA), 197 (APA), 237 (*Chicago*), 257 (CSE)
he, him, his, sexist use of, 17, 31, 265
Helping verbs
  defined, 272
  and forming verb tenses, 28–29
  multilingual concerns with, 45–47
her vs. *she*, 34–37
he said, she said, comma with, 60, 69–70
he/she, his/her, 74
he vs. *him*, 34–37
hisself (nonstandard), 265
hopefully, 265
however
  at beginning of sentence, 265
  comma with, 58–59
  semicolon with, 62
Humanities, writing in the. *See Chicago* papers; MLA papers
hung. See hanged, hung, 265
Hyphens, 85–86
  in URLs (Web addresses), 157, 158 (MLA); 198 (APA); 237 (*Chicago*); 258 (CSE)
  in word divisions at ends of lines, 86

I

I
  vs. *me*, 34–37
  point of view, 8
  shifts with *you, he,* or *she*, avoiding, 8
ibid., 218
Idioms (common expressions), 53
i.e. (meaning "that is"), 79–80
-ie, -ei, spelling rule, 83
if clauses, 30
illicit. See elicit, illicit, 264
illusion. See allusion, illusion, 261
Illustrated book, MLA citation of, 138
immigrate. See emigrate from, immigrate to, 264
immoral. See amoral, immoral, 261
Imperative mood, 30
imply, infer, 265
in, in idioms (common expressions), 53
Incomplete comparison, 7–8
Incomplete construction, 6–8
Incomplete sentences. *See* Fragments, sentence
Indefinite articles. *See a, an*
Indefinite pronouns
  agreement of verb with, 21
  as antecedents, 31
  apostrophe with, 65–66
  defined, 272
Indenting
  in APA reference list, 197
  in *Chicago* bibliography, 238
  in *Chicago* notes, 237
  in CSE reference list, 258
  of long quotations
    APA style, 170–71, 196
    Chicago style, 214, 236
    CSE style, 257
    MLA style, 112–13, 120–21, 156–57
    no quotation marks with, 68
  in MLA works cited list, 158
Independent clauses
  colon between, 63–64
  and comma with coordinating conjunction, 55
  defined, 272
  and run-on sentences, 42–45
  semicolon between, 62–63
Indexes to periodicals, print, 90. *See also* Databases, for finding sources
Indicative mood, 30
Indirect objects, 35, 272–73
Indirect questions, 71
Indirect quotations, 68, 71
Indirect sources, 128 (MLA), 178 (APA), 226 (*Chicago*)
infer. See imply, infer, 265
Infinitive phrases, 273

I

Infinitives
  case of pronouns with, 36
  defined, 273
  split, 12–13
Inflated phrases, avoiding, 2–3
Information, for essay. *See also* Sources
  finding, 89–94
  managing, 100–03
  working bibliography, 100–01
Information notes (MLA), 155
-ing verb ending. *See* Gerunds; Present participles
in, into, 265
in regards to, 265
Inserted material, in quotations. *See* Brackets
Integrating sources, 102–03; 110–21 (MLA); 169–73 (APA); 213–17 (*Chicago*)
Intensive pronouns, 273
Interjections (exclamations), 59–60, 273
Internet
  addresses. *See* URLs
  citation at a glance, 145 (MLA), 192–93 (APA), 232–33 (*Chicago*)
  citing in paper, 141, 143–54 (MLA); 187–95 (APA); 220–35 (*Chicago*); 250–56 (CSE)
  evaluating sources from, 99
  finding sources on, 92–94
  previewing sources on, 95, 98
  searching, 92
Interrogative pronouns, 37, 273
In-text citations. *See also* Footnotes or endnotes; Integrating sources
  APA style, 174–78
  CSE style, 245–47
  MLA style, 122–30
into. *See in, into*, 265
Intransitive and transitive verbs, 48, 276–77
Introductory word groups, comma with, 55–56
Inverted sentence order
  with expletives *there, it*, 22, 52
  and subject-verb agreement, 22
irregardless, 266
Irregular verbs, 24–27, 45–46, 275
is vs. *are*. *See* Agreement of subject and verb
is when, is where, avoiding, 10
it
  as expletive (placeholder), 52, 272
  indefinite use of, 33
  as subject of sentence, 51
Italics, 81–82; 126, 156 (MLA); 179, 196, 198 (APA); 236 (*Chicago*); 258 (CSE)
its, it's, 66, 67, 266

J

Jargon, 15–16
Journal articles. *See* Articles in periodicals
Journals. *See* Periodicals
jury. *See* Collective nouns
just, placement of, 10–11

K

Keywords. *See* Searching for information
kind of, sort of, 266

L

Labels, for visuals, 157 (MLA), 197 (APA), 237 (*Chicago*)
Language
  appropriate, 15–18
  biased, avoiding, 17–18
  borrowed. *See* Citing sources; Plagiarism, avoiding
  clichés, avoiding, 16
  direct, 2–3
  idioms (common expressions), 53
  jargon, 15–16
  offensive, avoiding, 18
  plain, 2–3
  sexist, avoiding, 17
  slang, 16
  wordy, 2–3
Latin abbreviations, 71, 79–80
lay, lie; laying, lying, 25
lead, led, 266
learn, teach, 266
leave, let, 266
less. *See fewer, less*, 264

let. See *leave, let,* 266
Letter in a published collection,
    Chicago citation of, 223
    citation at a glance, 224–25
Letters of the alphabet
    capitalizing, 76–78
    as letters, italics for, 82
    as letters, plural of, 67
liable, 266
Library resources, 89–92. *See also* Online sources
lie, lay, 25
like, no comma after, 61
like, as, 266
Limiting modifiers (*only, almost,* etc.), 10–11
Line spacing, 156 (MLA), 196 (APA), 236–37 (*Chicago*), 257 (CSE)
Linking verbs
    adjectives after, 38
    defined, 273
    pronoun after, 35
List of sources, in research papers. *See* Bibliography, *Chicago* style; Reference list (APA); Reference list (CSE); Works cited list (MLA)
Lists. *See also* Series
    with colon, 63–64
    with dash, 72
Literary present tense, 9, 29, 119
Literature, writing about. *See* MLA papers
Literature review (APA style), sample pages from, 199–201
Long quotations. *See* Indenting, of long quotations
loose, lose, 266
-ly ending, on adverbs, 38
lying vs. *laying,* 25

M

Magazine articles. *See* Articles in periodicals
Magazines. *See* Periodicals
Main clauses. *See* Independent clauses
Main point. *See* Thesis
Main verbs, 45–46, 277. *See also* Verbs
man, mankind, sexist use of, 17
Manuscript formats, 155–58 (MLA), 196–98 (APA), 235–38 (*Chicago*), 256–58 (CSE)
Maps. *See* Visuals
Margins, 156 (MLA), 196 (APA), 236 (*Chicago*), 257 (CSE)
Mass nouns. *See* Noncount nouns
mathematics (singular), 23
may. See *can, may,* 262
may, as modal verb, 47–48
maybe, may be, 266
may of, might of (nonstandard), 266
media, medium, 266
Medium of publication, in MLA works cited list, 130
Memo, sample, 205–06
me vs. *I,* 34–37
might, as modal verb, 47–48
might of (nonstandard). See *may of, might of,* 266
Minor ideas. *See* Subordination
Misplaced modifiers, 10–13. *See also* Modifiers
Missing words. *See* Needed words
Mixed constructions, 9–10
MLA Handbook for Writers of Research Papers, 121, 155
MLA papers, 104–62
    citation at a glance
        article from a database, 147
        article in a periodical, 136
        book, 138
        selection from an anthology, 142–43
        short work from a Web site, 145
    citations, in-text, 122–30
        directory to models for, 122
        models for, 123–30
    evidence for, 106–07
    footnotes or endnotes (optional), 155
    literary quotations in, 118–21
        citing and formatting, 120–21
        introducing, 118–19
        present tense for, 29, 119
        shifts in tense, avoiding, 119
    manuscript format, 155–58

MLA papers (*cont.*)
    numbers in, 81
    plagiarism, avoiding, 107–10
    sample pages, 159–62
    signal phrases in, 113–16
    sources in
        citing, 107–10, 122–54
        integrating, 110–21
        synthesizing, 116–18
        uses of, 107
    supporting arguments in, 106–07, 116–18
    tenses in, 29, 115, 119
    thesis in, 105–06
    URLs (Web addresses) in, 141, 144
    works cited list, 130–54
        directory to models for, 131–32
        formatting, 157–58
        medium of publication in, 130
        models for, 133–54
        sample, 160, 162
Modal verbs, 47–48, 273. *See also* Helping verbs
Modern Language Association. *See* MLA papers
Modifiers
    adjectives as, 38
    adverbs as, 39–40
    commas with, 56–58
    dangling, 11–12
    defined, 273
    of gerunds, 36–37
    limiting, 10–11
    misplaced, 10–13
    redundant, 2
    restrictive (essential) and nonrestrictive (nonessential), 57–58
    split infinitives, 12–13
    squinting, 10–11
Mood of verbs, 30
more, most (comparative and superlative), 39–40
moreover
    comma with, 58–59
    semicolon with, 62
Multilingual grammar concerns, 45–53
    articles (*a, an, the*), 48–51
    idioms (common expressions), 53

nouns, count and noncount, 48–50
omitted subjects, expletives, or verbs, 51
prepositions, 53
repeated subjects, objects, or adverbs, 52
verbs, 45–48
must, as modal verb, 47–48
must of (nonstandard), 267
myself, 35, 267

N

Name-year system
    in APA papers, 174
    in CSE papers, 244, 258
Narrowing a subject, 88
N.B. (meaning "note well"), 79–80
nearly, placement of, 10–11
Needed words, 6–8
    articles (*a, an, the*), 48–51
    in comparisons, 7–8
    in compound structures, 6–7
    it, 51–52
    in parallel structures, 6
    subjects, 51–52
    that, 7
    there, 52
    verbs, 51
Negatives, double. See *hardly*, 265
neither (singular), 21, 31
neither . . . nor, 5–6, 272
nevertheless
    comma with, 58–59
    semicolon with, 62
news (singular), 23
Newspapers. *See* Periodicals
News sites, 93
nobody (singular), 21, 31
Noncount nouns, 49–50
none (singular or plural), 21
Nonrestrictive (nonessential) elements, commas with, 57–58
Nonsexist language, 17
no one (singular), 21, 31
nor
    comma with, 55
    as coordinating conjunction, 55, 272

and parallel structure, 5–6
and subject-verb agreement, 21
not, placement of, 10–11
Notes. *See Chicago* papers, footnotes or endnotes; Information notes (MLA)
Note taking, 101–03
not only . . . but also, 5–6, 272
Noun clauses, 274
Noun equivalent, 274
Noun markers, 48
Nouns. *See also* Nouns, types of
 adjectives with, 38, 270
 articles with, 48–51
 capitalizing, 76–77
 defined, 273
 of direct address, comma with, 59
 plural of, 83–84
 renaming other nouns. *See* Appositives
 shifts between singular and plural, avoiding, 8
Nouns, types of. *See also* Nouns
 collective (*audience, family,* etc.), 22, 32
 common vs. proper, 76–77
 count, 48–49
 generic, 31–32
 noncount, 49–50
 possessive, 65–66
Novels
 capitalizing titles of, 77
 citing, 120
 italics for titles of, 81
 quoting from, 120
nowheres (nonstandard), 267
no, yes, commas with, 59
number. See *amount, number*, 261
Number and person
 shifts in, avoiding, 8
 and subject-verb agreement, 20–24
Numbering. *See also* Page numbers, in papers
 of *Chicago* footnotes and endnotes, 237
 of CSE references, 258
Numbers, 80–81
Numbers mentioned as numbers
 italics for, 82
 plural of, 66–67

Nursing practice paper, sample pages from, 202–04

O

Object complements, 274
Objective case
 of personal pronouns, 34–37
 whom, 37
Objects
 direct, 272
 indirect, 272–73
 of infinitives, 36
 objective case for, 34
 of prepositions, 275
 pronouns as, 34
 repetition of, avoiding, 52
Offensive language, avoiding, 18
off of (nonstandard), 267
Omissions, indicated by
 apostrophe, 66
 ellipsis mark, 74
on, in idioms (common expressions), 53
one of the, 23
Online sources. *See also* Internet
 archives, digital, 92–93
 avoiding plagiarism from, 101
 citation at a glance, 145 (MLA), 192–93 (APA), 232–33 (*Chicago*)
 citing, 141, 143–54 (MLA); 187–95 (APA); 231–34 (*Chicago*); 250–56 (CSE)
 databases, for periodical articles, 90–91
 evaluating, 99
 finding, 92–94
 library catalog, 91
 previewing, 95, 98
 saving copies of, 101
 search engines for, 92
only, placement of, 10–11
only one of the, 23
or
 comma with, 55
 as coordinating conjunction, 55, 272
 parallelism and, 5–6
 and subject-verb agreement, 21

Organization, of papers, 106–07 (MLA), 165 (APA), 209 (*Chicago*)
ought to, as modal verb, 47–48
Ownership. *See* Possessive case

P

Page numbers, in papers, 156 (MLA), 196 (APA), 236 (*Chicago*), 257 (CSE)
Paired ideas, parallelism and, 5–6
Parallelism, 5–6
Paraphrases
  avoiding plagiarism and, 109–10 (MLA), 168–69 (APA), 212–13 (*Chicago*)
  integrating, 102–03; 114 (MLA); 171–73 (APA); 215–17 (*Chicago*)
  no quotation marks for, 68
  and note taking, 101–03
Parentheses, 73
  no comma before, 61
Parenthetical citations. *See* In-text citations
Parenthetical elements
  commas with, 59
  dashes with, 72–73
Participial phrases, 274. *See also* Past participles; Present participles
Participles. *See* Past participles; Present participles
Parts of speech, 274
  adjectives, 270
  adverbs, 270
  conjunctions, 271
  interjections (exclamations), 273
  nouns, 273
  prepositions, 275
  pronouns, 275
  verbs, 277
passed, *past*, 267
Passive voice
  vs. active voice, 3–5, 48, 270
  appropriate uses of, 4–5
  forming, 48
past. See *passed*, *past*, 267
Past participles
  defined, 274
  of irregular verbs, 24–27
  and passive voice, 48
  and perfect tenses, 47
  of regular verbs, 24
Past perfect tense, 28, 29, 47
Past progressive forms, 29, 46
Past tense, 28
  in APA papers, 172, 174
  and -*d*, -*ed* endings, 24
  of irregular verbs, 24–27, 46
  vs. past perfect, 29, 46–47
  of regular verbs, 24, 46
Percentages, numerals for, 80
Perfect tenses, 28–29, 47
Periodicals. *See also* Articles in periodicals
  capitalizing titles of, 77; 156 (MLA); 196, 198 (APA); 258 (CSE)
  italics for titles of, 81; 156 (MLA); 198 (APA); 236 (*Chicago*); 258 (CSE)
Periods, 71
  with ellipsis mark, 74
  to end a sentence, 71
  with quotation marks, 69
Personal pronouns
  case of, 34–37
  defined, 274
Personal titles. *See* Titles of persons
Person and number
  shifts in, avoiding, 8
  and subject-verb agreement, 20–24
Persons, names of. *See* Nouns
Photographs. *See* Visuals
Phrases, 274
  absolute, 270
  appositive, 271
  empty or inflated, 2–3
  fragmented, 41–42
  gerund, 272
  infinitive, 273
  participial, 274
  prepositional, 275
physics (singular), 23
Places, names of. *See* Nouns
Plagiarism, avoiding
  in APA papers, 166–69
  in *Chicago* papers, 210–13
  and integrating sources, 102–03
  and Internet sources, 101
  in MLA papers, 107–10
  and taking notes, 101–03
  working bibliography for, 100–01

Plays
  capitalizing titles of, 77
  citing, 121
  italics for titles of, 81
  quoting from, 121
Plurals. *See also* Agreement of pronoun and antecedent; Agreement of subject and verb; Singular vs. plural
  of abbreviations, 66–67
  of compound nouns (*father-in-law* etc.), 84
  of letters used as letters, 67
  of numbers used as numbers, 66–67
  spelling of, 83–84
  of words used as words, 67
plus, 267
p.m., a.m., PM, AM, 79
Podcast, citing in paper, 150 (MLA), 189 (APA), 234 (*Chicago*), 256 (CSE)
Poems
  capitalizing titles of, 77
  citing, 120–21
  quotation marks for titles of, 68; 156 (MLA); 196 (APA); 236 (*Chicago*)
  quoting from, 120–21
Point, main. *See* Thesis
Point of view, 8
politics (singular), 23
Popular sources, vs. scholarly, 97
Possessive case
  apostrophe and, 65–66
  with gerund, 36–37
Possessive pronouns
  defined, 275
  no apostrophe in, 67
precede, proceed, 267
Predicate, 275
Predicate adjective. *See* Subject complements
Predicate noun. *See* Subject complements
Prefixes, hyphen after, 85
Prepositional phrases, 275
Prepositions
  at, in, on, to show time and place, 53
  defined, 275
  in idioms (common expressions), 53
  repeating, for parallel structure, 6

Present participles
  defined, 274
  and progressive verb forms, 46, 47
Present perfect tense, 28, 47; 115 (MLA); 172, 174 (APA); 216 (*Chicago*)
Present progressive form, 28, 46
Present tense, 28, 46
  in *Chicago* papers, 216
  in MLA papers, 115
  subject-verb agreement in, 20–24
  in writing about literature, 29, 119
  in writing about science, 29
Pretentious language, 15–16
Primary source from a Web site, *Chicago* citation of, 232–33
principal, principle, 267
Print indexes, of periodicals, 90. *See also* Databases, for finding sources
proceed. See *precede, proceed,* 267
Progressive verb forms, 28–29, 46, 47
Pronoun/adjectives, 48
Pronoun-antecedent agreement, 30–32
Pronoun case, 34–37
  I vs. *me*, etc., 34–37
  who vs. *whom*, 37
  you vs. *your*, etc., 36–37
Pronoun reference, 32–34
Pronouns
  agreement of verbs with, 20–24
  agreement with antecedent, 30–32
  as appositives, 35
  case (*I* vs. *me*, etc.), 34–37
  defined, 275
  as objects, 34
  reference of, 32–34
  shifts in person and number, avoiding, 8
  singular vs. plural, 30–32
  as subjects, 34
  who, whom, 37
Proof. *See* Evidence
Proper nouns
  capitalizing, 76–77
  the with, 51

Publication Manual of the American Psychological Association, 173, 195. *See also* APA papers
Punctuation, 54–74
   apostrophe, 65–67
   brackets, 73; 112 (MLA); 170 (APA); 214 (*Chicago*)
   colon. *See* Colons
   comma. *See* Commas
   dash, 72–73
   ellipsis mark, 74; 111–12 (MLA); 169–70 (APA); 213–14 (*Chicago*)
   exclamation point. *See* Exclamation points
   parentheses, 61, 73
   period, 69, 71, 74
   question mark. *See* Question mark
   quotation marks. *See* Quotation marks
   with quotation marks, 68–70
   semicolon. *See* Semicolons
Purpose and audience, evaluating, 99

Q

Quantifiers, with noncount nouns, 50
Question mark, 71
   and MLA citations, 123
   no comma with, 61
   with quotation marks, 69
Questions, research, 88–89
Quotation marks, 67–71. *See also* Quotations
   to avoid plagiarism, 109 (MLA), 167–68 (APA), 211 (*Chicago*)
   with direct quotations (exact language), 67–68
   misuses of, 70–71
   not used with indented (long) quotations, 68
   not used with paraphrases and summaries, 68
   other punctuation with, 68–70
   single, 68
   with titles of works, 68; 156–57 (MLA); 196 (APA); 236 (*Chicago*); 258 (CSE)
   with words used as words, 68

quotation, quote. *See quote, quotation*, 267
Quotations. *See also* Quotation marks
   in APA papers
      accuracy of, 169–70
      appropriate use of, 169–71
      brackets with, 170
      context for, 172–73
      dropped, avoiding, 171
      ellipsis mark with, 169–70
      embedding, 172–73
      integrating, 169–73
      long (indented), 170–71
      quotation marks for, 167–68
      sic for errors in, 170
      with signal phrase, 171–73
   capitalization in, 77–78
   in *Chicago* papers
      accuracy of, 213–14
      appropriate use of, 213–14
      brackets with, 214
      context for, 216–17
      dropped, avoiding, 215
      ellipsis mark with, 213–14
      embedding, 216–17
      integrating, 213–17
      long (indented), 214, 236
      quotation marks for, 211
      sic for errors in, 214
      with signal phrase, 215–17
   citing. *See* Citing sources
   direct and indirect, 68
   ellipsis mark to indicate cuts in, 74
   literary, 118–21
   long (indented), 68
   in MLA papers
      accuracy of, 111–12
      appropriate use of, 111–13
      brackets with, 112
      context for, 116
      dropped, avoiding, 113
      ellipsis mark to indicate cuts in, 74, 111–12

embedding, 116
integrating, 102–03, 111–16
long (indented), 112–13, 120–21, 156–57
quotation marks for, 67–68, 109
sic for errors in, 112
with signal phrase, 113–16
punctuation of, 68–70
within quotations, 68
synthesizing, 116–18
quoted in (*qtd. in*), for a source used in another source, 128 (MLA), 226 (*Chicago*). *See also* cited in
quote, quotation, 267
Quotes. *See* Quotations

R

Ratios, colon with, 64
Reading
active and critical, 98–99
evaluating sources, 94–99
previewing sources, 95–98
real, really, 267
reason . . . is because (nonstandard), 10
reason why (nonstandard), 267
Redundancies, 2
Reference list (APA), 179–95. *See also* Bibliography, *Chicago* style; Reference list (CSE); Works cited list (MLA)
directory to models for, 179–80
formatting, 197–98
models for, 181–95
sample, 201, 204, 206
Reference list (CSE), 247–56
directory to models for, 247
documentation systems for, 244
models for, 248–56
numbering, 244, 257–58
organizing, 257–58
Reference of pronouns, 32–34
Reference works, 89–90
Reflexive pronouns, 273
Regular verbs, 24, 45–46, 275. *See also* Verbs

Relative adverbs, 275
introducing adjective clauses, 52
Relative pronouns
agreement with verbs, 22–23
defined, 275
introducing adjective clauses, 52
who, whom, 37
Repetition
of function words, for parallel structure, 6
unnecessary, 2, 52
Requests, subjunctive mood for, 30
Researched writing. *See also* Researching a topic
APA papers, 163–206
Chicago papers, 207–42
CSE papers, 243–58
MLA papers, 104–62
sample pages, 159–62 (MLA), 199–206 (APA), 239–42 (*Chicago*)
Researching a topic, 87–103. *See also* Researched writing
bibliography, working, 100–01
catalog, library, 91–92
databases and indexes, 90–91
evaluating sources, 94–99
getting started, 88–89
keeping records and copies of sources, 101
keyword searches, 91
library resources, 89–92
managing information, 100–03
and note taking, 101–03
online resources, 92–94, 99
reading critically, 98–99
reference works, 89–90
research questions, 88–89
respectfully, respectively, 267
Restrictive (essential) elements, no commas with, 57–58, 61
Review of the literature, sample pages from, 199–201
Run-on sentences, 42–45

S

-s
- and apostrophe, 65–66
- and spelling, 83–84
- as verb ending, 20

Scholarly sources
- identifying, 95, 96
- vs. popular sources, 96–97

Science, writing about. *See* CSE papers

Scientific facts, and verb tense, 29

Scientific Style and Format: The CSE Manual for Authors, Editors, and Publishers, 244, 256. *See also* CSE papers

Scores, numerals for, 80

Searching for information. *See also* Researching a topic
- in databases, 91
- keywords for, 91
- in library catalog, 91
- scanning results, 95, 98
- in search engines, 91, 92

Second-person point of view, 8

Semicolons, 62–63
- with commas, 62–63
- to fix run-on sentences, 43, 44
- and independent clauses, 62–63
- misuse of, 63
- with quotation marks, 69
- with series, 63
- transitional expressions with, 62

sensual, sensuous, 268

Sentence fragments, 40–42

Sentences. *See also* Sentence types
- choppy, coordination and subordination for, 13–14
- defined, 276
- fragments, 40–42
- incomplete, 40–42
- logical, 10
- run-on, 42–45
- variety in, 13–14
- wordy, 2–3

Sentence structure
- mixed constructions, 9–10
- multilingual concerns with, 51
- simplifying, 3

Sentence types
- complex, 271
- compound, 271
- compound-complex, 271
- simple, 276

Series
- comma with, 56
- parallelism and, 5
- parentheses with, 73
- semicolon with, 63

set, sit, 268

Sexist language, avoiding, 17

shall, as modal verb, 47–48

she, her, hers, sexist use of, 17

she said, he said, comma with, 60, 69–70

she vs. *her,* 34–37

Shifts, avoiding, 8, 119

Short stories
- capitalizing titles of, 77; 156 (MLA); 196 (APA); 236 (*Chicago*)
- citing, 120
- quotation marks for titles of, 68; 156 (MLA); 196 (APA); 236 (*Chicago*)
- quoting from, 120

should, as modal verb, 47–48

should of (nonstandard), 268

sic, 112 (MLA), 170 (APA), 214 (*Chicago*)

Signal phrases, 113–16 (MLA), 171–73 (APA), 215–17 (*Chicago*)

Simple sentences, 276

Simple tenses, 28, 46

since, 268

Singular vs. plural
- antecedents, 30–32
- nouns, 20–24
- pronouns, 30–32
- subjects, 20–24

sit. See set, sit, 268

site. See cite, site, 262

Slang, avoiding, 16–17

Slash, 74

so. See Coordinating conjunctions

Social sciences, writing in the. *See* APA papers; *Chicago* papers

Software. *See* Word processing programs

some (singular or plural), 21

somebody, someone, something (singular), 21, 31
Songs, quotation marks for titles of, 68
sort of. See kind of, sort of, 266
Sources. *See also* Internet; Online sources
   citing. *See* Citing sources
   documenting. *See* Documenting sources
   evaluating, 94–99
   finding, 89–94
   integrating, 102–03; 110–21 (MLA); 169–73 (APA); 213–17 (*Chicago*)
   introducing. *See* Signal phrases
   keeping records of, 101
   list of. *See* Bibliography, *Chicago* style; Reference list (APA); Works cited list (MLA)
   popular, 97
   quoted in another source, 128 (MLA), 178 (APA), 226 (*Chicago*)
   scholarly, 95, 96
   synthesizing, 116–18
   uses of, 94–95; 107 (MLA); 165–66 (APA); 209–10 (*Chicago*)
Spacing. *See* Line spacing
Specific nouns, *the* with, 49
Spelling, 82–84
Split infinitives, 12–13
Sponsor, of Web site
   in *Chicago* notes and bibliography, 231
   and evaluating sources, 99
   in MLA works cited, 141, 143
Squinting modifiers, 10–11. *See also* Misplaced modifiers
Statements contrary to fact, 30
State of publication, in MLA works cited list, 130
statistics (singular), 23
Stereotypes, avoiding, 17–18
Subject, grammatical
   and agreement with verb, 20–24
   case of, 34, 37
   defined, 276
   following verb, 52, 276
   identifying, 20–21
   of infinitive, 36

naming the actor (active voice), 4, 48
naming the receiver (passive voice), 4–5, 48
pronoun as, 34
repeated, avoiding, 52
required in sentences, 51
separated from verb, 20–21
singular vs. plural, 20–24
understood (*you*), 51, 277
Subject, of research paper, narrowing, 88
Subject complements
   adjectives as, 38
   case of pronouns as, 34, 35
   defined, 276
   with linking verbs, 276
Subjective case, of pronouns, 34
who, 37
Subject-verb agreement. *See* Agreement of subject and verb
Subjunctive mood, 30
Subordinate clauses
   adjective (beginning with *who, that,* etc.), 270
   adverb (beginning with *if, when,* etc.), 270–71
   avoiding repeated elements in, 52
   defined, 276
   fragmented, 41
   with independent clauses, 271
   noun, 274
Subordinating conjunctions, 276
Subordination
   for fixing sentence fragments, 40–42
   for sentence variety, 13–14
Subtitles of works. *See* Titles of works
such as
   no colon after, 65
   no comma after, 61
Suffixes, hyphen with, 85
Summary
   avoiding plagiarism and, 109 (MLA), 168 (APA), 212 (*Chicago*)
   integrating, 102–03; 114 (MLA); 171 (APA); 215–17 (*Chicago*)

Summary (*cont.*)
no quotation marks for, 60
and note taking, 101–03
Superlative form of adjectives and adverbs, 39–40
Support. *See* Evidence
suppose to (nonstandard), 268
sure and (nonstandard), 268
Synthesizing sources, 116–18

T

Tables. *See* Visuals
take. See *bring, take*, 262
teach. See *learn, teach*, 266
team. *See* Collective nouns
Tenses, verb, 27–29
and agreement with subject, 20–24
in APA papers, 172, 174
in *Chicago* papers, 216
in literature papers, 9, 29, 119
in MLA papers, 115, 119
multilingual concerns with, 46–47
in science papers, 29
shifts in, avoiding, 9, 119
than
in comparisons, 7–8
no comma before, 61
parallelism with, 5–6
pronoun after, 36
than, then, 268
that
agreement of verb with, 22–23
needed word, 7
vague reference of, 33
vs. *which*, 58, 268, 269
vs. *who*, 269
the, multilingual concerns with, 48–51
with geographic names, 51
omission of, 49–51
with proper nouns, 51
their
misuse of, with singular antecedent, 30–32
vs. *there, they're*, 268
theirselves (nonstandard), 268
them vs. *they*, 34–37
them vs. *those*, 268
then, than. See *than, then*, 268
there, as expletive (placeholder), 272
and subject following verb, 22, 52
therefore
comma with, 58–59
semicolon with, 62
there, their, they're, 268
Thesis
in APA papers, 164–65
in *Chicago* papers, 208–09
in MLA papers, 105–06
they
indefinite use of, 33
vs. *I* or *you*, 8
misuse of, with singular antecedent, 30–32
vs. *them*, 34–37
they're. See *there, their, they're*, 268
Third-person point of view, 8
this, vague reference of, 33
Time
abbreviations for, 79
colon with, 64
numerals for, 80
Title page
for APA papers, 196, 199, 202
for *Chicago* papers, 236, 239
for CSE papers, 257
for MLA papers (optional), 156
Titles of persons
abbreviations with names, 78–79
capitalizing, 77
comma with, 60
Titles of works
capitalizing, 77
APA style, 196, 198
Chicago style, 236
CSE style, 258
MLA style, 156
in citations with unknown authors
APA style, 176, 182
Chicago style, 218, 222
MLA style, 124, 134
italics for, 81–82
APA style, 196
Chicago style, 236
CSE style, 258
MLA style, 156

quotation marks for, 68
APA style, 196, 198
Chicago style, 236
CSE style, 258
MLA style, 156
treated as singular, 23–24
to, too, two, 268
toward, towards, 269
Transitional expressions
commas with, 58–59
list of, 62
semicolon with, 62
Transitive verbs, 276–77
Trite expressions. *See* Clichés, avoiding
troop. See Collective nouns
try and (nonstandard), 269
two. See to, too, two, 268

U

Underlining. *See* Italics
Understood subject (*you*), 51, 277
unique, 40
Unknown author
citing in APA papers, 176, 177, 182
citing in *Chicago* papers, 222
citing in MLA papers, 124, 134
URLs (Web addresses)
breaking, 86; 157, 158 (MLA); 198 (APA); 237 (*Chicago*); 258 (CSE)
citing, 141, 144 (MLA); 187 (APA); 231–34 (*Chicago*)
Usage, glossary of, 260–70
use to (nonstandard), 269
Using sources, 94–95
in APA papers, 165–66
in *Chicago* papers, 209–10
in MLA papers, 107
us vs. *we,* 34–37
utilize, 269

V

Vague reference of *this, that, which,* 33
Variety
in sentences, 13–14

in signal phrases, 115 (MLA), 172 (APA), 216 (*Chicago*)
Verbal phrases, 277
dangling, 11–12
Verbs. *See also* Verbs, types of
active, 4–5, 270
adverbs as modifiers of, 39
agreement with subjects, 20–24
be, forms of, vs. active, 3–4
in conditional sentences, 30, 47–48
-d, -ed ending on, 24
defined, 277
forms of, 45–46
mood of, 30
multilingual concerns with, 45–48
needed, 51
without objects, 48, 276–77
passive, 3–5, 270
separated from subjects, 20–21
-s form of, 20
shifts in tense, avoiding, 9, 119
in signal phrases, 115 (MLA), 172 (APA), 216 (*Chicago*)
with singular vs. plural subjects, 20–24
standard forms of, 24–25
strong, vs. *be* and passive verbs, 3–4
before subjects (inverted sentences), 22, 52
tenses of. *See* Tenses, verb
Verbs, types of. *See also* Verbs
irregular and regular, 24–27, 275
linking, 38, 273
modal (*can, might,* etc.), 47–48, 273
transitive and intransitive, 276–77
Video clip, online, citing in paper, 149 (MLA), 191 (APA), 234 (*Chicago*), 255–56 (CSE)
Visuals
in APA papers, 197
in *Chicago* papers, 236–37
in CSE papers, 257
in MLA papers, 157

Voice
 active vs. passive, 3–5, 48
 appropriate, in writing, 15–18

W

wait for, wait on, 269
was vs. *were*
 and subject-verb agreement, 20
 and subjunctive mood, 30
ways, 269
we
 vs. *us*, 34–37
 vs. *you* or *they*, 8
weather, whether, 269
Web, World Wide. *See* Internet; Online sources
Weblog. *See* Blog
well, good, 39
were vs. *was*. *See was* vs. *were*
where vs. *that*, 269
whether . . . or, 5–6, 272
whether, weather. See *weather, whether*, 269
which
 agreement of verb with, 22–23
 vs. *that*, 58, 268, 269
 vague reference of, 33
 vs. *who*, 269
while, 269
who
 agreement of verb with, 22–23
 omission of, 6–7
 vs. *which* or *that*, 269
 vs. *whom*, 37
who's, whose, 269
Wiki
 citing in paper, 149–50 (MLA), 191 (APA)
 as source, 94
Wikipedia, 94
will, as modal verb, 47–48
Wishes, subjunctive mood for, 30
Word groups. *See* Independent clauses; Phrases; Subordinate clauses

Wordiness, 2–3
Word processing programs
 and hyphenation, 86
 and keeping track of files, 101
Words
 compound, 84, 85
 confused. *See* Glossary of usage
 division of, 86
 foreign, italics for, 82
 needed. *See* Needed words
 spelling of, 82–84
 unnecessary repetition of, 2–3, 52
 using your own. *See* Paraphrases; Summary
Words as words
 italics for, 82
 plural of, 67
 quotation marks for, 68
 treated as singular, 23–24
Working bibliography, 100–01
Works cited list (MLA)
 directory to models for, 131–32
 formatting, 157–58
 models for, 133–54
 sample, 160, 162
World Wide Web. *See* Internet; Online sources
Worn-out expressions. *See* Clichés, avoiding
would, as modal verb, 47–48
would of (nonstandard), 269

Y

yes, no, commas with, 59
yet. *See* Coordinating conjunctions
you
 indefinite use of, 33–34
 vs. *I* or *they*, 8
 and shifts in point of view, avoiding, 8
 understood, 51, 277
 vs. *your*, 36–37
your, you're, 270
YouTube. *See* Video clip

Documentation Directories

Directory to MLA works cited models

LISTING AUTHORS (PRINT AND ONLINE)
1. Single author — 133
2. Two or three authors — 133
3. Four or more authors — 133
4. Organization as author — 133
5. Unknown author — 134
6. Two or more works by the same author — 134

ARTICLES IN PERIODICALS (PRINT)
7. Article in a journal (paginated by volume or by issue) — 135
   Citation at a glance 136
8. Article in a monthly magazine — 135
9. Article in a weekly magazine — 135
10. Article in a daily newspaper — 135
11. Article with a title in its title — 135
12. Editorial or other unsigned article — 137
13. Letter to the editor — 137
14. Review — 137

BOOKS (PRINT)
15. Basic format for a book — 137
    Citation at a glance 138
16. Book with an author and an editor — 137
17. Book with an author and a translator — 139
18. Book with an editor — 139
19. Graphic narrative or illustrated book — 139
20. Entire anthology — 139
21. One or more selections from an anthology — 139
    Citation at a glance 142
22. Edition other than the first — 140
23. Multivolume work — 140
24. Encyclopedia or dictionary entry — 140
25. Sacred text — 140
26. Foreword, introduction, preface, or afterword — 141
27. Book with a title in its title — 141
28. Book in a series — 141
29. Republished book — 141
30. Publisher's imprint — 141

ONLINE SOURCES
31. Entire Web site — 143
32. Short work from a Web site — 144
    Citation at a glance 145
33. Article in an online journal — 146
34. Article in an online magazine — 146
35. Article in an online newspaper — 146

Continued >

Directory to MLA works cited models
(*Continued*)

ONLINE SOURCES (*CONTINUED*)

36.	Article from a database	146
	Citation at a glance 147	
37.	E-book (electronic book)	146
38.	Online book-length work	148
39.	Part of an online book	148
40.	Digital archives	148
41.	Online poem	148
42.	Entire blog (Weblog)	149
43.	Entry or comment in a blog (Weblog)	149
44.	Online video clip	149
45.	Online review	149
46.	E-mail message	149
47.	Posting to an online discussion list	149
48.	Entry in a wiki	149

AUDIO AND VISUAL SOURCES (INCLUDING ONLINE VERSIONS)

49.	Digital file	150
50.	Podcast	150
51.	Musical score	150
52.	Sound recording	151
53.	Film	151
54.	DVD or Blu-ray Disc (BD)	151
55.	Special feature on a DVD or Blu-ray Disc (BD)	151
56.	CD-ROM	151
57.	Computer software or video game	151
58.	Radio or television program	151
59.	Radio or television interview	151
60.	Live performance	152
61.	Lecture or public address	152
62.	Work of art	152
63.	Cartoon	152
64.	Advertisement	152
65.	Map or chart	152

OTHER SOURCES (INCLUDING ONLINE VERSIONS)

66.	Government document	153
67.	Historical document	153
68.	Legal source	153
69.	Pamphlet or brochure	154
70.	Unpublished dissertation	154
71.	Abstract of a dissertation	154
72.	Published proceedings of a conference	154
73.	Published interview	154
74.	Personal interview	154
75.	Personal letter	154
76.	Published letter	154

Directory to APA reference list models

GENERAL GUIDELINES FOR LISTING AUTHORS (PRINT AND ONLINE)

1. Single author — 181
2. Two to seven authors — 181
3. Eight or more authors — 181
4. Organization as author — 181
5. Unknown author — 182
6. Two or more works by the same author — 182
7. Two or more works by the same author in the same year — 182

ARTICLES IN PERIODICALS (PRINT)

8. Article in a journal paginated by volume — 183
9. Article in a journal paginated by issue — 183

   Citation at a glance   184

10. Article in a magazine — 183
11. Article in a newspaper — 183
12. Letter to the editor — 183
13. Editorial or other unsigned article — 183
14. Review — 183

BOOKS (PRINT)

15. Basic format for a book — 185

    Citation at a glance   186

16. Book with an editor — 185
17. Book with an author and an editor — 185
18. Book with an author and a translator — 185
19. Edition other than the first — 185
20. Article or chapter in an edited book or an anthology — 185
21. Multivolume work — 187
22. Book with a title in its title — 187

ONLINE SOURCES

23. Article in an online journal — 187
24. Article in an online magazine — 187
25. Article in an online newspaper — 188
26. Article from a database — 188

    Citation at a glance   190

27. Online book — 188
28. Chapter in an online book — 188
29. Report or long document from a Web site — 188
30. Section in a Web document — 189

    Citation at a glance   192

31. Short work from a Web site — 189
32. Podcast — 189
33. Blog (Weblog) post — 191
34. Online audio or video file — 191

Continued >

Directory to APA reference list models (*Continued*)

ONLINE SOURCES (*CONTINUED*)

35.	Entry in a wiki	191
36.	Data set or graphic representation	191
37.	E-mail	193
38.	Online posting	193

OTHER SOURCES (INCLUDING ONLINE VERSIONS)

39.	Dissertation from a database	194
40.	Government document	194
41.	Report from a private organization	194
42.	Conference proceedings	194
43.	Map, chart, or illustration	194
44.	Advertisement	194
45.	Lecture, speech, or address	194
46.	Brochure, pamphlet, or fact sheet	195
47.	Film or video (motion picture)	195
48.	Television program	195
49.	Computer software or video game	195

Directory to *Chicago*-style notes and bibliography entries

BOOKS (PRINT AND ONLINE)

1.	Basic format for a print book	220
	Citation at a glance 221	
2.	Basic format for an online book	220
3.	Basic format for an e-book (electronic book)	220
4.	Two or three authors	222
5.	Four or more authors	222
6.	Unknown author	222
7.	Multiple works by the same author	222
8.	Edited work without an author	222
9.	Edited work with an author	222
10.	Translated work	223
11.	Edition other than the first	223
12.	Volume in a multivolume work	223
13.	Selection in an anthology	223

Directory to *Chicago*-style notes and bibliography entries (Continued)

BOOKS (PRINT AND ONLINE) (*CONTINUED*)

14.	Letter in a published collection	223
	Citation at a glance *224*	
15.	Work in a series	226
16.	Encyclopedia or dictionary entry	226
17.	Sacred text	226
18.	Source quoted in another source	226

ARTICLES IN PERIODICALS (PRINT AND ONLINE)

19.	Article in a print journal	226
	Citation at a glance *227*	
20.	Article in an online journal	229
21.	Journal article from a database	229
	Citation at a glance *228*	
22.	Article in a print magazine	230
23.	Article in an online magazine	230
24.	Magazine article from a database	230
25.	Article in a print newspaper	230
26.	Article in an online newspaper	230
27.	Newspaper article from a database	231
28.	Unsigned newspaper article	231
29.	Book review	231

ONLINE SOURCES

30.	Web site	231
31.	Short work from a Web site	233
	Citation at a glance *232*	
32.	Online posting or e-mail	233
33.	Blog (Weblog) post	233
34.	Podcast	234
35.	Online audio or video	234

OTHER SOURCES (INCLUDING ONLINE VERSIONS)

36.	Government document	234
37.	Unpublished dissertation	235
38.	Personal communication	235
39.	Published or broadcast interview	235
40.	Video (DVD, Blu-ray Disc)	235
41.	Sound recording	235

Directory to CSE reference list models

BASIC GUIDELINES
1. Single author — 248
2. Two or more authors — 248
3. Organization as author — 248
4. Two or more works by the same author — 249
5. Two or more works by the same author in the same year — 249

BOOKS
6. Print book — 250
7. Online book — 250
8. Book with an editor — 250
9. Edition other than the first — 251
10. Article or chapter in an edited volume — 251

ARTICLES
11. Article in a print journal — 251
12. Article in an online journal — 251
13. Article in a print magazine — 252
14. Article in an online magazine — 252
15. Article in a print newspaper — 252
16. Article in an online newspaper — 252
17. Article from a database — 253

OTHER SOURCES
18. Home page of a Web site — 253
19. Short work from a Web site — 253
20. Report from a government agency (print and online) — 254
21. Conference presentation (print and online) — 254
22. DVD or Blu-ray Disc (BD) — 255
23. Online video — 255
24. Podcast — 256
25. E-mail — 256

Charts and Lists for Quick Reference

Clarity

Inflated vs. concise phrases   2–3
Jargon with plain English translations   15
Clichés   16
Sexist language and appropriate alternatives   17

Grammar

Common irregular verbs   25–27
Commonly used noncount nouns   50
At, on, and *in* to show time and place   53

Punctuation

Conjunctive adverbs and transitional phrases   62

Mechanics

Proper vs. common nouns   76
Italics for titles of works   81

Research

Refining keyword searches   91
Determining if a source is scholarly   95
Scholarly vs. popular sources   96–97
Evaluating all sources   98
Evaluating Web sources   99
Integrating and citing sources to avoid plagiarism   102–03

MLA

Using signal phrases in MLA papers   115
Citation at a glance: Article in a periodical   136
Citation at a glance: Book   138
Citation at a glance: Selection from an anthology   142–43
Citation at a glance: Short work from a Web site   145
Citation at a glance: Article from a database   147

APA

Using signal phrases in APA papers   172
Citation at a glance: Article in a journal or magazine   184
Citation at a glance: Book   186
Citation at a glance: Article from a database   190–91
Citation at a glance: Section in a Web document   192–93

Chicago

Using signal phrases in *Chicago* papers   216
Citation at a glance: Book   221
Citation at a glance: Letter in a published collection   224–25
Citation at a glance: Article in a journal   227
Citation at a glance: Journal article from a database   228–29
Citation at a glance: Primary source from a Web site   232–33

Checklist for Global Revision

Focus
- Is your thesis stated clearly enough? Is it placed where readers will notice it?
- Does each idea support the thesis?

Organization
- Can readers easily follow the structure? Would headings help?
- Do topic sentences signal new ideas?
- Do you present ideas in a logical order?

Content
- Are your supporting ideas persuasive?
- Do you fully develop important ideas?
- Is the draft concise enough — free of irrelevant or repetitious material?

Style
- Is your tone appropriate — not too stuffy, not too casual?
- Are your sentences clear, direct, and varied?

Use of sources
- Which sources inform, support, or extend your argument?
- Have you varied the function of sources — to provide background, explain concepts, lend authority, and counter objections? Do you introduce sources with signal phrases that indicate these functions?
- Is it clear how your sources relate to your argument?
- Do you analyze sources in your own words?
- Is your own argument easy to identify and to understand, with or without your sources?
- Is the draft free of plagiarism? Are summaries and paraphrases in your own words? Is quoted material enclosed in quotation marks or set off from the text?
- Have you documented source material that is not common knowledge?

List of Excerpts from Student Papers

MLA

RESEARCH PAPER   159–60

"Online Monitoring: A Threat to Employee Privacy in the Wired Workplace" by Anna Orlov

LITERATURE PAPER   161–62

"The Transformation of Mrs. Peters: An Analysis of 'A Jury of Her Peers'" by Dan Larson

APA

LITERATURE REVIEW   199–201

"Can Medication Cure Obesity in Children? A Review of the Literature" by Luisa Mirano

NURSING PRACTICE PAPER   202–04

"Acute Lymphoblastic Leukemia and Hypertension in One Client: A Nursing Practice Paper" by Julie Riss

BUSINESS PROPOSAL   205–06

"Proposal to Add a Wellness Program" by Kelly Ratajczak

Chicago

RESEARCH PAPER   239–42

"The Massacre at Fort Pillow: Holding Nathan Bedford Forrest Accountable" by Ned Bishop

For full texts of these and other student papers, including annotated bibliographies and papers in CSE style, visit **hackerhandbooks.com/pocket** and click on Model papers.

Visiting the Writing Center

Step 1: Gather your materials.

- Gather materials your instructor has provided: the assignment, sample papers, your syllabus.
- Gather your own materials: a copy of your draft, copies of texts you have cited in your paper, previous papers with instructor comments.

Step 2: Organize your materials and prepare questions.

- Reread the assignment. If you are confused, ask your instructor to clarify the assignment before you visit the writing center.
- Look at previous papers with instructor comments. Can those comments help you think about your current paper?
- Create a list of specific questions to focus your writing center conversation.

Step 3: Visit the writing center.

- Be on time and treat your tutor or consultant with courtesy and respect.
- Participate actively by asking questions and taking notes.
- Understand the limitations of your visit. Be prepared to cover one or two major issues.
- Understand the purpose of your visit. Most writing center staff are trained to give you suggestions and feedback, but they will not write or edit your paper for you.

Step 4: Reflect on your visit.

- As soon as possible after your visit, make sure you understand your notes from the session and add anything you didn't have time to write during your visit.
- As you revise, apply your notes to your entire paper. Don't focus only on the parts of your paper you looked at in the session.
- Do not feel obligated to follow advice that you disagree with. Writing center staff are trained to provide helpful feedback, but you are the author; you decide which changes will help you best express your meaning.
- As you revise, keep track of questions or goals for your next writing center visit.

Revision Symbols

abbr	abbreviation **23a**	" "	quotation marks **20**
adj/adv	adjective or adverb **13**	.	period **21a**
add	add needed word **4**	?	question mark **21b**
agr	agreement **10, 12a**	!	exclamation point **21c**
appr	inappropriate language **9**	—	dash **21d**
art	article **16b**	( )	parentheses **21e**
awk	awkward	[ ]	brackets **21f**
cap	capital letter **22**	. . .	ellipsis mark **21g**
case	case **12c, 12d**	/	slash **21h**
cliché	cliché **9b**	*pass*	ineffective passive **2b**
cs	comma splice **15**	*pn agr*	pronoun agreement **12a**
dm	dangling modifier **7c**	*ref*	pronoun reference **12b**
-ed	*-ed* ending **11a**	*run-on*	run-on sentence **15**
ESL	English as a second language/multi-lingual writers **16**	*-s*	*-s* ending on verb **10, 16a**
frag	sentence fragment **14**	*sexist*	sexist language **9d, 12a**
fs	fused sentence **15**	*shift*	confusing shift **5**
hyph	hyphen **24b**	*sl*	slang **9c**
irreg	irregular verb **11a**	*sp*	misspelled word **24a**
ital	italics **23c**	*sv agr*	subject-verb agreement **10**
jarg	jargon **9a**	*t*	verb tense **11b**
lc	use lowercase letter **22**	*usage*	see glossary of usage
mix	mixed construction **6**	*v*	voice **2**
mm	misplaced modifier **7a–b, 7d**	*var*	sentence variety **8**
mood	mood **11c**	*vb*	problem with verb **11, 16a**
num	numbers **23b**	*w*	wordy **1**
om	omitted word **4, 16c**	//	faulty parallelism **3**
p	punctuation	∧	insert
ˆ,	comma **17a–i**	x	obvious error
no ,	no comma **17j**	#	insert space
;	semicolon **18a**	⌒	close up space
:	colon **18b**		
ʼ	apostrophe **19**		

Detailed Menu

Clarity   1

1 Wordy sentences 2

2 Active verbs 3
  a vs. *be* verbs
  b vs. passive verbs

3 Parallelism 5
  a Items in a series
  b Paired ideas

4 Needed words 6
  a In compound structures
  b *that*
  c In comparisons

5 Shifts 8
  a Point of view
  b Tense

6 Mixed constructions 9
  a Mixed grammar
  b Illogical connections
  c *is when, is where, reason . . . is because*

7 Misplaced and dangling modifiers 10
  a Misplaced words
  b Misplaced phrases and clauses
  c Dangling modifiers
  d Split infinitives

8 Sentence variety 13
  a Combining choppy sentences
  b Varying sentence openings

9 Appropriate voice 15
  a Jargon
  b Clichés
  c Slang
  d Sexist language
  e Offensive language

Grammar   19

10 Subject-verb agreement 20
  a Words between subject and verb
  b Subjects with *and*
  c Subjects with *or, nor*
  d Indefinite pronouns such as *someone*
  e Collective nouns such as *jury*
  f Subject after verb
  g *who, which, that*
  h Plural form, singular meaning
  i Titles, company names, words as words

11 Other problems with verbs 24
  a Irregular verbs
  b Tense
  c Mood

12 Pronouns 30
  a Agreement
  b Reference
  c Case (*I* vs. *me* etc.)
  d *who* or *whom*

13 Adjectives and adverbs 38
  a Adjectives
  b Adverbs
  c Comparatives and superlatives

14 Sentence fragments 40
  a Clauses
  b Phrases
  c Acceptable fragments

15 Run-on sentences 42
  a Revision with comma and coordinating conjunction
  b With semicolon (or colon or dash)
  c By separating sentences
  d By restructuring

16 Grammar concerns for multilingual writers 45
  a Verbs
  b Articles (*a, an, the*)
  c Sentence structure
  d Prepositions showing time and place

Punctuation   54

17 The comma 55
  a Independent clauses with coordinating conjunction
  b Introductory elements
  c Items in a series
  d Coordinate adjectives
  e Nonrestrictive elements
  f Transitions, parenthetical expressions, absolute phrases, contrasts
  g Direct address, *yes* and *no*, interrogative tags, interjections
  h *he said* etc.
  i Dates, addresses, titles
  j Misuses